THE UNKNOWN NOSTRADAMUS

If anyone in the world could
discover the "truth" about the seer it would
be Peter Lemesurier.

MARIO GREGORIO,
Archivist of the International
Nostradamus Research Group

THE UNKNOWN NOSTRADAMUS

The essential biography for his 500th birthday

PETER LEMESURIER

New Age Books

ISBN: 81-7822-195-0

First Indian Edition: Delhi, 2005

(Originally published in the UK by John Hunt Publishing Ltd., 46A West Street, Alresford, Hants SO24 9AU)

Published in 2004 under Licence from John Hunt Publishing Ltd.

Disclaimer

Neither the author nor the publishers are responsible for the expressed views or predictions of Nostradamus, nor do they necessarily subscribe to them. Reader's reactions to the prophecies are entirely their own responsibility. While all interpretations are offered in good faith, no guarantee is implied or should be inferred regarding their predictive validity.

Superscript numbers and lower-case letters refer to the Reference-Bibliography at the end of the book.

Superscript 'P' denotes an illustration in the color-plate section.

Published by

NEW AGE BOOKS

A-44 Naraina Phase-I

New Delhi-110 028 (INDIA)

Email: nab@vsnl.in

Website: www.newagebooksindia.com

For Sale in Indian Subcontinent Only

Printed in India

at Shri Jainendra Press

A-45 Naraina Phase-I, New Delhi-110 028

Contents

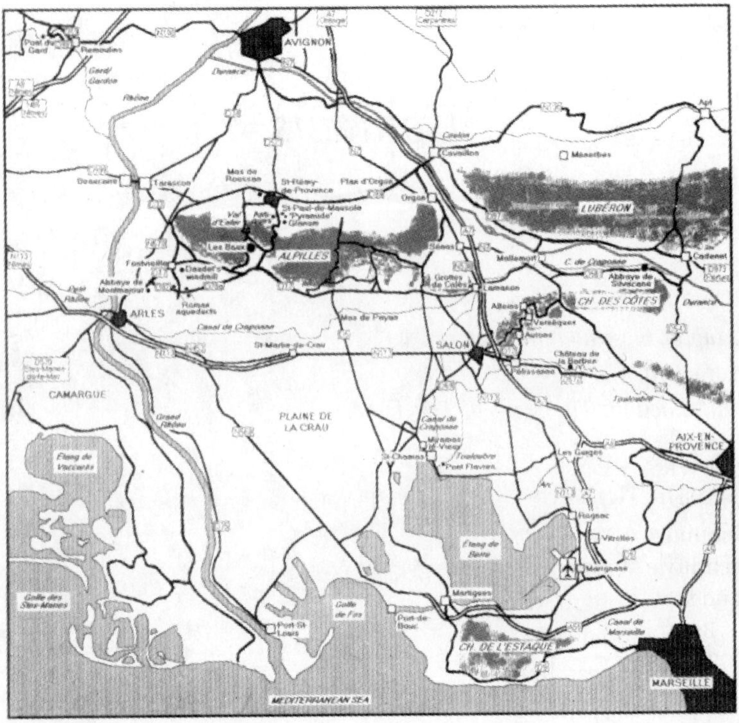

Map of Nostradamus's Provence as it is today

Foreword

After five hundred years more heed they'll take
Of him who was th' adornment of his age.
Then light effulgent suddenly shall break
Such as that time's great pleasure to engage.[52a]

SO WROTE MICHEL NOSTRADAMUS in the very first edition of his *Propheties*, evidently anticipating their eventual success some half a millennium later. The implication is clear. At some point during our own century people would finally be convinced of his prophetic powers, and see that he was right.

But today, 500 years after his birth, is there any sign of it?

That is one of the things that this book is designed to examine. Tracing his life story from his childhood, through his time as a student, to his activities as an apothecary, his production of annual almanacs, his subsequent efforts to set himself up as a prophet and his eventual fame – and notoriety – as mage and royal adviser, we shall see him as he really was, rather than as the professional spinners of tall tales have for centuries sought to portray him. Roping in all the findings of modern research, we shall attempt to lay bare the facts of the case, in the process translating into English for the first time many relevant contemporary texts, including private letters to, from and about the seer. And finally, we shall try to assess his accuracy, gauge his legacy, judge his continued relevance as a prophet today.

The answers to such questions are not necessarily the same as they were even a few years ago. As new texts are discovered and new archives unearthed, many of the former assumptions, often based more on rumor and hearsay than on actual contemporary evidence, have to be discarded. The dogmas have to go, the myths to be jettisoned. And, in the process, the real man who emerges from the mists of historical obfuscation turns out to be a lot more interesting, and his legacy a lot less fearsome, than we have long been taught to suppose.

But there is, of course, no better way of gaining insight into a man's mind than reading what he himself wrote. And so the Appendices that conclude the book present a selection of key texts both by and about Nostradamus (by no means all of them prophetic), most of which have never before been published in English.

In all of this I have been grateful for the support and advice of Michel Chomarat who, as 'guardian of the Nostradamus texts' at the Bibliothèque Municipale de Lyon, has generously supplied me with numerous facsimiles and other documents from his unparalleled collection of over 2000 original items: to Jacqueline Allemand and the staff of the Maison de Nostradamus at Salon-de-Provence for much guidance, encouragement and friendly conversation; to Bernard Chevignard, Professor of Language and Communication at the University of Burgundy in Dijon for his supporting documentation and comradely advice; to Dr Jennifer Britnell, Head of French at the University of Durham, for kindly making available her painstaking research into the *Mirabilis liber*; to Roger Prévost for his inspiration and assistance; to the late Vlaicu Ionescu for his stimulating insights; to Mario Gregorio for his unstinting documentary research and long-term on-line collaboration; to Jason Jamieson for his work on Nostradamus's astrology; to Monique Roussy for her French textual research; to Samuel Oak and Erin Pittenger for their collaboration in translating parts of the *Mirabilis liber* and Nostradamus's private correspondence; to the late and much lamented Ted Johnson for his bequest of valuable historical materials; and to my many other Internet correspondents who, even when they have not been particularly informative, have never ceased to question and provoke.

Introduction: The Signs of The Times

NEVER WAS THERE A TIME MORE RIPE FOR A PROPHET OF DOOM. All those wonderful Renaissance hopes of a glittering renewal of ancient classical learning and culture in fifteenth- and sixteenth-century Europe were all very well, but they were only for the learned and the cultured. For the rest of society it was still the Middle Ages.

And the Middle Ages were showing worrying signs of turning very nasty indeed.

Merely consider the weather. Far more than today, this was of absolutely crucial importance at the time for everybody's health and wealth. Yet ever since the 1470s it had been taking a distinct turn for the worse. By the 1520s, what we now know as Europe's Little Ice Age was in full swing. As a result, winters were tending to become more arctic, summers colder and wetter. Even when the plowing and sowing could be done at all, the crops would often rot in the fields. No crops meant no food, and no food meant no survival. France alone would suffer no fewer than thirteen major famines during the course of the century. Peasants – the vast majority of the population – either starved where they stood in their tens of thousands or migrated to the smelly and overcrowded towns, where they were merely confronted with the next threat to their miserable existence.

For the Plague, too, was on the loose all over Europe, especially in the towns and cities. True, it came and went, depending on the ever-more-unpredictable weather and on the time of year. But for it to come even once was once too often. Nobody knew what caused it. Nobody had a cure for it. Already in the fourteenth century it had wiped out up to a third of the population of Europe. And so, given everybody's total ignorance of what to do about it, there was every prospect that it might well do so again.

Yet these major threats to existence still did not manage to dissuade the rulers of Europe from continually making war on each other (or, indeed, the peasants themselves from staging intermittent catastrophic revolts), so causing even more widespread death and destruction. The French King François I and his Burgundian contemporary, the Holy Roman Emperor Charles V, were particularly prominent in this, and Germany, Italy, Spain, the Netherlands and England would all eventually be sucked in – to say nothing of the powerful North African pirate fleets that continually ravaged the Mediterranean coasts, let alone the invading hordes of the Turkish Ottomans under Suleiman the Magnificent who, flooding in from the south-east, were threatening to overrun Vienna itself by 1526. Later in the century, too, the grisly Wars of Religion would cost at least 1,600,000 lives in France alone, out of a population of only ten million or so.

War, Plague, Famine and Death, then – the dreaded Four Horsemen of the Apocalypse – were starkly and unmistakably abroad in sixteenth-century Europe. And, to top it all, by 1536 (following Martin Luther's explosive Protestant initiative of some twenty years earlier), there was something even worse. There in Geneva, insidiously spreading his seditious message all over Europe and undermining many of the most cherished and ancient teachings of the Church, sat the man whom many Catholics saw as the Antichrist himself in flesh and blood – none other than John Calvin, the embodiment of everything that threatened to torpedo even the one hope that was left, namely the Catholic religion and its promise of eternal salvation.

There was nothing sudden about all this, of course. Thinking people had seen it coming for decades, and naturally they had sought to understand it and work out what it all meant. But since most thinking people were religiously inclined, if not actual Church dignitaries, they groped for the one source of understanding that they had always been taught to value most – namely the Bible. And they deduced from it that all this was the vengeance of an angry God against a humanity that had gone badly astray.

However, the Bible was not yet widely available to Catholics in the vernacular. Even those lay people who could read it in the Latin Vulgate translation were not encouraged to do so by the Church. Such knowledge was considered dangerous. And so reading the Bible was mainly for clerics and monks, and finding out what exactly it said meant either listening to their sermons or reading what they had written.

Thus arose the vogue for collecting anthologies of ancient prophecies (themselves largely written by clerics and monks on the basis both of Bible prophecies and of well-known Bible stories) in an attempt to explain the events of the time. And in particular, since current events seemed to have all the grisly trademarks of the Last Times – that direst of periods described by the Bible as leading up to the End of the World and the Last Judgment – people sought authoritative literature that would confirm them in that belief.

This may seem strange to us now. Yet the desire to know the worst is a strong human urge. Even today, it is gloom-and-doom that most readily makes the newspaper headlines. And every generation likes to think that it stands at the climax of world history.

By the middle of the fifteenth century such anthologies of apocalyptic prophecies were almost two-a-penny. Some of them were purely private collections. One such was the half-assembled *Book of Prophecies* on which no less a man than Christopher Columbus was working towards the end of his life, and which had convinced him that the New World promised by the Bible would dawn in his own time on the very continent that was, as we now know, eventually to bear that name.[72] 'God made me the messenger of the new heaven and new earth of which he spoke in the Apocalypse of St John after speaking of it through the mouth of Isaiah, and he showed me the place to find it,' he wrote to a Spanish courtier in 1500, after being ignominiously sent back in chains to Spain.

Other anthologies of prophecies, though, were printed, published and perfectly well known. Prime among these was the anonymous *Mirabilis liber* of 1522, a huge and oft-reprinted compendium of prophecies, mainly in Latin, taken from various religious writings dating back as far as the seventh century, though sometimes claiming an even earlier origin. Granted, whoever compiled it introduced a few slight changes, evidently designed to promote the election of François I of France as Holy Roman Emperor in 1520.[10] But even after the failure of that attempt and the election of Charles V instead, the book still retained most of its prophetic force – whence, no doubt, its numerous reprints. For its main subject was the Last Times that were destined to lead up to the End of the World – an event that now seemed almost catastrophically imminent. Its language was therefore suitably disturbing, menacing, even blood-curdling.

Moreover, since it would go on to supply the prophetic blueprint for virtually all later religious prophecies right down to the present day, including those of the Prophet of Provence himself – to say nothing of a good many of his actual, detailed predictions – we shall do well to spend a few minutes here tracing in some detail the grand prophetic scenario that it envisaged.

* * *

The first, most vivid and most influential of the prophecies reprinted in the *Mirabilis liber* was attributed to 'Bishop Bemechobus' (evidently a misreading of the fourth-century *Beatus Methodius*, or 'Blessed Methodius'), though the text is known to be a seventh-century one that merely attributes the prophecy to him, and whose author is therefore nowadays better known as 'Pseudo-Methodius'. It announced itself as:

> The Book of Bemechobus, bishop and martyr of Christ, translated through his efforts from Hebrew and Greek into Latin; treating of the beginning of the world, of kingdoms, of nations, and of the end of the ages, and praised by the most illustrious and blessed Jerome in his works.

The text started with a summary of biblical history. On the basis of historical analogy, it then started to apply it to the future:

> So God delivered the sons of Israel from the slavery of the children of Ishmael. These [i.e. the Arabs] shall, however, renew their enterprise, they shall destroy the land, shall invade the globe from the East unto the West, from the South to the North, as far as Rome. Their yoke shall weigh heavy on the heads of the people. There shall be no nation or realm that can fight against them, until the Times shall be accomplished. Only then shall they be defeated by the Christians; and the Roman empire, in its turn, shall take captive the children of Ishmael.

This, clearly, was intended as some kind of general template for much of what was to follow:

> This new invasion of the Ishmaelites shall be a punishment without measure or mercy. The Lord shall deliver all the nations into their hands because of the transgressions that we have committed against his laws. That is why God delivered us into the arms of the barbarians [another code-word for the Arabs], because we have forgotten his divine precepts.
>
> For the Christians shall give themselves up to a host of unlawful acts and shall defile themselves with the most disgraceful depravities, and that is why the Lord has delivered them [in advance] into the hands of the Saracens. Cappadocia, Licilia, the land of Syria, once subjected to the devastation, shall become a desert; their inhabitants shall be dragged off into captivity, while others shall perish by the sword. Massacre and

> captivity await the Greeks. [North] Africa shall be made desolate, the Egyptians, Orientals and Asians shall be made to offer tribute in gold and silver. The Spanish shall perish by the sword. France, Germany and the land of the Goths, eaten up by a thousand scourges, shall see a host of their inhabitants carried off. The Romans shall be killed or put to flight; and pursuing their enemies as far as the islands of the sea, the sons of Ishmael shall invade at one and the same time the North and the East, the South and the West... All the treasures and ornaments of the churches made of gold, silver and precious stones shall become their property; the desolation shall be great, the churches burnt, and the corpses of the faithful shall be thrown where no one shall be able to find them to bury them.

The text continued to pile on the agony:

> Thus it is that all the earth shall be delivered to the children of Ishmael [i.e. the Arabs still], who shall bring dissolution in their wake. That is why the Lord called Ishmael, their father, the Instrument of War; and many cities shall be made desolate, for the sons of the desert shall come, and they are not men, but beings odious to men. They shall even be seen putting pregnant women to the sword-point and immolating the priests in the sanctuary. They shall desecrate their churches, cohabiting there with women, and they shall bedeck themselves, both themselves and their spouses, with sacred ornaments. They shall attach their horses to the tombs of the faithful as though to a bush. There shall be a general tribulation among the Christians who inhabit the earth...
>
> There shall emerge from Gaul [a patriotic interpolation by the sixteenth-century French editor!] a race of Christians who shall make war on them and shall pierce them with the sword, shall take away their women captive and shall slaughter their children. In their turn, the sons of Ishmael shall encounter both sword and tribulation. And the Lord shall return to them the evil that they shall have done in sevenfold measure. The Lord shall deliver them into the clutches of the Christians, whose empire shall be elevated above all empires. The yoke that the Christians shall impose on them shall be hard, and those that shall remain shall be slaves. The earth, previously laid waste by them, shall then be pacified. The prisoners they had taken shall once again see their homelands, and the population shall grow and multiply.
>
> The king of the Romans shall show great indignation against those who have denied Christ in Egypt or in Arabia. Peace and tranquility shall be reborn on earth, a peace such as there has never been, and such as there shall never be: happiness and rejoicing shall be everywhere. The world shall rest from its tribulations. That shall be the peace of which the

> Apostle said: 'When tranquility shall be achieved there shall be a sudden mortality: men shall be as they were in the days of Noah, eating and drinking, and becoming betrothed: fear shall be banished from their hearts.'

For everything was far from over yet:

> In the very midst of this calm, there shall suddenly emerge from the north with Gog and Magog a nation that shall make the whole world tremble. Horrified, all men shall hide themselves in the mountains and among the rocks in order to flee their presence. They are not of the race of Japheth. The plague of the North, they shall devour human flesh and snakes, women and little children. No one shall be able to stand up against them. Seven years later, when they have taken the city of Joseph, the Lord shall send one of his princes against them, and, in a trice, shall strike them with the fire of the thunderbolt: the emperor of Greece shall come and shall rule over Jerusalem for seven years.
>
> It is then that the Son of Perdition shall appear, the Antichrist. He shall be born in Chorazin, shall be brought up at Bethsaida, and shall reign in Capernaum, as the Lord said in the Gospel: 'Woe to you, Chorazin; woe to you, Bethsaida; woe to you, Capernaum, if you are exalted to the skies, for you shall descend into hell.'
>
> Next the king of the Romans and Greeks shall go up to Golgotha, where the Lord condescended to suffer the torment of the cross for us. The king of the Romans shall take off his crown, then he shall place it on the head of Christ, shall raise his hands to Heaven, and shall give up his soul to the Lord, the king of the Christians; then shall appear the sign of the cross in Heaven; the child of perdition shall come in his turn, thinking that he is God. He shall perform a thousand miracles on earth. Through him the blind shall see, the lame shall walk, the deaf shall hear, the dead shall revive, such that, if it is possible, the elect themselves shall be deceived. He shall enter into Jerusalem, and shall seat himself in the temple as if he were the Son of God, and his heart, drunk with pride, shall forget that he is the son of a man and a woman of the tribe of Dan; deceiver and forger, he shall seduce through his miracles many credulous folk.
>
> Then God shall send two of his most faithful servants, Enoch and Elias, preserved so that they may bear witness for him against his enemy. Then the first who shall believe in Judah shall be last. Elias and Enoch shall attack him in the face of all the people, and shall convict him of imposture and falsity. The Jews of all the tribes of Israel shall then believe and shall be killed for Christ. The Antichrist, seized with rage, shall order the death of the saints of God, and of those that shall have added faith

> to their words. Then shall come the Son of God in person, our Lord Christ, carried on the clouds of heaven, surrounded by legions of angels and by celestial glory: immediately they shall put to death the Antichrist, the beast, the enemy, the seducer, and those that shall have lent him their support.
>
> This shall be the consummation of the ages, and the Judgment shall commence before thousands of angels and hundreds of thousands of archangels and seraphim. The saints, the patriarchs, the prophets, the martyrs, the confessors, the virgins and all the saints together shall be grouped around Christ. Then both the just and the sinners shall give an account of their actions in the presence of the Lord.
>
> The righteous shall be separated from the wicked. The righteous, radiant as the sun, shall follow the lamb of life and the King of heaven, whose radiance shall always be visible to them, and in whose company they shall remain for ever. The wicked shall descend into hell with the beast. The righteous shall live in eternity, and shall be endlessly glorified with the King of Heaven, while the wicked shall suffer without end. May the Lord save us from a like fate! The Lord who liveth forever and ever. Amen.[45]

This, Pseudo-Methodius's hugely influential account of the expected Apocalypse and the events leading up to it, was the overall template on which most of the rest of the *Mirabilis liber* was to be based – as, indeed, were most other religious prophecies from that time to this. Many other contributions merely served to fill in the details on particular stages of the scenario, while attempting to relate them to current religious, political and military developments. Thus, the prophecy that the *Mirabilis liber* went on to attribute to the ancient Tiburtine Sibyl (based on a Syrian text of the ninth century) was more specific about the later events mentioned by Pseudo-Methodius, but similar in tone, and many of its details were similarly to find their way into the later prophecies of the man from Provence:

> Then shall emerge from Babylon a king, a henchman of Satan who, in his infernal power, shall put the saints to death, and shall destroy the churches. There shall be many wars and tribulations. The children of Hagar [i.e. the Arabs again] shall seize Taranto, and spreading through Apulia, shall sack a host of towns. They shall be determined to enter Rome, and nobody in the world shall be able to resist them, unless it be the Lord God himself... Swarms of grasshoppers and an immense host of caterpillars shall devour all the trees and their fruits in Cappadocia and Sicily, and the people shall starve to death... There shall be earthquakes

> in divers places. The cities and provinces of the Islanders shall be swallowed up by floods. To the plague which shall devastate some places shall be joined the fury of enemies, and nothing shall be able to comfort them...

The Sibylline text went on to expand on the earlier, interpolated 'Gallic' reference:

> Then shall emerge in Gaul a king of the Greeks, Franks and Romans, of lofty stature and handsome appearance; his body and limbs shall have the most beautiful proportions; he shall reign a hundred and twelve years; he shall carry written on his forehead: 'This man, verily, is destined to avenge Christendom, snatch it away from the yoke of Ishmael, conquer it from the Saracens; none of the Saracens shall thereafter be able to reign.' Seven times over, he shall cause them the greatest ill, shall ruin their whole empire, shall strike them; after that, peace shall reign for Christians up until the time of the Antichrist.

And so, after elaborating further on Pseudo-Methodius's description of the dreaded peoples of Gog and Magog and of the Antichrist, the sibyl's account concluded with a truly dramatic depiction of the End of the World:

> On the day of judgment, the earth shall be covered with sweat; the king shall come from heaven for all eternity. He shall come in flesh and in person to judge the world. Believers or unbelievers, all shall then see the Lord in the midst of the legions of his saints who have already completed their race. All shall appear, body and soul, to be judged. Fire shall devour the land, the sea, and the sky at a single stroke. The doors of dark Avernus [Hell] shall burst. Everyone shall appear in the full light of day. Every people shall tell of deeds until then unknown; and the Lord shall bring to light the secrets of every conscience. Then shall commence the desolation and the anguish. The sun and the stars shall lose their brightness, and the moon its light. The hills shall be laid low, and the valleys raised up. There shall no longer be on earth any eminence or unevenness, for the azure waters of the sea shall roll in level with the mountaintops. All shall cease to be; the shattered earth shall perish. The waves and flames shall descend in destructive torrents, and from heaven shall suddenly come the gloomy sound of trumpets. The shattered globe, the gaping earth shall be no more than a horrible chaos, and the face of the Lord shall appear to all the kings of the earth. A rain of fire and sulfur shall descend from heaven.
>
> Then God shall judge everyone according to his works: the impious

> shall go to eternal torment, condemned forever to the flames. The just shall receive eternal life; there shall be a new heaven and a new earth that shall exist forever. The sea shall cease to be, God shall reign over the saints, and the saints shall reign with God for ever and ever, amen.[45]

Meanwhile another source, the fourteenth-century Swedish Saint Brigid, was quoted as issuing a variety of further prophecies in decidedly mysterious language that will, like much of the foregoing, be extremely familiar to connoisseurs of the later Nostradamus:

> Under the great eagle that shall nourish the fire in its breast [the Holy Roman Empire?], the Church shall be ravaged and trampled underfoot. For the Lord is capable, in his just judgments, of summoning the proud Germans against his Church in order to chastise its disobedience; and then the barque of Peter, attacked by powerful enemies, shall be shaken. Terrified, Peter [i.e. the Pope] shall be forced to flee, in order not to incur the infamy of servitude.[45]

And again:

> There shall come out of the soil of the West a lily [France?] that shall grow in an astonishing manner on virgin soil; its perfume shall absorb all poisons, its stem shall be stronger than the cedar... The lily, partner of the great eagle, shall sweep from the West to the East against the lion; the lion, defenseless, shall be overcome by the lily, which shall spread its perfume over Germany, while the eagle, in its flight, shall carry its fame afar.[45]

Such accounts – and these were merely one or two of the veritable cornucopia of prophecies contained in the *Mirabilis liber* – were nothing if not dramatic. If anything, they vastly outdid for effect even the original biblical accounts on which they were based. They supplied a wonderful background commentary on the dire developments that were currently devastating early sixteenth-century Europe, and they threatened even more and worse to come.

The result was a horrifying catalogue of war, plague, famine, fire, floods, droughts, unbearable heat, earthquakes, comets, strange celestial phenomena, wholesale deaths of livestock, virtual boilings alive of fish in the rivers and seas, plagues of grasshoppers or locusts, Muslim invasions, Christian counter-invasions, bloody oppressions, brutal occupations, religious persecutions, murders of innocents, rapes of virgins, slaughters of infants, cannibalism, sexual depravity, official corruption, priestly immorality, monkish decadence, papal treachery, the enforced flight of the Pope from Rome and, perhaps worst of all in the eyes of the contemporary religious, the desecration and destruction of holy sanctuaries and the eventual decay and collapse of the Church itself. Only rank genocide seems to have been missing from the list.

There was a problem, however. Nearly all of these absolutely seminal prophetic texts were *in Latin*. Not only that, but they were printed in inscrutable gothic script and replete with scholarly abbreviations. As a result, it was only the educated – mainly lawyers and doctors and clerics – who could even hope to understand them.

What was therefore needed now was some gifted, if adventurous, soul to tie together at last all these hopes, fears and expectations in succinct and memorable form, and in 'a language understanded of the people'. That, after all, was what the Protestants and Reformers, in their newfangled hymns and Bible translations, were already doing with the Latin texts of the Bible itself.

Cometh the hour, cometh the man...

1. The Child

IT IS A HOVEL. THERE IS NO OTHER WAY TO DESCRIBE IT. Not much bigger inside than a two-story airing cupboard, young Michel's birthplace just inside the ancient ramparts of St-Rémy-de-Provence seems quite astonishingly lowly.

True, the tumbledown frontage (recently renovated) has a few stone moldings, especially around the single window over the door. It must once have been in better repair – but it can never have been much bigger.

The rather incongruous municipal plaque over the door, illustrated on the right (and none too accurate, as we shall see), reads in English translation, 'Here was born, on 14 December 1503, Michel de Nostredame, known as Nostradamus, *astrologer*'.

It is all too easy, of course, for unsuspecting visitors to deduce that this is where the child actually grew up – grew up, that is, into a man whose influence, already great in his own lifetime, would in due course spread world-wide and last right down to our own day. If so it would have been a real story of rags to riches. Those same visitors might well smell a rat – and they would be right.

For the truth is that this was merely where his mother's parents lived. Women at the time usually went back to their mothers to have their babies, and Reynière de Saint-Rémy was no exception. As December wore on, she would have gathered together a few belongings and made her way around to her humble parental abode in what is now the Rue Hoche,[P] to be welcomed and sat in front of the fire by her mother Beatrice Tourrel. Already ensconced there, feet toasting in the hearth, would probably have been an aged, beady-eyed, black-clad figure with a long beard. Rarely moving, he would have seemed almost a fixture. When he spoke at all, it was in Provençal rather than French. He was Jean de Saint-Rémy, Béatrice's ancient father-in law. Having long since lost her husband, and he his wife, Béatrice was caring for him in his declining years as tradition required. But the old, retired doctor and town treasurer probably had less than a year to live. Indeed, winter already had him in its grip.

And so the various brothers and sister who followed would seemingly never meet him. Jehan, the first of the male siblings, didn't arrive until 1507. He would eventually go on to become a distinguished lawyer and local author, serving as attorney to the provincial parliament at Aix, a day's ride to the east. Bertrand, born perhaps a dozen years later, would become a rich merchant, landowner and captain of the local militia, and would settle down with his wife Thomine Rousse and their six children on their delightful country estate (now the Château de Roussan) on the road to Tarascon, just to the west of the town. Antoine, born in 1523, would become a lawyer and consul of St-Rémy itself and, with his wife Loyse Berle, produce no fewer than ten offspring. Then there was Pierre, and the future landowner Hector, and Louis, and apparently another Je(h)an, not to mention the determinedly virginal Delphine, possibly the eldest of all of them, who would remain an eccentric and crotchety spinster for the rest of her life, preferring to live alone rather than endure the agony of having to speak daily to her sister-in-law Loyse Berle...[42]

But live here? No, the family was not merely too numerous, but far too distinguished and energetic, ever to have tolerated being bottled up together in this dark, cramped hole. Even Jaume de Nostredame, their father, was no mere down-and-out such as the house might suggest, but a flourishing merchant of the town. The latest archival evidence suggests, in fact, that he and his family may well have lived in a rather ampler property which he is known to have owned next door.

Moreover, within a couple of years of the infant's birth he was putting his occasional brushes with the legal profession to good use by launching himself as a home-grown lawyer. For a suitable fee, or even a regular commission from the future Cardinal Alessandro Farnese – the Papal Legate at Avignon who would go on to become the notoriously nepotistic Pope Paul III, and who had a splendid residence nearby – he could be relied on to draw up handwritten legal deeds and other documents in the regulation Latin as the occasion demanded. At least one of them still exists. Now in the Nostradamus museum at Salon-de-Provence, the parchment bears at the bottom his characteristic 'seal' – a hand-drawn image of what appears to be either an ancient Hebrew altar built of stones or a typical alchemist's furnace, with a cross and the keys of St Peter growing out of the receptacle on the top of it, and inscribed at the base with the name *Ja. de nostradomin*. And alongside it a large, florid 'A', the first letter of his typical signing-off piece: *A me Jacobo de nostra domina...* – or 'By me, James of Our Lady...'[P]

The name is a curiosity. For it was not the family's original name. The records show a succession of surnames that sound ever stranger and more alien as they stretch back closer and closer towards the Spanish frontier. None of them bears any relation to the name 'Our Lady'. But then surnames were in any case something of a novelty at the time. People were commonly named after the place where they lived (take the Saint-Rémys themselves, for example), or after some distinguishing personal characteristic – in which case their names were *literally* 'surnames', or nicknames. And so there had apparently been an Astruge de Carcassonne, followed two generations later by an Arnauton de Velorgues, who, at Avignon, had married a Venguessonne – presumably the daughter or former wife of one Venguesson, or Ben Guesson.

And all of them were Jews.

Conceivably, then, they had been among the so-called *Marranos* (so-called because the word, ironically, meant 'pigs'). These were Spanish Jews who for at least a century had been either persecuted or forced in their tens of thousands either to flee abroad or ostensibly to convert to Christianity while continuing to pursue their ancestral religion in secret. Somehow managing to survive in this way, many of those who stayed had grown rich, and even intermarried with the Spanish nobility. But in 1473 violent riots against them broke out in Cordoba, and quickly spread to other cities. Soon the Inquisition was joining in, allegedly burning them in their hundreds. Thousands, too, were massacred by the mobs. And eventually, on 31 March 1492 – the self-same year when Columbus at last set out for America – the survivors were finally expelled from Spain by royal edict. Similar edicts quickly followed in Portugal and Navarre. Even as they fled, however, they continued, like those who had already moved abroad, to follow their ancestral religion and to preserve it in their new homelands.

Could this, then, be why the later Nostradamus would write so sympathetically, if secretively, of what he expected to be the eventual triumph of what he called the *religion du nom des mers*, or 'religion named after the seas'?[55a] Could this be a word-play on the fact that between the sound of French *marins* (sailors) and Spanish *Marranos* there was not a lot of difference? For him, after all, such word-plays were to become meat and drink. And meanwhile could 'Venguessonne' (i.e. 'Ben Guesson') originally have been some such Spanish-Jewish name as *Ben Guason*, 'Son of the Wit', or 'Son of the Joker', perhaps – a 'Joker' who was himself known to his friends as *El Guason*? And could this in turn have been why Arnauton's son had been called Guy *Gassonet* – or 'Little Gasson'?

Nobody can be sure. But that, certainly had been the original name of the infant Michel's paternal grandfather, a grain-merchant and money-lender of Avignon (by the look of it, then, a descendant of the first wave of *Marrano* refugees). But then, in response to yet further anti-Jewish edicts, he had been forced to convert and take a new, 'Christian' name in around 1455. He was not alone in this. At nearby Carpentras, whose ancient synagogue still stands and whose Jewish cemetery (only recently desecrated) is the oldest in France, the former cathedral of St-Siffren preserves to this day the name *la Porte des Juifs*, and features the statue of a standing Christ welcoming the Hebrew converts with open arms...

So it was, then, that Guy Gassonnet, perhaps taking his new 'Christian' name from that of the presiding bishop and his 'surname' from the saint whose day it was, had suddenly become first 'Pierre de Sainte Marie', then 'Pierre de Nostredame'. And at the same time, his new third wife (he had legally repudiated his second, Jewish one when she refused to convert) had insisted on continuing to call herself 'Blanche de Sainte Marie'.

Evidently, then, the women of the future prophet's family were nothing if not strong-willed...

In due course the name – together with its Latin form, *de nostra domina* – was inherited in turn by Pierre's son Jaume, who (as we have seen) would duly inscribe it on his handwritten 'seal'. In this way it reflected with wonderful aptness the symbols of Christian truth growing triumphantly out of the melting pot of ancient Jewry and medieval alchemy. And so it was, too, that *his* eldest son, the religiously-inclined and someday-to-be-famous Michel, would grow up signing himself, in similar Latin style, *Michaletus de nostra domina*, or 'Mickey of Our Lady'.

For just as Latin was the universal language of religion and the law, so it was the language of learning, too. And never was it more appropriate than now.

For this, as we noted in our Introduction, was the time of the French Renaissance. Thanks largely to the advance of the Turkish Ottomans into Europe and their capture of Constantinople in 1453, Italy in particular had suddenly been overwhelmed with a flood of fleeing Greek scholars from the east. These had borne with them whole libraries of precious manuscripts that bore witness to the glories of ancient Greek and Roman art, science and scholarship – glories of culture that for centuries had been all but forgotten in the West. This was a positive revelation. Suddenly medieval Western Europeans were faced with the dizzying realization that there had once been a positive golden age on earth – even if they too easily overlooked the fact that it had been only for a privileged few. Surely, then, what had been achieved once could be achieved again? All that was needed, presumably, was sufficient human will and effort, and humanity could, in the words of Petrarch, 'walk back into the pure radiance of the past'.

But what kind of effort? Basically, the effort of deliberate imitation. And so Latin in particular – which had never ceased to be the medium of communication in religious and scholarly circles – must be studied with new fervor. Greek and Roman literature must be drummed into the young, classical styles of art and architecture (and even of entertainment) must be revived, classical medicine rediscovered, classical astronomy re-explored and re-applied, classical mythology resurrected, classical history studied as though it had happened only yesterday. Writers such as Homer and Herodotus, Hippocrates and Galen, Virgil and Horace, Ovid and Cicero, Seneca and Livy, Pliny and Suetonius, Plutarch and Tacitus became the veritable men of the moment, whom not to know was ignorance indeed.

Thus, when the young Michel started his education, if not at the feet of old Jean de Saint-Rémy, possibly at his father's – given the absence of definite information, the various accounts differ over this – we may be sure that these were among the major stars in his firmament, not least because they would constantly resurface in his later writings. And not only would he have been taught Latin and perhaps some Greek, but astrology, too (though whether the lad's actual application to the subject ever measured up to his enthusiasm for it may, as we shall see, be doubted), for we know that, long after his aged great-grandfather's death, Michel still treasured the astrolabe that he had inherited from him,[3a, 21a] while happily giving away the one that would later be presented to him by the Governor of Provence.[3b, 21b] Indeed, when death eventually came for him in turn, he likewise would pass on the precious instrument to his own son César.[41a]

But, for the growing Michel, an even more direct and vivid form of classical education lay close at hand. Only a few hundred yards to the south of St-Rémy, just to the left of the road leading up into the low, balding limestone range of local mountains known as the Alpilles, stood an ancient Augustinian priory[P] that would at some point be taken over by the Franciscans. It was known as St-Paul-de-Mausole, or 'St Paul of the Mausoleum'.[42a] It was so called because just opposite it stood two actual Roman monuments in a remarkable state of preservation. One of them was the massive ceremonial town gate of the long-since ruined Graeco-Roman city of Glanum. The other was a towering edifice that was, as the name implied, a mausoleum.[P]

There can be no doubt at all that the young Michel spent many days of his youth exploring the site during the years before he finally left his hometown, for he would constantly refer back to it in his writings. And with good reason. For here was concrete evidence, if evidence was

Glanum: relief panel on the mausoleum of the Julii

needed, that the Romans had been real people, that their achievements had been real achievements – and larger-than-life ones, too. Merely to be in the presence of these mighty monuments was to imbibe something of the aura of those glorious ancient times of which others could only speak and write. Merely to play in the shadow of the arch, or to chase his friends around the mausoleum, was to bathe directly in the overpowering aura of a race of giants.

Sculpted into the corners of the arch were groups of dejected-looking prisoners surmounted by victory-trophies. Around the arch itself ran exquisite friezes of fruit and flowers, and its ceiling was decorated with a marvelously preserved hexagonal motif. But it was the mausoleum itself that was the real marvel. Tall, four-square, and almost as pristine as on the day when it was built long ago during the reign of the Emperor Augustus, it bore around its base four huge, sculptured panels showing scenes of battle and of the hunt. Above them, four massive arches carried a frieze with a maritime theme. Above that again, a cage of classical columns surmounted by a cupola contained two life-sized human figures representing the parents whom their sons Sextus, Lucius and Marcus had so lovingly commemorated here all those years ago.

Of particular delight to the budding young scholar in his breeches, jaunty cap and short gown, though, was the inscription just above its decorated north arch:

SEX.L.M.IULIEI.C.F.PARENTIBUS.SUEIS

or 'Sextus, Lucius, Marcus, sons of Caius Julius, to their parents'.[P] Whether the fact bears witness to the boy's somewhat facetious sense of humor or not, he would refer for ever after to the 'arch of SEX'[52b] – thereby revealing at the same time that his memory was none too clear as to which building the inscription was actually on. This extraordinary mental vagueness was to accompany him for the rest of his life – but, paradoxically, it was also to serve him in good stead when, as we shall see, it came to writing his future prophecies.

At all events, both this part of the site and his memory of it would still be very much in his mind when, some forty years later, he would sign off the *Proem* to his popular medical cookbook with the rather surprising words: *Toy disan à Dieu, de Saint-Remy-de-Provence, dite Sextrophea*[57a], or, literally, 'Bidding you adieu from St-Rémy-de-Provence, called Six-Monuments'. It would still be there, too, when in 1555, he referred to this self-same mausoleum as the *temple d'Artemide,*[52b] so revealing to anybody who cared to know it that he was perfectly well aware of the origin of the world 'mausoleum'. For the very first 'mausoleum', long known as one of the Seven Wonders of the World, had been built by Queen *Artemisia* of Caria in 353 BC as a tomb and memorial for her dead husband King *Mausolus*.

But then such academic showing-off, combined with a pronounced taste for word-play, was very much a characteristic of the age.

However, the youngster had not finished with Glanum yet – or rather *it* had not yet finished with *him*. Just across the road, he had only to follow the south wall of the monks' enclosure for a few hundred yards to reach the vast, sunken wilderness which was all that now remained of the city's ancient stone quarry. Perhaps, indeed, it was the Brothers themselves who befriended him and guided him to it. Once he had pushed his way into it through the undergrowth, or climbed down the precipices that surrounded it, he would have found himself hemmed in on almost all sides by mighty cliffs, at the foot of which dark, man-made galleries led yet further into the underworld.[P] From their echoing depths indescribable smells emerged – for these caves were nowadays used for shelter by goatherds and their animals. Meanwhile, at the very center of the quarry, an extraordinary, isolated pinnacle of rock (evidently left by the Romans as a last refuge for the genius of the place, rather like the last swathe of corn in a harvest field) still marked the various levels from which the stones of the city had been quarried. *La Pyramide*, the locals called it[P] – possibly from some such expression as *La pierre-en-mi* ('the rock in the middle') – and so, consequently, did Nostradamus.[52b] But then he would also refer in his later *Propheties* not merely to the various features of the site in general,[53a, 53b] but even to the *caverne caprine* or 'goat cave' itself.[55b]

But if the quarry, what of the city itself? Only a little more southward clambering, after all, would have brought the young Nostredame to the edge of the sheltered valley where ancient Glanum had once lived and flourished. It had long since collapsed into ruins, of course,[P] and most of its lower parts had become buried under the silt washed down from the valley sides by the rains of centuries. But here and there, possibly, some ancient piece of quarried stone still poked out of the dirt or nestled half hidden among the scrub, especially on the upper slopes. A piece of ruined aqueduct, a tumbled column drum from some former temple or public building, the odd ancient tombstone with the obligatory letters *D.M.* (*Dis manibus*, or 'Into the hands of Pluto', god of the underworld) carved near the top of it,[P] or even one of the many altars to Hercules, who seemed to have been one of the prime gods of the place...[P]

Certainly the future seer would mention the discovery of a tombstone bearing the inscription 'D.M.', accompanied by suggestions of yet-to-be-discovered buried treasure,[55c] in his *Propheties* – which would also go on to contain yet other suggestions of unsuspected riches at Glanum.[53b] He would mention Hercules constantly, whether in his Roman incarnation[52c, 53c, 55d] or in his Gallic one as *Ogmion*.[53d, 55e] He would also mention the oddly-shaped mountain known as the *Mont Gaussier* that overlooked the city, and that the later Vincent Van Gogh would one day feel moved to paint.[53a] Yet the main 'buried treasure' for the young Michel was undoubtedly the site itself and all that it symbolized for him. Here, after all, was the former age of Greece and Rome writ large – not merely inscribed in the pages of some old and dusty tome, but real, solid, almost alive.

But Hercules – what on earth was *he* doing here? Far from being either solid or alive, he, surely, was just a myth?

The question no doubt continued to revolve in his mind as he trotted happily and full of enthusiasm back down the hill and through the town gate into St-Rémy, forgetting completely to brush the dust off his breeches before bursting in at the front door. And had he raised the subject with his father, as he undoubtedly did, Jaume would have told him a curious story...

Only a mile or two to the west of the *Antiques*, as the then-visible ruins of Glanum were (and still are) known, a parallel but quite different route, entirely unsuitable for children, led from St-Rémy up into the rocky fastnesses and bleached precipices of the Alpilles. Tortuous, even terrifying, and known to this day as the *Val d'Enfer*, or 'Valley of Hell', this narrow trackway, flanked by menacing cliffs and forbidding caves haunted only by goat-herds and God knew what else, snaked its way up into the mountains until it was weaving its way among the peaks themselves. Barely had it started to descend again after reaching the summit pass, when it brought the traveler to the gates of the formidable rock-fortress of Les Baux, long renowned as one of the great courts of love frequented by the thirteenth-century Troubadours. And from this point an incredible vista stretched away southwards all the way to the Mediterranean coast – a vista over a vast and salty plain that

The rock-hewn fortress of Les Baux

was remarkable chiefly for the fact that it was covered almost entirely with *large pebbles*.

The story went that the mighty hero Herakles (Hercules' former Greek incarnation) had been on his way back from his Tenth Labor of rustling the cattle of King Geryon of Tartessos, hard by the straits of Gibraltar (where Herakles had, of course, set up the celebrated 'Pillars of Herakles', including the Rock of Gibraltar, to guard the entrance to the Mediterranean), when he had been ambushed here amid this marshy wilderness by the local Ligurian tribes. Soon he had run out of arrows to defend himself with and so, finding nothing beneath his feet but soft ground, he had knelt down in tears (whence, of course, the salt!) to implore the aid of his father Zeus. Zeus, taking pity on him, had called up a storm out of which a shower of stones had promptly pelted down. With these, Herakles had finally managed to put his enemies to flight.

And the result was what the Greeks had called the 'stony plain', and what the sixteenth-century inhabitants of Provence knew as the desert of the *Craux* (from Latin *gravidus*, 'loaded, burdened').[P]

No more than the ancient Greeks, of course, did Jaume or anybody else know the real reason for the huge expanse of stones, which it would take much later geologists to unravel. The idea that the river Durance might once have flowed southward through the Lamanon gap and, skirting Salon to the west, have emptied into the sea via what was now the Étang de Berre would never have occurred to him (see Frontispiece). The idea that the river subsequently changed its mind and decided to flow westwards to empty itself into the Rhône at Avignon instead, leaving behind it, strewn across the plain, the vast cargo of pebbles that for millennia it had been wrenching from the very heart of the distant Alps, would have seemed to him frankly bizarre. Even more bizarre, however, would have been the idea that his young son might one day have a considerable hand in helping at least partially to reverse the effects of that ancient disaster...

But such developments would be for a long time in the future. First, the young boy had to complete his basic education. Then he would have to go to college.

2. *The Herbalist*

GOING TO COLLEGE AT SIXTEEN was not particularly unusual at the time. Life expectancy in the sixteenth century was not so high as to encourage putting off anything important longer than it needed to be. Nor was it at all surprising that a bright, well-off boy from St-Rémy should attend university at Avignon.

Contemporary Avignon was celebrated not so much for the Pont St-Bénézet that has since become so famous in song as the 'bridge of Avignon', as for its strong papal connections. Ever since the great Western Church Schism of the fourteenth century, when rival Italian and French popes had reigned in Rome and Avignon, the huge, fortified papal palace had dominated the city from its lofty height as though determined to crush the whole region underfoot.[P] The Popes had also thrown strong fortifications around the growing city. Yet inside its walls the atmosphere was curiously cosmopolitan and easy-going. Jews were tolerated and protected, provided that they wore yellow hats and badges, paid certain dues, attended obligatory Christian sermons and restricted their activities to tailoring, commerce, second-hand dealing and money-lending. Others milled freely about its narrow streets, too – foreigners, artists, students, pilgrims, penitents, sellers of indulgences, barrow-boys, litigants, political refugees, adventurers, outlaws, smugglers, counterfeiters... In consequence, the Italian poet Petrarch, himself one of the political refugees, had described the place as 'the Babylon of the West' – not merely because, like the original Babylon, it had ruled over a land of two rivers (the Rhône and the Durance), but also because of its flagrant immorality, hedonism and corruption. It was, he had written, 'a sewer where all the filth of the world comes together'.

Even when supreme Church power had returned to Rome in 1378, Avignon's power had remained considerable. Now ruled over by a Vatican legate, it remained the capital of a papal enclave with laws and dispensations of its own. It had a growing printing industry. And it had a huge university, which since 1511 had even had its own medical faculty.

Since the diocese of Avignon included St-Rémy, it was therefore to this major seat of learning that young Nostredame was duly packed off in the fifth year of the reign of King François. It is unlikely, though, that he actually studied medicine there. The normal procedure was for undergraduate students to follow the standard curriculum made up of the *trivium* (whose 'trivia' were routinely made up of grammar, rhetoric and logic) followed by the *quadrivium*, comprising geometry, arithmetic, music and astronomy. Given that virtually no real astronomy had been done in the non-Arab world since classical times, this last was all but indistinguishable from astrology. 'Astronomy' was simply the name for the general body of knowledge inherited from the ancients, and particularly from the second-century Egyptian astronomer Claudius Ptolemy: 'astrology' was the interpretation and application of it in terms of alleged planetary 'influences' on terrestrial events.

We do not know how well Michel did at his studies. All we have is an apocryphal report that he had a good memory and was a cheerful and witty student, if also a caustic and facetious one.[12] He was also reputed to be keen on astrology. However, the signs are that he never even got to that part of the curriculum. Late in 1520 the Plague struck, as it regularly did at the time, forcing the university to close its doors. Bearing what few possessions they had, the students fled into the countryside. Whether they were hurriedly awarded the degrees towards which they had been working is not known.

Consequently the semi-qualified Michel was now out on his own, and decided to make the best of the situation. Certainly he never attempted to return. Instead, as he would later write, he

> ... spent most of my young years from the year 1521 to the year 1529, O KINDLY READER, on pharmaceutics and the knowledge and study of natural remedies across various lands and countries, constantly on the move to hear and find out the source and origin of plants and other natural remedies involved in the purposes of the healing art.[57a]

Typical of the man's prose style, this was rather a lot of words for something quite simple. Moreover, by a possibly Freudian error, the original text actually said *planetes* (planets) instead of *plantes* (plants). What it clearly meant, though, was that he had become a wandering student –

and later, as we shall see, a peddler – of herbal remedies, constantly on the lookout for new cures to add to his repertoire.

But where had this evident zest for herbal healing come from, and which were the 'lands and countries' through which it took him?

To the first question, most of the proposed answers center around old Jean de Saint-Rémy, who must have picked up at the very least a traditional folk-remedy or two during his long years as a local physician. To the second, a whole raft of areas have been proposed, though the south-west of France – from Narbonne, through Carcassonne and Toulouse, to Bordeaux – is generally thought to have been his most likely stamping-ground.

But of course a lot can happen in eight years – and a lot did. For a start, this was the great age of world exploration. Granted, Columbus was already dead, and Vasco da Gama on his last legs. But it was in 1521 that the Spanish adventurer Hernando Cortés finally succeeded in capturing what was to become Mexico City amid a welter of native blood, and Ferdinand Magellan, in the midst of his attempt to circumnavigate the globe for the first time, was killed by natives in the Philippines. 1522 saw the return of his last surviving ship to Seville. Within a couple of years Francisco Pizarro in turn was starting out on the first of his rampages of exploration and bloody conquest down the north-west coast of South America.

Some of these developments were, with hindsight, already dire enough, but at home it was clear that even worse things were happening. There was of course the Plague itself, which made its usual periodic devastating inroads, especially across the south of the country. Then there was the awful winter of 1523, a dreadful harbinger of the Little Ice Age that was even then tightening its grip on Europe and leading to failed harvests, widespread starvation and the desertion of the land by the peasants in favor of the already overcrowded, plague-ridden towns and cities. On the religious front, there was the excommunication of Martin Luther and the 1521 condemnation by the Sorbonne in Paris of the ninety-five theses that he had so famously nailed to the church door at Wittenberg in 1517 – the first act in a long religious conflict that would eventually bring terrible death and destruction right across France. In the same year, too, there was the death of the great Medici Pope Leo X – the patron *par excellence* of Renaissance art and letters – and in 1523 that of his immediate successor, too. Meanwhile all attempts to reconcile Catholics and the newly dubbed 'Protestants' in

France were finally scotched by the French parliament in 1525.

But to this dire mix of pestilence, starvation and religious upheaval yet more ghastly ingredients were steadily being added. Abroad, the marauding Turkish forces of Suleiman the Magnificent, who had just succeeded to the Ottoman throne, overwhelmed Belgrade in 1521. The following year saw the capture of the island of Rhodes by the Ottomans, who in 1526 went on first to defeat the Hungarian Christian army at the battle of Mohacs, then to sack Budapest. By 1527 Suleiman had moved yet further west, and was laying siege to Vienna itself.

Meanwhile the coronation of the Holy Roman Emperor Charles V in 1520 had led to the first of a series of wars between France and the Empire the following year, with huge taxes being levied to pay for it by the affronted King François, who had wanted the Imperial crown for himself. In 1522, in the course of it, France lost most of its possessions in Italy, while Henry VIII of England declared war on it from the north, and the strangely named and somewhat bone-headed young Anne de Montmorency, Lord of Les Baux and a major future player on the political, religious and military fronts, was appointed Marshal of France. In 1524 the former Lord Constable, Charles de Bourbon, who had defected to the Empire in a fit of pique when he was not allowed to inherit his dead wife's lands, invaded the south-east of France from Italy on its behalf, taking Aix-en-Provence and very nearly Marseille too. In 1527 he went on to sack Rome itself, with the Pope a virtual prisoner in the Castel Sant'Angelo. Worst of all, at the disastrous battle of Pavia of 1525, King François himself was captured in the course of a foolish piece of military bravado and carted off to exile in Madrid, not returning until March the following year after a huge ransom had been paid that almost ruined the country – and after his two sons (the younger of them the future Henri II) had been detained as hostages into the bargain.

Not merely pestilence, starvation and religious upheaval, then, but murderous military threats, widespread slaughter abroad, national defeat, royal disgrace and imprisonment, financial near-ruin and the sacking of the Vatican itself: it was an extraordinary and worrying time for a young man to be alive, let alone starting out on his career. With the traditional Four Horsemen of the Apocalypse – War, Pestilence, Famine and Death – all very much in evidence, people could be excused for assuming that the End of the World must finally be at hand...

But just how much of all this tumultuous series of events did the wandering Michel de Nostredame know about? The answer is probably

'A very great deal'. He was, after all, one of a vast army of regular travelers swarming all over the countryside – peddlers, mountebanks, merchants, couriers, students, pilgrims – who were, in effect, the only news media of the day. True, they were only the *un*official grapevine – but since there was no official one, what they didn't know probably wasn't worth knowing, even though it took at least a month or two for news to arrive along non-existent roads and boggy dirt-tracks from other parts of Europe, let alone from further afield.

One piece of apocalyptic news, however, Nostredame knew all about well in advance, as did everybody else – and it was so overwhelming as to put all the others in the shade. It was that there was to be an ominous major line-up of all the known planets in the sign of Pisces between 13 and 25 February, 1524. Even the full moon would be in alignment on 19 February, if on the other side of the earth. There could be no doubt about it. Countless astrologers had calculated it. Over 130 books and pamphlets had been published about it in Europe, many of them lavishly provided with astrological diagrams, confirmatory biblical quotations, poems and lurid woodcuts designed specifically to alarm the credulous.[8] Now the End-of-the-Worlders could *really* give free reign to their imaginations.

In his *Almanach noua* for 1524 in particular, the well-known astrologer Johannes Stöffler had written:

> This year we shall see no eclipse either of Sun or Moon. But in the current year the dispositions of the planets shall be most worthy of astonishment: for in the month of February, 20 conjunctions, from the least to the most ordinary, shall befall, of which 16 shall occupy a Water sign. The which shall signify for the whole world, for regions, kingdoms, provinces, states and conditions, together with brute beasts and sea monsters and whatever be born on earth, an indubitable change, variation and alteration, such indeed as we have barely seen for many generations from our historians or forebears. Therefore lift up your heads, O Most Christian men![8a]

This last expression particularly seemed to suggest that something truly apocalyptic was at hand, if not the End of the World itself, and the reference to Water signs suggested that, like that of Noah, it would be by flood. Many of the other publications affirmed the point specifically. And at the time the dreaded word 'change', so often used by the astrologers, was taken to imply the overthrow of the existing order.

It had long been anticipated. Even Chaucer's notorious *Miller's Tale* of well over a century earlier seems to have referred in advance to the occasion, in the course of its racy tale of the astrologically minded student Nicholas and the gullible carpenter whom he persuades to build three mini-arks against the dreadful day:

> 'Now John,' quod Nicholas, 'I wol nat lye:
> I have y-founde in myn astrologye,
> As I have loked in the mone bright,
> That now, a Monday next, at quarter-night
> Shall fall a reyn, and that so wilde and wood
> That half so greet was never Noës flood.
> This world,' he seyde, 'in lasse than in an hour
> Shal al be dreynt, so hidous is the shour.
> Thus shal mankynde drenche and lese her lyf.'

And thereby (to coin a phrase) hangs a tale…

But what of the young Nostredame? Rebel that he seems to have been by instinct, did he accept the general view? We have no direct evidence on this. But his later activities and attitudes suggest a very different response. We know, for example, that he had long since developed a passion for reading every learned tome he could lay his hands on – books on astrology, on medicine, on history – and not least the recently reprinted medieval chronicles.[60] He would thus have known that this was far from the first time that the planets had lined up in this way. Merely from the astrological works of Abraham ibn Ezra (whom the French preferred to call Avenezra) he would have known that an almost identical line-up of planets had occurred in Libra in September 1186. And from the chronicles he would also have discovered that absolutely nothing of note had happened in that year.

But if nothing in particular had happened before, why should it this time either? The very Renaissance itself, after all, was based on the idea of history repeating itself, of the past being resurrected anew. What, then, if the principle were a universal one, and the future could simply be predicted on the basis of past events? What if King Solomon had been right when, in the book of Ecclesiastes, he had written:

> To everything its season, and to every activity under heaven its time…
> Whatever is has already been, and whatever shall be has already been, and God recalls each event in its turn.

With this decisive scriptural backing, then, it seems quite likely that the wandering herbalist stuck his brash young neck out of his fashionable collar and doublet and came right out with it. 'Calm down,' we can imagine him saying, 'nothing is going to happen.' The *Mirabilis liber*,[45] after all – the dramatic new anthology of ancient, Bible-based prophecies whose Latin he at least could understand – made it perfectly clear that a very great deal had to happen before the End of the World could dawn...

No doubt the people around him were incredulous. Probably they accused him of being off his rocker. Possibly they even branded him some kind of agent of the Devil. 'But everybody knows,' they would have protested, 'that the stars are presaging the imminent End of the World. All the great astrologers are saying so. Who are you to deny it?'

Nostredame no doubt reflected that he was somebody who knew that what 'everybody knows' wasn't always either factual or truthful. Like most intellectuals of the day, he had a healthy contempt for popular culture. As he would later write quite openly and publicly – and with a hint of long-suppressed rage and frustration:[57b]

> Here where I am resident, I am living... among brute animals and barbarous folk, the mortal enemies of all good learning and worthwhile scholarship.

But he held his tongue and bided his time, however difficult it proved. It was safer, after all.

And so preparations duly began. By 24 January 1524, when the planet Mars was already joining Jupiter and Saturn in Pisces, thousands of people were fleeing the cities for higher ground. By the time Venus also joined in on 2 February, the first of some 20,000 Londoners were starting to imitate the Prior of St Bartholomew's and head for areas such as Harrow-on-the-Hill – though they were of course unable to join him in the secure fortress that he was just then in the process of stocking up with essential supplies for his own exclusive survival. In Toulouse, a local inhabitant was putting the final touches to a biblical ark. In Germany, it is reported that one Count von Igelheim was doing the same. In his case it was a magnificent, three-storied affair. All over Europe, others were preparing their own rather less ostentatious boats and water-borne contraptions.

On 10 February the sun, too, joined the celestial line-up, followed only two days later by Mercury. Now the fat was really in the fire. No fewer then seven planets (including, as current tradition maintained, the sun and moon) were evidently plotting the downfall of humanity. Quite what everybody would have done, had they realized that, in addition, the yet-to-be-discovered planet of Neptune (a watery giant if ever there was one!) had also been there in Pisces all along, only waiting for the rest to join it, hardly bears thinking about.

As 20 February loomed, tension mounted. In Germany, the Elector of Brandenburg hurriedly made for the nearest mountain-top. As the sun, Mercury, Jupiter and Saturn all took up station within around four degrees of each other, and Mars and Venus became similarly locked together less than ten degrees away in the same sign, people held their breaths. Not that anybody could actually *see* the planets in question. Since they included the sun, and were thus (with the exception of the moon) overhead at noon, all except the sun itself were completely invisible. But the astrological charts said that that was where they were, and the astrologers had predicted the inevitable result. People duly stepped aboard their makeshift craft, or hovered anxiously nearby, oars or paddles at the ready.

The moment came – and went. And nothing whatever happened.

No doubt it rained somewhere. No doubt somebody's cat was sick. No doubt somebody's grandmother dropped dead – from sheer excitement, if nothing else. But otherwise everything carried on exactly as before. People started to breathe again, ignoring the hurriedly revised protestations of the astrologers that they wouldn't be safe for another hundred days at least. Nostredame must have felt pleased with himself. People no doubt slapped him on the back, congratulated him and told him they had of course believed him all along. For others around him, it was almost as if he personally had been responsible for humanity's unexpected salvation, and so should be regarded with awe as one who had the gift of prophecy. Perhaps he was even convinced. Certainly, once such convictions have taken hold, they are usually there for life...

And probably nobody even recalled the great scare of 1524 when, almost exactly a year later, at the disastrous battle of Pavia, King François was captured, and almost the entire flower of French chivalry slain.

Or possibly Michel de Nostredame did. Possibly he reflected that the great conjunction had, after all, produced a result. Possibly he rechecked the history-books and was astonished to discover that the 1186 alignment, too, had been followed only two years later by the destruction by Saladin of the Frankish crusader kingdoms in the Middle East.

And perhaps the germ of an idea was thus planted in his mind – the idea that, by referring back to history and applying the principles of simple astrology (albeit with a certain amount of in-built delay), it might one day be possible not only to predict the entire future of humanity on the basis of celebrated collections of prophecies such as the *Mirabilis liber*,[45] but even to calculate the dates of individual events and developments within it...

3. The Apothecary

THERE WAS AN OLD TRADITION IN PROVENCE that a married son could, on reaching the age of 25, claim his share of the paternal inheritance even while his father was still alive.[42] In Nostredame's case that might not have amounted to very much, given the number of his brothers and sisters. Besides, so far as we know he was not yet married. Yet somehow or other he seems to have come into some money at this point in his life. For on 3 October 1529 he paid his subscription to be enrolled in the student body of the Medical Faculty at Montpellier, and on 23 October enrolled in the Faculty itself to study for his medical doctorate.

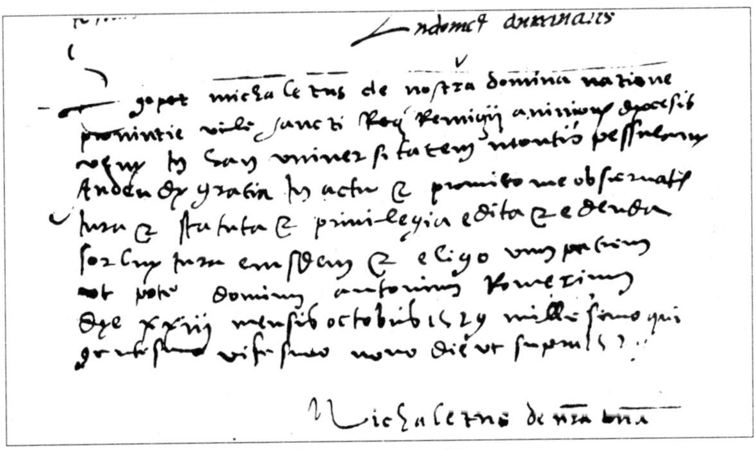

Nostradamus's handwritten enrolment at Montpellier

His chaotic handwritten Latin enrolment, complete with errors and abbreviations, still exists in the Faculty library. In translation it reads:

> I, Mickey of Our Lady of the nation of Provence, of the town of St-Rémy, of the diocese of Avignon, have come to this university of Montpellier to

> study in its jurisdiction by the grace of God and promise to observe the laws and statutes and ordinances both laid down and to be laid down; I have paid its dues and choose one Antonio Romerio as my patron, so far as is possible, on the 23rd day of the month of October 1529, the one thousand five hundred and twenty-ninth, on the day as above, 1529.
>
> Michaletus de nsa dma

The reason for the evident schoolboy flannel – and especially for the ludicrous piece of gobbledygook at the end – is unknown. But it looks rather as if, on enrolment, freshmen were expected to compose a piece of some sixty words of their own invention, perhaps to test how literate they were in Latin. If so, Nostredame can barely have passed. Certainly, when the 35-year-old classical scholar and renegade monk François Rabelais[P] enrolled there the following year, his piece was of similar length, but much more controlled and literary:

> I, François Rabelais of Chinon, in the diocese of Tours, have come here for the sake of medical studies, and I have chosen as my patron the distinguished Master Jean Schyron, doctor and regent of this venerable university. I promise, moreover, to observe whatever is laid down in the said Medical Faculty and observed by those who give their name in good faith, having sworn on oath as is the custom. I append my name with my own hand on the seventeenth day of the month of September in the Year of Our Lord fifteen-thirty.
>
> Rabelaesus

An entry in the margin reads 'Paid 3 pounds' (around $90 today).

But these two future contrasting giants of the age were seemingly never to meet at Montpellier. The reason stares vividly out at us from the page of the *liber scolasticorum* on which Nostredame had originally inscribed his name for enrolment in the student body. Angrily, the student registrar, Guillaume Rondelet, has scratched out his entry, adding in the margin:

> He whom you here see crossed out – mark well, reader – has been an apothecary or quack. We have established this through Chante., an apothecary of this city, and through the students who have heard him speak ill of doctors. Wherefore as laid down by statute I have been enjoined to strike him out from the book of students.
>
> Guillelmus Rondelletus registrar

Worse, there is absolutely no record of his re-admission.

Evidently young Michel had been as controversial as ever. Vastly over-confident, he had poked fun at the revered members of the very profession that he was trying to join. Disaster had been the inevitable result. He was out on his ear.

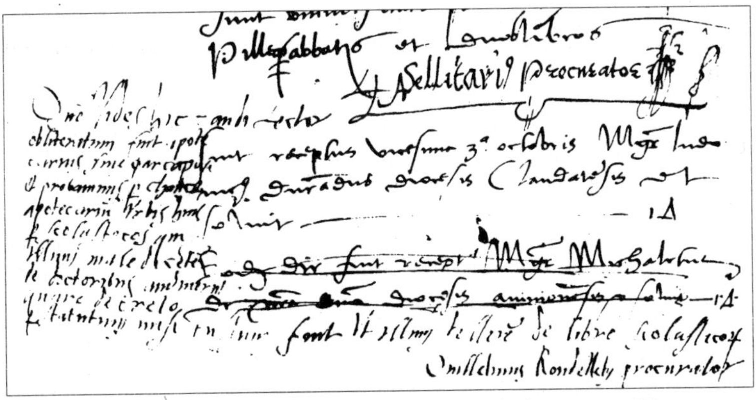

Nostradamus's handwritten expulsion from the student body at Montpellier

Rabelais' baccalaureate is duly recorded for 1531, and his doctorate (following a spell of absence) for 1537. But for Nostredame there is no such record, either here or at any other known medical faculty. Moreover, whereas Rabelais (when he wasn't writing rumbustious, risqué novels under the anagrammatical pseudonym 'Alcofribas Nasier') would constantly sign himself as a doctor from then on, Nostredame seems never to have done so. Suitably red-robed as Rabelais appears in his official portrait,[P] Nostredame (of whom no official portrait or other memorial exists at Montpellier) would later be painted by his own son César merely in humble black.[P] So it is difficult to avoid the conclusion that he never in fact obtained his doctorate at all.[38a]

And so the young Nostredame, expelled from his would-be *alma mater*, was left to wander the highways and byways of Europe, still as an apothecary – or, at best, as a simple physician or medico – seeking an appointment here, a position there, as chance befell, and always on the lookout for new remedies. As he would frankly admit much later:

> When I finally reached the end of my eight years, I found myself unable perfectly to attain the summit of the supreme doctrine [of medicine], and so I did what the one who represented the summit of the Latin tongue said: *Et egressus sylvis vicina coegi*, and proceeded to complete my studies up to the present time, which is the thirty-first year of my profession, which we know as 1552.[57a]

The Latin expression, taken from the celebrated *Aeneid* of Nostradamus's favourite Roman poet Virgil, means (at least as re-applied by Nostredame to his own context): 'And having got out of the woods, I collected whatever I found around me.' And curiously enough, it mirrors almost exactly what another great healer of the time would write:

> The universities do not teach everything, so a doctor must seek out old wives, gypsies, magicians, wandering tribes, former brigands and similar outlaws, and learn from them. A doctor must be a traveler.

Indeed, in this he in turn was merely echoing the famous comment by Hippocrates, the ancient Greek 'father of medicine', that every young physician, once having qualified, should first set out to travel from town to town in order to become 'not merely a physician in name, but a physician in deed.'

Even more curiously, it was in that very same year – 1529 – that that other prominent healer of the time took his own advice and set out to wander the roads of Europe as a physician and apothecary. But then, at 36, Theophrastus Bombastus von Hohenheim (he must have been a noisy child!) had already acquired Europe-wide fame as a chemist and physician. He had even been appointed lecturer in medicine at Basel in Switzerland on the strength of it, notwithstanding his apparent lack of a doctorate – at least until he scandalously threw open his lectures to all and burned the almost 'sacred' medical textbooks of Avicenna and Galen in front of the very university itself. At some point, indeed, his subsequent journeys, it is said, even took him through Montpellier.

Yet his path and Nostredame's never crossed, or the Frenchman, who could never resist the temptation to drop the names of famous people he had met, would have mentioned the fact. Nowhere in his writings, in fact, does the name 'Paracelsus' ('Greater than Celsus') occur at all.

Which is odd, for their approaches were strikingly similar. Both valued ancient folk remedies at least as highly as the currently approved medical practices. Both traveled widely in search of medical knowledge. And just as the irrepressible, erratic Paracelsus had spent much of his youth seeking out famous teachers at the various universities (even though later he did typically wonder aloud how it was that 'the great colleges managed to produce so many great asses'), so Nostredame now seems to have set out on a determined bid to 'collect' as many famous doctors and healers as he could. This was not merely in order to learn from their experience, but also, no doubt, in the hope that some of their prestige would rub off on him as well. His travels, he writes, took him to Bordeaux, to Toulouse, to Narbonne, to Carcassonne...

Quite what he did with the remainder of his presumed inheritance in the meantime is not known. Possibly, incorrigible bibliophile that he was, he blew it all on rare and expensive books. Certainly it was not long before he was drawn to another collector of such literary treasures who also happened to be a prominent physician, scholar and researcher, his house a veritable hub of intellectual activity in the south-west...

Giulio Cesare della Scala, born in 1484 in the Republic of Venice, had migrated in 1525 to Agen, in the south-west of France, to take up a post as physician to the local bishop. Here he now styled himself first 'Jules Cesar de l'Escalle' and finally 'Julius Caesar Scaliger'. By his own account he had been a soldier, scholar, poet, grammarian, physician, scientist and astrologer, and would be outdone only by his son Joseph Justus, the most eminent of his fifteen children, who learned thirteen languages and became the most brilliant polymath of the age. Certainly, whatever he had been, Scaliger senior was a violent polemicist, continually disagreeing with other prominent scholars. Not merely Erasmus and Cardano, but Rabelais, too, would eventually feel the sharp edge of his pen. But Nostredame evidently found in this larger-than-life Renaissance figure who was some twenty years his elder something of a kindred spirit – or perhaps it was the other way around – and so in 1531, after some years of correspondence, he made his way to Agen to join the great man's intimate but illustrious circle and presumably become his personal apothecary.

He now married one Henriette d'Encausse and with her had two children, a boy and a girl (whose names have not come down to us), and for a while he seems to have been happy here. Certainly he would apparently name the first son even of his *second* marriage after his former patron, and years afterwards was still describing the latter as

> Julius Cesar Squaliger [a Freudian slip, perhaps?] of whom I doubt but that his soul might not have been father to the eloquence of Cicero [a writer whom the Italian had in the meantime brutally torn apart!], in his perfect and supreme poetry another Virgil, in his medical teaching worth any two of Galen, and to whom I remain more indebted than to anybody else in this world.[57b]

Yet the fact is that in the end they quarreled – violently. Nostredame always seems to have retained the ability to write generously – perhaps over-generously – of those with whom he disagreed, at least when decorum or political correctness demanded it, and especially after the event. Even on the subject of the current idol of the medical profession, the great Graeco-Roman physician Galen (about whom, on the evidence of the above, he would later become distinctly unenthusiastic) he could be almost effusive when it suited him. However, the later writings of the Scaligers reflect rather more accurately the true nature of the catastrophic relationship that eventually developed between them. According to a late collection of their devastating epigrams, the future prophet was a 'mad babbler', a 'bandit', an 'inane, vile scoundrel', a 'criminal beggar' and a purveyor of 'falsities'.[8b]

But then there were other reasons for Nostredame's sudden departure, too. By 1534 or so his wife and young son and daughter were all dead – apparently victims of the Plague. As if to make matters worse, the wife's family were suing him, possibly for the return of her dowry. Other unconfirmed reports suggest that he had fallen foul of the Inquisition of Toulouse, too, apparently thanks to an incautious remark to a bronze-founder casting a statue of the Virgin Mary to the effect that he was 'doing the devil's work'. This was a basically iconoclastic, rather than irreligious, remark directed against the prevalent cults of the saints, and one which, if genuine, testifies to the stern, rather austere view of Catholicism which would later draw him towards the Franciscans. But it was still controversial enough to raise the Inquisition's interest.

Not that the Inquisition of the time was half as red in tooth and claw as the more lurid semi-fictional accounts would have us believe. The Inquisitors, after all, were basically lawyers and scholars, and wanted nothing better than to achieve their ends through legal argument, not torture or public burnings. The various lay authorities were much more adept and experienced at such activities than they were. Nevertheless, an interview with the Inquisition was not something to be looked forward to with much relish.

And so Nostredame set out on his travels again with nothing better to do than to 'collect' yet more eminent medical men with a view to picking their brains and reputations. He would later comment very favorably, for example, on the skills of well-known doctors he had met such as Antoine Saporta, Jacques Dubois, Franciscus Marius of Vienne and Jerome de Monteux. He even took good care to praise Guillaume Rondelet,[57] the very man who had expelled him from the student body at Montpellier in the first place, and who would one day become its Chancellor, famous above all for using the body of his own dead son as the subject for the one annual dissection that was permitted at the Faculty. All of these were figures on whose skills he is unlikely to have been in a position to comment unless he had actually worked for them. Moreover, the fact that they were all *alumni* of Montpellier rather suggests that he was deliberately attempting to perform a piece of what today is known as 'association marketing' – presenting himself as if he were himself a member of their 'magic circle', and so hanging on to their professional coat-tails for all he was worth.

Nobody, it has to be said, ever accused Nostredame of being commercially inept, whatever his other failings!

But his travels at this time may not have been limited to France. He also mentions, for example, the celebrated German doctor Leonard Fuchs – though it is possible that he had merely read one of his works that had been published in Lyon. Some apocryphal accounts have him visiting Orval, on the frontier between France and the Low Countries – though this is unlikely, given that it was a war-zone between France and the Empire at the time. Besides, the writings that he is sometimes alleged to have left there are obvious nineteenth-century forgeries.[41b]

But then contemporary events would have been impinging on him in other ways, too. There had been further periods of terrible weather, leading to widespread starvation and social upheaval. Further disease epidemics merely made a bad situation even worse. In Geneva, John Calvin was starting his campaign of Protestant reform, leading to increasingly bitter conflicts, sectarian wars and persecutions (these last especially in Provence, at the behest of the Aix parliament). For a while all bookstores were closed and all printing banned throughout France. Even afterwards, the book trade, which was held to be directly responsible for spreading the new, seditious religious ideas, was placed under strict parliamentary supervision, and rules laid down whereby in future books could be published only after receiving a royal *privilege*, or imprimatur, and religious ones only with the permission of the Sorbonne in Paris – even assuming that the printers were not on strike anyway, as happened in Lyon in 1539. Nevertheless, in the teeth of opposition from the Sorbonne's theological faculty, the restored King François, ever keen on the new classical learning, set up the first chairs of Latin,

Greek and Hebrew at what would become the Collège de France, the second of which would be occupied by the eminent classicist Jean Dorat, who would later become a keen Nostradamian enthusiast. Both the Jesuits and a national police force were set up – in the former case to preserve the purity of the Catholic faith, and in the latter to prevent treason, theft, begging, vagabondage and brigandage.

The wars between France and the Empire continued. In an attempt to end them, King François, having nearly ruined the country all over again to pay off the ransom for his two captured sons, allowed the Emperor Charles V to stage a royal progress through France. Then he met him in state at Aigues-Mortes, a superb fortified port on the coast not far from Montpellier, in the presence of François Rabelais, who was by now a famous novelist, doctor and diplomat. Meanwhile the Dauphin François, newly rescued from Spain, had died, leaving as heir-apparent his younger brother Henri, who had just married Catherine de' Medici, daughter of the pre-eminent Florentine banking family that had long since become the city-state's powerful rulers. And in the background the ever-menacing Ottomans had taken Tunis and occupied Algeria, and were mounting increasingly ferocious sea-borne raids all along the Mediterranean coast.

Quite what effect all this had on Nostredame's travels we do not know. Perhaps he escaped much of it by visiting Italy, as some accounts suggest, where he would naturally have been attracted to Florence. It was, after all, the very power-house of the Renaissance, too. Other attractions might have been Naples (where according to some accounts Virgil had retired to die, and where the Sibylline Oracle had formerly practiced) and possibly even Sicily, where the huge ruins of numerous ancient Greek temples still stood.

If so, it would have been natural for his return journey of 1544 to bring him back into France again via Marseille, where possibly the most famous of the Montpellier *alumni*, the now elderly but vastly respected Louis Serre, was currently fighting a major outbreak of the Plague. And possibly in working for him, as he now evidently did, Nostredame positively welcomed the chance to avenge the deaths of his wife and children by working to fight the dread contagion. He may even have assumed that, having escaped its former ravages, he himself was somehow immune to it. Besides, there was also the sheer classical lure of the place, which had formerly been a major Greek and Roman port (and one to which he would frequently refer by its classical name of *Phocaea* in his later writings), even though the ruins of the original Greek harbor that have once more become accessible in our own day were almost certainly still unrediscovered in his.[P]

Certainly in this case the 'association marketing' seems to have paid off. As soon as the Plague struck the provincial capital of Aix in the spring of 1546, we can fairly safely assume that all the local doctors immediately fled in panic, in accordance with the well-known advice of the celebrated Toulouse doctor Augier Ferrier (another Montpellier *alumnus*): 'Get out fast, stay well away, come back late.' And since the only reputable doctor who could be relied upon to stay and fight the pestilence was still engaged in Marseille, and either couldn't or wouldn't come, the only thing left to do was to invite his second-in-command. If the organ-grinder refused to perform, there was nothing for it but to settle for the monkey.

The city's financial accounts for June 1546 still record the engagement:

> *Me Micheou de Nostredame, dix ecus d'or sol pour son entrée dans la convention faicte comme appert plus a plain au mandement et acquit cy produits, cy XXXVII fs VIs*

– or 'Master Michel de Nostredame, ten golden crowns (i.e. some $900 today) for entering the agreement made as appears more fully in the order and receipt herewith, in the sum of 37 florins and 6 shillings.'[6a] Not a word, note, about his being a doctor – though the abbreviation *Me* (*Maistre*) does suggest that they assumed he was at least competent in his field.

For what actually transpired, we can do no better than take Nostredame's own account in his best-selling medical cookbook of 1552, first published in 1555, entitled *Excellent & moult utile opuscule...* and better known as the *Traité des fardemens et des confitures*.[57] This comes in chapter 8 of Book I, in which in typical apothecary's style he gives the recipe for his famous rose-pills for repelling the Plague:

> Take one ounce of the sawdust or shavings of cypress-wood, as green as you can find, six ounces of Florentine iris [the root, presumably], three ounces of cloves, three drams of sweet calamus, and six drams of aloes-wood. Reduce the whole to powder before it spoils. Next, take three or four hundred in-folded red roses, fresh and perfectly clean, and gathered before dewfall. Pound them vigorously in a marble mortar with a wooden pestle. When you are half through pounding them, add to them

> the above-mentioned powder and immediately pound it all vigorously, while sprinkling on it a little rose-juice. When everything is well mixed together, form it into little flat lozenges, as you would pills, and let them dry in the shade, for they will smell good.
>
> And note that from this mixture may also be made aromatic soaps, cypress powder, violet root powder, aromatic balls, perfumes, 'Cyprus birds' and perfumed waters. And in order to make the mixture even more excellent, add as much musk and ambergris as you either can or wish. If these two are added I do not doubt that you will produce a superbly pleasant perfume. Pulverize the said musk and ambergris, dissolving it with rose-juice, then mix it in and dry in the shade.
>
> Quite apart from the goodness and scent that this mixture lends to the items and mixtures mentioned above, you only have to keep it in the mouth a little to make your breath smell wonderful all day. Or if the breath has been stinking, whether as a result of the teeth being rotten or because of bad smells emerging from the stomach, or because the person involved has some stinking ulcer somewhere, or some other odd case that has obliged him to flee people's company, keep a little of it in the mouth without chewing, and it will give out such a good odor that nobody will be able to tell where it is coming from. And in time of Plague, keep it often in the mouth, for there is no fragrance better for keeping away the bad and pestiferous air.

There was admittedly a positive addiction to roses at the time. Nostredame's preparations are full of them, and the poet Ronsard would constantly write about them. But the recent claim that this preparation has been reconstituted at the Pasteur Institute in Paris and found to kill the Plague bacillus, at least in a Petri dish, unfortunately seems to have no basis in fact. Besides, even if true, it would merely have indicated that it could have offered some protection against the disease, and would in no sense have constituted a cure.

Nostredame now goes on:

> And as proof of this, in 1546 I was recruited and hired by the city of Aix-en-Provence, by whose senate and people I was appointed to save the city at a time when the Plague was so great and horrific. It started on the last day of May and lasted nine whole months, and from it died an extraordinary number of ordinary, walking, talking [the original says 'eating, drinking'] people of all ages, such that the churchyards were so full of dead bodies that nobody knew of any further consecrated ground in which to bury them. Most of them fell into a delirium on the second day, and those who went into a delirium did not get any spots. Those who did

get the spots died suddenly in mid-sentence, their mouths frozen in position, but after death their whole body was covered with black spots. And the urine of those who were dying in delirium was thin, like white wine, and after they died half of their entire body was sky-blue and gorged with purple blood.

The infection was so violent and malignant that one had only to approach within five paces of one of those with the Plague to be infected. Many had bright red spots in front and behind, and even all over their legs. And those who had them on their backs found that they made them itch, and most of these escaped, but of those who had them on their fronts not one escaped. There were a few who had the marks behind the ears in the early stages of the outbreak, and they lived up to six days, and I was at a loss to know why they should have died on the sixth day rather than the seventh, other than because of the severity of the disease.

Towards the beginning and middle [of the outbreak] not one escaped. Neither blood-lettings, restorative medicines, sacred hymns nor anything else had any more effect than doing nothing at all, and [even] the Tyriac of Andromacus, correctly and truly prepared, had no role to play, for the disease raged with such violence that not one of them escaped.

Once the whole city had been visited and the Plague victims had been thrown out, there were even more the next day than before, and no medicine in the world was found to offer better protection against the Plague than this composition [above]. All those who carried and retained some of it in the mouth were protected, and towards the end there was clear evidence that many people were preserved by it from the infection.

And although this fact is not relevant to the subject that we are discussing, it is nevertheless no bad reason for reporting how helpful it was for us in time of Plague. For this particular Plague outbreak was so malignant that it was a sheer horror. Many insisted that it was a Divine punishment, for at a distance of a league all around there was nothing but good health, yet the whole city was so infected that a mere glance from someone who had been infected would quickly give it to another.

There were plenty of provisions of every kind at virtually dirt-cheap prices, but death came so suddenly and so frenziedly that fathers took no care of their sons, and many abandoned their wives and children as soon as they realised that they had been infected by the Plague. Many who were covered with Plague spots threw themselves down wells in their delirium, others cast themselves from their windows on to the cobbles, others who had carbuncles behind the shoulder and on their breasts suffered violent nosebleeds that lasted day and night to the point where they died, pregnant women aborted and at the end of four days died, and the child, too, died suddenly, and its whole body was

> found to be stained a purple color, as if the blood had spread to all corners of the body.
>
> In short, the desolation was so great that even with gold and silver in their hands, people often died for want of a glass of water, and if I prescribed some medicine or other for those who were afflicted, it was taken to them, but badly administered, such that many died with it actually in their mouths.
>
> Among the [most] admirable things I saw, I think, was a woman who, even while I was paying a visit on her and calling to her through the window, replied to what I was saying – still through the window – while sewing herself unaided into her own shroud, starting with the feet. And when the *alarbes* arrived (which is what we in Provence call those who take the Plague victims away and bury them) and went into this woman's house, they found her dead, lying in the middle of the house with her sewing half-finished.
>
> The above is what happened in three or four parts of the city, one of which I saw for myself. And I would happily have recounted more about the whole Plague outbreak that happened in the city, but this would be to confuse the present work...

Perhaps deliberately, the gruesome and remarkably clear account reads rather like one of the sets of detailed case-notes from Hippocrates' treatise *On Epidemics*, which Nostredame actually mentions later on in his text. Nevertheless, this is no mere fictional imitation. His description is clearly founded on brutal fact – which suggests that Nostredame certainly earned his money, even though he must have had helpers. Nevertheless, he himself admits that none of his methods worked – not even the regulation bleeding that so many commentators insist that he never used. Even his rose-pills were only a prophylactic, no doubt intended for his own use as much as anybody else's.

Yet at the end of nine months the outbreak subsided of its own accord, as such outbreaks usually did – and Nostredame naturally got all the credit for it, and apparently a great many gifts, too. In the process, he came to be popularly perceived as the 'Plague Doctor' *par excellènce*. After all, he had been the man in charge of the regional capital itself. And so, when a further outbreak occurred in nearby Salon the following year, he was summoned there too, only to be sent for by the city of Lyon in its turn. True, the local archives cast some doubt on whether the Lyon outbreak was really the Plague at all. Indeed, some modern medical experts who have examined his description above doubt whether the Aix one was, either. Nevertheless, the fact that it was Nostredame who was sent for suggests (if true) that it probably was, or at least was so regarded.

Some kind of *contretemps* seems to have followed. At all events, one apocryphal account suggests that a local doctor, a Protestant sympathizer called Philibert Sarrazin (and yet another graduate of Montpellier), who preferred to be known as *Sarracenus*, and who was technically in charge, was incensed at having his patch taken over by the unqualified newcomer with his unfamiliar and strangely fundamentalist medical ideas that were more redolent of Hippocrates than of Galen (*mes premiers principes*, as the newcomer would later call them). So incensed was he, in fact, that would-be patients were obliged to come to Nostredame at night in order to consult him in secret. Nevertheless, Nostredame would typically later write of him that he bore him no grudge,[57b] even though it seems that his rival promptly left Lyon in a huff for the Protestant stronghold of Villefranche, just to the north, and went on to become official doctor to Calvin himself.

The outbreak once over, Nostredame returned to Salon, where he appears already to have struck up a close friendship with one Anne Ponsarde, known to her friends as *Gemelle* ('Twinny'), whose husband, the rich lawyer Jean Beaulme, had seemingly died during the recent outbreak there, leaving her a large house and a lot of money. And so on 11 November 1547, in front of her own cousin the lawyer Maître Estienne Hozier, the young, newly rich widow and the newly successful 43-year-old apothecary were married.

The Plague, which had lost him one wife, had now brought him another. Might it now bring him another family as well?

4. *The Water Bearer*

CURIOUSLY, THE INITIAL ANSWER SEEMS TO HAVE BEEN 'NO'. Almost the first of Nostredame's actions after getting married was to leave home and set out on an extended tour of Italy. The first child of his new family, consequently, would not even be conceived until around 1550. One can only assume that his disappointed and possibly enraged wife went back to her mother's for the duration.

We do not know the reason for Nostredame's sudden departure, though we do know that he would acquire yet further recipes from well-known apothecaries en route, two of which (both for laxatives involving rhubarb) he would in due course include at the end of his medical cookbook.[57] Perhaps that was the real purpose of the trip.

Alternatively, it is possible that he was already sensing the first stirrings of the prophetic impulse that was to drive much of the rest of his life. In which case, a renewed visit at the very least to Florence would have been called for, to peruse the most recently acquired ancient occult manuscripts in the Medici library of San Marco. Naples would once again have beckoned, too. Not merely was there the nearby cave of the ancient Sibyl of Cumae, whose prognostications had become part of the Roman state archives, where they were consulted without fail in time of doubt or crisis. There were also the city's associations with the great Roman poet Virgil, whom Nostredame and his contemporaries idolized, and who had come to be regarded by the Romans as a prophet in his own right, so lending his writings something of a similar status. The great Greek temples of Sicily would likewise have continued to exercise their spell, redolent as they were of all the magic of the immemorial theurgic rites to which ancient writers such as Iamblichus[30] had attributed supreme power to summon up knowledge of the future.

Yet the only remotely factual reports we have of his travels are of visits to Venice, Genoa and (by his own admission[57]) Savona. Manifestly these are unlikely to have filled the two years or so that the trip took him, and certainly they cannot have justified it.

Evidently, then, even more compelling and immediate circumstances were in play. And these seem to have revolved around two principal themes. One of these was his newly acquired house. The other was the ancient Greek healer Hippocrates. And the single factor that seemingly linked the two was his new, young architect.

Quite where Nostredame first came across the 22-year-old Adam de Craponne[P] is not entirely clear. He was, admittedly, a native of Salon, but his name suggests (after the fashion of the day) that he had a family origin in the village of Craponne. But *which* Craponne – Craponne-sur-Arzon, in the Auvergne, some distance to the south-west of Lyon, or the other Craponne, much closer to the city, in the foothills of the Lyonnais mountains? And what was it about either place that would encourage a young lad possibly living there temporarily with his grandparents or other relations (following the known death of his father on a commercial trip to the Middle East in 1537) to develop the passion for architecture and especially hydraulic engineering that would come to dominate the rest of his life? Certainly Salon amid its stagnant salt marshes can scarcely have encouraged such an obsession.

About Craponne-sur-Arzon there was nothing particularly unusual or hydrological, apart from the fact that it of course stood on the river Arzon. About the other Craponne, however, there was something very significant indeed. Within walking distance of the village lay the crumbling remains of an ancient Roman aqueduct.[P] A couple of hours further away were the colossal ruins of a much bigger one built by the emperor Hadrian. To the growing boy, if that was where he really was, they must have looked like a broken line of stone teeth as they marched away into the distance across the dips in the landscape.

Once upon a time the great, sweeping curves of both aqueducts had collected the water from the streams that ran off the eastern flank of the Lyonnais mountains, and then funneled them through protected, sediment-trapped culverts and conduits and siphons and overhead canals into the mighty city of Lugdunum, as Lyon was called in those days – the very birthplace of the three Emperors Claudius, Marcus Aurelius and Caracalla. There were at least four such aqueducts originally, all now long-since decayed. And as young Adam played as a boy in the shadow of their ruins, possibly rather like Nostredame at ancient Glanum, no doubt he would have imagined the whole network as it once was, bringing the laughing waters rushing into the city from all the country around. In they would flow, supplying the fountains and public baths, filling the storage tanks and perpetually flushing the sewers. Day and night, winter and summer the waters continued to flow, with never the help of human hand. It was like some mighty machine lying open to the sky and proclaiming the typical Renaissance dream of the final mastery of man over nature.

And so, whereas Nostredame and his ilk had found their inspiration and passion for Roman antiquity in classical books and monuments, for young Craponne it would have been aqueducts. No wonder if, in consequence, he determined there and then that he wanted to be a hydraulic engineer and architect when he grew up, so as to build such marvelous systems and structures for himself.

Such, at any rate, is one possible scenario. What more natural, then, in that case, than that in 1547 the now 22-year-old Adam, hearing that the latterly famous apothecary Michel de Nostredame not only had a passion for the teachings of Hippocrates, but was about to set off again for Lyon to apply them there, should have decided to meet up with him with a view to helping him do so?

Hippocrates, after all, had written not merely a famous treatise *On Epidemics*, but an equally well-known one on communal and municipal health entitled *On Air, Water and Places*. True, Nostredame knew perfectly well that not all the works attributed to the celebrated Physician of Cos had actually been written by him in person. As he himself would later put it in his medical cookbook:[57a]

> Nevertheless that Phoenix of the Doctor's craft who was Hippocrates wrote so divinely that it is impossible for a mere man to know how to imitate him... even though so many possible works are attributed to him that if he were still alive he would deny the greater part, despite the fact that there is not one of those works that is not redolent of the Hippocratic teaching.

And so what did the Hippocratic texts (whoever had actually written them) actually have to say about water in particular? The Latin version of the ancient treatise that Nostredame would have seen[26] was extremely clear on the subject. In translation, it read:

> Likewise I shall now tell you which waters are better or more wholesome, and which worse or more harmful, and what benefit or harm can be attributed to them, as is well known, as regards the state of bodily health.

> Thus, waters that are muddy, stagnant, salty and marshy are hot in summer, thick, and have an almost pungent smell because they do not flow, but are supplied only by the rains, and the rays of the sun constantly burn them up. Therefore they are bound to be bad, and to cause red choler in summer. Likewise in winter they are frozen, congealed and muddy from the snows and from the ice that they form, and as a result produce phlegm, hoarseness and choler...

Elsewhere it asserted:

> Truly that water that is found in high places or that comes from the dusty mountains is best, most healthy of all, and tastes so good that it does not need to be mixed with much wine. It is warm in winter and cold in summer. Similarly that which flows from deep springs, which is even better if it flows from the east, and best of all if it flows clear in summer...

But:

> All water obtained from snow and the like is worse for everybody and causes many stranguries among its drinkers, stones in the bladder, pain under the kidneys and in the hips, and hernia of the testicles, and even more so that which comes from great rivers or stagnant lakes, or which flows from many and diverse streams, even including those flowing from high places. For they are not all alike: they include not only sweet-tasting water, but cold, salty water and water from hot springs. Therefore all of them are mixed with each other in such a way that either the stronger or the lesser wins, depending on the wind-direction.

It followed, then, that a good local supply of clear, clean running water must be of absolutely prime importance in municipal health-care, and Nostredame, in his new role as (basically) a community health-care worker, was therefore bound to look first of all at a town's water-supply before he could so much as begin trying to treat its epidemics and communal diseases. (Even in his later published recipes, he would always specify spring water, not well water.) After all, Hippocrates had specifically laid down exactly how peripatetic physicians should approach the task:

> Verily, whoever shall approach a strange city, let him inquire as to its situation. It is meet, therefore, to find out what sort of winds it experiences and how it is situated relative to the sunrise, for not all of them are alike... But those cities that are facing the east and are exposed to the north wind and have good-tasting water, just like the other places mentioned above, can be harmed by acidity, just as much as those that are in wet places and

> whose drinking water is salty or marshy... And it is likewise most important to study whether they are drinking beneficial or harmful water...

So what had been the water-supply situation in the towns and cities in which Nostredame had actually worked of late? In Marseille, fresh running water was plentiful thanks to the hills with which it was surrounded, and aqueducts had existed ever since ancient Greek times to bring it into the city. Aix was positively overflowing with water, being plentifully supplied both with streams and with natural springs: indeed, its very name was based on the Latin word for 'waters'. As for Lyon, its site at the confluence of the mighty Saône and Rhône might seem to make access to fresh water easy. But both rivers could be muddy, and under the terms of Hippocrates' prescription they were in any case not ideal, being, as he had put it, great rivers that contained water *ex multis & diversis rivis fluentibus* ('flowing from many and diverse streams') – quite apart from the fact that their waters necessarily lay *below* the level at which they would have to be used. This was presumably why the Romans had thought it necessary to construct four mighty aqueducts to bring in crystal-clear water from high ground much further afield. And, that being so, Nostredame, operating in the city in 1547, had no doubt thought along similar lines. At which point, possibly, enter the young Adam de Craponne, with the commission to restore such of the old high-level water-distribution system as he could from the few relics of the Roman system that still remained.

Following which, later in 1547, it looks as if they were both at Salon – Nostredame in the Rue Farreyroux with his new wife and house, and Craponne staying with his elder brother Frédéric just around the corner, seemingly already with a copy of an official edict in his pocket dated that very year concerning the dues that canal-builders were expected to pay to the landowners across which they cut their waterways.

But why would the edict be dated that same year, unless some proposal for a canal-building project was already afoot? Could it be that he and Nostredame were already plotting the major irrigation project that was to become Salon's and the Craux's *Canal de Craponne*?[P]

Salon, after all, was in a much less satisfactory situation than the other cities – from the Hippocratic point of view, at least – as far as its water supply was concerned. The original settlement had been a natural rock-citadel atop a mountain just to the east of the present town, its impregnable cliffs glowering southwards towards the distant Mediterranean,[P] and accessible only from the north. Its few inhabitants had probably lived mainly off their goats and other animals, but of it not much more than an isolated troglodyte dwelling and the ruins of an ancient chapel now remained. In its day it had had limited access both to underground water and to the little stream that cascaded down a nearby ravine now known as the *Val de Quech* in the wet season or after rain.

To the west of this lay the salt marshes of the eastern *Craux*, and beyond them the highest part of the vast, stony plain itself for which Herakles and Zeus (later, Hercules and Jupiter) had between them been blamed since time immemorial. When the Romans came, they ran their *Via Domitia* – the Empire's arterial link between Italy and Spain – around the edge of the marshes to where the spur known as the *Via Aurelia* turned off left to head straight as an arrow across the plain towards the city of *Arelate*, which would later become Arles (see frontispiece). And to guard the junction they built a strong fort atop the rocky eminence now known as the *Rocher du Puech* that jutted high and dry out into the middle of the morass.

In time, just as nearly always happened with such military complexes, the local inhabitants, no longer needing (thanks to the *Pax Romana*) to defend themselves from tribal marauders in their mountain fastness, ventured down to settle just outside the fortifications in order to profit from the new opportunities for civilized living and trade, both with the garrison and with travelers along the road. Once there, their numbers grew. And since there was nothing much else to trade with, they traded in the thing that was most freely available – namely *salt*.

Indeed, given that the Latin for 'to sprinkle with salt' was *salo* or *sallo*, it is not at all impossible that it was this word that lay at the root of the town's very name.

This was all very well, of course, but the very presence of the salt meant that all the surface water supplies were irredeemably contaminated – *turbulente stagnantes salinares & palustres... & grosse: austeri odoris propue qui non currunt* ('muddily stagnant, salty and marshy... and of almost pungent odor because they are not flowing'), as the Latin translation of Hippocrates put it. Deeper down, however, there was plenty of crystal-clear, if mineral-laden water, some of it thermal. There was even a well in the courtyard of Nostredame's new house. Whether this underground water was really enough to satisfy the needs of the local inhabitants, now some 5000 strong, may be doubted, though. Some at least of them may have had either to rely on the unreliable waters of the *Val de Quech* or to trek all the way to the little river Touloubre, some way to the south, for their fresh water.[P] And given that the latter's course had already taken it beneath the walls of the lofty castle of La Barben and through the fortified town of Pélissanne, where all kinds of filth had been deposited in it, this water was more than a little suspect.

The urgent need for some kind of additional fresh water supply for the town of Salon had thus long been known about. It was not just that, according to Hippocrates' prescription, the ideal source of drinking water would be a running-water supply taken directly from high hills, rather than static water from underground sources. Over time, the inhabitants had diversified their activities to include the growing of olives, as well as of saffron crocuses. With the aid of running water they might be able to install water-driven mills, presses and other machinery to process them and so expand the trade. And then there was all that stony, salty desert just to the west, currently inhabited only by snakes, scorpions, birds of prey and lonely goatherds with their skinny flocks. If only *that* could be irrigated and brought into use, too!

Yet, even though there was no real river as such, the *potential* for one had been there for millennia – a potential that, had Nostredame and his contemporaries but known it, had once upon a time been vigorous and healthy actuality. And it was this potentiality that had been recognized as early as 1167 in a royal charter:

> Furthermore I, Alphonso King of Aragon... grant and concede in perpetuity, entirely without reserve, to the Church of Arles and to you the Most Reverend Archbishop of the same Church the channel and water of the River Durance for collecting and redirecting from the Durance as far as Salon and thence to the sea.[7a]

In Nostredame's day, the Archbishop of Arles was his near neighbor, being the latter-day lord of the lofty medieval castle that now occupied the site of the Romans' original fort atop the *Rocher du Puech*.[P] But his sovereignty over such matters had now been devolved to the parliament in Aix, from whom any authorization to proceed must now be obtained.

For whatever reason, then – Hippocratic, philanthropic, commercial or all three at once – Nostredame seems to have talked, persuaded or cajoled the young Craponne into undertaking the mighty project himself. So, at least, we are tempted to assume, if only from the fact that the future seer himself would invest 200 crowns in it in 1556, a further 288 crowns in 1560, and yet another 100 crowns in 1562, to say nothing of a further 100 from his wife Anne on her own behalf the year before he died – 688 crowns in all, in fact, or over $60,000 today, amounting to around a thirteenth share in the entire project. Clearly, this was a personal commitment of the first order.

But then there was also the matter of Nostredame's house to consider. A persistent tradition maintains that one of the first things he did on settling in Salon was to convert its top floor into a study – hardly a point worth making, one would have thought, had it merely meant shuffling a few sticks of furniture around. What is more likely to have been involved was a complete remodeling of the top story, or even the conversion of the loft into an extra one, possibly incorporating not only the typical alchemist's furnace, but also the construction of a small turret at one corner, from the top of which he could observe the

Nostradamus's original house at Salon, after Leroy

stars. We know for a fact that professional astrologers of the time often possessed such an 'observatory', as it was generally called, and we also know from Nostredame's later writings that he was positively addicted to being out under the stars at night – though more as a kind of romantic attachment based on the conviction that they were in some sense the very mind and thoughts of God than as a means of studying them scientifically. He was, as he himself said, an *astrophile*, or 'lover of the stars'.

But if such major rebuilding work was to be undertaken, then Nostredame needed an architect. And young Craponne was, of course, not merely a budding hydraulic engineer, but an accomplished architect, too...

And so the scenario that starts to suggest itself is that, while Craponne was largely rebuilding Nostredame's house, the latter would set out for Italy, while his wife possibly went back to her mother's for the duration. The sound of sawing and hammering, after all, would hardly be conducive to academic study and reflection, still less prophetic meditation, and all the dust and dirt involved would hardly inspire the keeping of a clean and tidy house, either. Then Nostredame would return to his newly rebuilt house, collect his wife from her mother's, make a proper start on his new, married life, settle down to some serious prophetic study and the writing of books, and at last start work with Craponne on the great canal project whose route the young man had in the meantime roughly surveyed.

Unfortunately, though, when Nostredame finally returned home from his travels in around 1549, Craponne was no longer there. His outstanding engineering abilities had, it seems, been noticed by none other than the King who, convinced that such strategic potential was too good to waste, had conscripted him into a responsible position in the army. Either that, or Craponne, impatient for his patron's return, had in the interim sought out such military experience and promotion on his own account. At all events, when we next hear of him, in 1552, he is with the army at Metz, far away in the north east.

For much had happened in the meantime. King François had died in 1547 at age 53, to be succeeded by his surviving son Henri, then 28, who had promptly started reorganizing the national administration and finances before setting out on a triumphant progress through the country, where he had been welcomed as the 'Gallic Hercules'. In particular, a swingeing salt-tax had been imposed, causing serious riots, especially in the south west. These had been put down (though with only partial success) by Montmorency, who had now been appointed Constable of France, Governor of Languedoc and Head of the Privy Council. Protestantism, following Jean Calvin's installation in Geneva, had made further energetic inroads into France, and so had started to attract official persecutions of equal vigor and fanaticism. Indeed, now that Calvin – regarded by many Catholics as the Antichrist in person – had been added to the grisly mix of War, Pestilence, Famine and Death, the stage now seemed set (as we noted in our Introduction) for nothing less than the biblical Apocalypse itself.

Nearer home, and on a less dramatic note, Nostredame's own younger brother Jehan had been appointed attorney to the parliament at Aix, while at Lyon Iamblichus's famous account of the ancient mysteries known as the *De Mysteriis Aegyptiorum* had been republished in Latin. In Paris, Joachim du Bellay, with Ronsard's help, had published his hugely influential manifesto for remodeling the French language after classical models entitled *La Deffense et Illustration de la Langue Françoyse*, which their teacher, the eminent classical scholar Jean Dorat, had enthusiastically supported and encouraged. Rabelais had meanwhile gone to work as secretary to Du Bellay's cousin, Cardinal Jean du Bellay, who had been appointed French ambassador in Rome.

But young Henri II was now gearing up for renewed war with the Empire to the east. In 1549 he imposed a new war-tax to pay for increased numbers of soldiery, and in early 1552 borrowed a further 450,000 pounds (some $27 million today) from French and Italian bankers. By the spring, French forces were on the rampage again both in Italy and in the north east, where Montmorency had taken command in the Rhineland and Duke François de Guise in Lorraine. The bishoprics of Metz, Toul and Verdun were soon overrun and recaptured. But the advance was pursued much too far into Germany, and soon the Emperor Charles V was staging a huge counter-attack. However, Guise led a heroic resistance at Metz for almost three months, eventually throwing the imperial forces back in late December.

And for this, Adam de Craponne was at least partially responsible. Placed in charge of the engineering works there, he had strengthened the fortifications, then hit on the somewhat drastic idea of tearing down many of the city's houses in order to strengthen them even more. Drastic or not, it had worked. The city's ten thousand defenders had succeeded in beating off an Imperial force of some 100,000, and the cold, wet, disheartened Imperial troops had withdrawn in disarray. Some historians even identify this battle as marking the beginning of the end for the increasingly worn-out and gout-ridden Charles V, who finally abdicated only three years later.

Adam de Craponne, then, had every reason to feel satisfied – not least because now at last he could return home to his beloved, warm Provence and the long-neglected canal project. Evidently his enthusiasm for it had reached such a pitch in the interim that it was almost as if the water was already coursing through his very veins – for his first act was to set off in the wake of Nostredame to Italy in order to study the systems of sluices used on Italian canals, some of them designed by Leonardo da Vinci himself.

And so it was that, by 1554, Craponne was finally in a position to petition the Court of the Exchequer at Aix for permission to start work. Whether or not because Nostredame's brother Jehan was now attorney to the parliament there, he got his reply within three weeks, authorizing him

> to take the water from the River Durance... and to divert it via a head-bay and ditch... through the territories of Laroque... Lamanon... as far as and within the territory of Salon... to discharge it into the sea... [and] he shall be permitted to retain mills, water-engines, applications and such other utilities as he may see fit to construct for his profit... as much for himself as for his successors, as proper to themselves.[7]

At the same time the local council determined that he

> shall undertake to provide a sufficiency of water for irrigating Salon and the places to which he shall be able to take his water.[7]

Craponne therefore started work at once. Borrowing the first of the 8,775 crowns (some $800,000 today) that he would eventually need to finance the initial part of the project, he surveyed the route, engaged the necessary engineers (notably the brothers Ravel) and took on the manual workforce. By dint of choosing for his initial sluice a point on the Durance a long way upstream, some distance above the Abbey of Silvacane, he contrived to produce an overall 'fall' of as much as 2 in 1000 – a much steeper gradient than was usual – which would produce a flow so rapid as perpetually to scour the bed of the waterway, while keeping the water as fresh as possible and at the same time providing the motive power for innumerable water-mills and other engines *en route*.

To start with, though, it was merely a matter of a pilot canal some four feet wide and 2½ feet deep. Through it the first trickle of water finally reached Salon on 13 May 1557, to the astonishment of an assembled crowd who had been sure that they would never see such a miracle of modern technology.

This was now the cue for Craponne to start work on widening the canal to its designed width of some 18 feet. After innumerable financial crises, the work was finally completed on Sunday 20 April 1559, and all the town turned out to celebrate it, including that year's three Consuls, the militia and no doubt Nostredame himself. Even before the year was out, a report by the local council reckoned that the various concessions connected with the canal had brought in over 8000 crowns (some $750,000 today) to the town's coffers. And meanwhile Craponne was already working to continue the canal to the sea at St-Chamas, while watering Lançon and Pélissanne on the way. By 1561, he was promising the Consuls of Arles that another branch of the canal would shortly be taken right across the northern Crau to empty into the Rhône there as well.

But he himself was never to see the day, and it would be left to his brother Frédéric and to the brothers Ravel to complete the mighty project.[P] For at some point he seems to have been re-conscripted into the royal service, then set to work on checking and improving the fortifications of far-away Nantes in Brittany. Having established that the Italian engineers then working on them had based them on sand instead of rock, he proposed to demolish them and start again. Then, sometime after 1576, he disappeared, never to be seen again. One apocryphal report suggests why. He had allegedly been poisoned by the same engineers.[7]

By then Nostredame, as we shall see, was long dead, too. What was certainly not dead, though, was the great canal project. Over the decades and centuries it was extended and improved. While some parts of it were closed down or allowed to decay, other local waterways were cannibalized to supply it anew. A whole network of irrigation canals gradually extended across the whole of the northern Craux, where they still remain in operation today. In our own time, huge hydroelectric canals have joined them – to the point where there is even a hydroelectric station in Salon itself. And as a result the Craux (or the *Crau*, as it is nowadays known) is triumphantly green and flowering, if still remarkably stony,[P] all the way from Salon in the east to Arles in the west.

Yet, curiously, for all the prophetic work into which he would plunge after 1549, Nostredame never seems to have foreseen this magnificent vindication of, and lasting practical memorial to, what were evidently his own ideas. Or at least, he never seems to have predicted it in writing. Which raises the interesting question whether, for him, predicting and foreseeing were ever quite the same thing...

5. *The Ephemerist*

SO IT WAS THAT NOSTREDAME, AFTER HIS RETURN FROM ITALY IN 1549, was left more or less twiddling his thumbs. But that was only as far as the great canal -project was concerned. There was, after all, his house to organize. There were his new wife and, hopefully, future family to attend to. There were no doubt letters to respond to.

More to the point, there was a huge amount to do on the academic and prophetic fronts. It was not merely a matter of catching up with all the important esoteric books that he had almost certainly acquired on his travels. There were his now-completed apothecary's notes to assemble and write up into some kind of medical cookbook for profitable future publication.[57] With literacy now widespread, especially among the moneyed and aristocratic classes, there seemed, after all, to be a ready market for such practical manuals. His notes on Egyptian hieroglyphs (a verse translation of earlier, none-too-reliable works on the subject, and seemingly written up before he had even started out for Italy) possibly deserved a publisher too (see overleaf).[50]

Even more important, though, were the latest seminal books that had only just been published. There was Du Bellay's already-mentioned literary manifesto of 1549 to catch up with – an epoch-making blueprint for revitalizing the French language by importing classical, regional, foreign and newly invented words and applying them within a syntactical framework largely borrowed from Latin. This was currently electrifying the whole literary establishment from Ronsard downwards with its revolutionary message that the much-despised French language could, after all, be developed to the point of rivaling Latin as the language of culture, scholarship and poetry if only contemporary writers cared to apply themselves to making it so. As Du Bellay put it:

> Let him who would enrich his language therefore apply himself to imitating the best Greek and Latin authors... Do not fear, future poet, to invent a few terms, in a long poem especially, yet always with modesty,

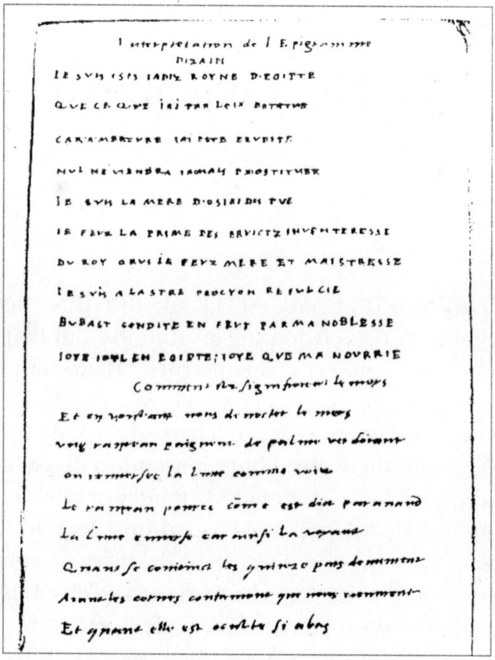

Manuscript page from the Orus Apollo: note complete absence of accents or punctuation

> analogy and aural judgment... For the rest, use words that are purely French, yet neither too common nor too unusual... I would also enjoin you to keep company not only with the scholars, but with all sorts of workers and artisans...[5]

Most vital of all to Nostredame, though, was Richard Roussat's literally epoch-making new survey of current astrological, cosmological and apocalyptic ideas, the *Livre de l'estat et mutations des temps* (the 'Book on the Nature of the Times and their Changes'), also just published.[67] This treatise, shamelessly plagiarized from the earlier (if, admittedly, hopelessly printed) work of the astrologer Pierre Turrel, claimed to cover the 'four seasons of the world' that allegedly made up the 7000 predestined years of its existence – terminating respectively with the Flood, the crossing of the Red Sea, the sack of Jerusalem in AD 70 and the End of the World – which, given that it had allegedly begun in 5199 BC, would apparently occur on a Friday in AD 1791 (a miscalculation, of course, for 1801 – even ignoring the fact that, technically, given that there was never a 'year zero', the figure ought to have been 1802). It also covered the various 'ages' of 354 years and 4 months each that were supposed to succeed each other within that overall framework according to the medieval astrologer Avenezra or Ibn Ezra, as well as the 'triplicities' or 'trigons' of planets that repeated themselves every 240 years to varying effect – to say nothing of the ten revolutions of Saturn that took place every 300 years or so, with all their highly significant, largely dire and of course inevitably cyclic consequences for life on earth.

World history, on this model, was said to comprise three great celestial cycles of 2480 years each, whose constituent ages (each ruled over by a different planet and archangel) were, for the current 'third cycle', listed as:

Archangel	*Planet*	*Start*
Caffiel	Saturn	239 BC
Annael	Venus	AD 116
Satkiel	Jupiter	AD 470
Raphael	Mercury	AD 824
Samael	Mars	AD 1179
Gabriel	Moon	AD 1533
Michael	Sun	AD 1887
[Finish		AD 2242

The fact that these datings made a fairly poor fit with the overall 7000-year framework seems not to have been regarded at the time as of any great significance. If the one didn't apply, the other certainly would. The scientific method not yet having been invented, contemporary scholarship was not nearly so exact as we have nowadays come to expect it to be.

And meanwhile, as far as the planetary ages of the current 'third cycle' were concerned, it followed that the age of Mars had come to a close, and that of the moon begun, some seventeen years before Roussat had written his book and Nostredame had consequently read it hot off the presses. Moreover, during it Roussat naturally expected a repetition of the developments during former lunar ages (history repeats itself, in other words). In particular, he warned of the birth of 'monsters' – i.e. deformed animals and/or children. However, he broke new ground (and upset many contemporary astrologers, too) by hinting that there could be eventually a *fourth* age of Saturn (possibly a golden age this time). The whole system, in other words, could conceivably extend into a 'fourth cycle' that would eventually conclude in 4368. This, it has to be said, represented an enormous extension of the timescale assumed in the *Mirabilis liber*, most of whose prophecies had assumed that the End was almost catastrophically imminent. But then Roussat's model was basically astrological, whereas they had been much more strongly Bible-based.

In part 3 Roussat went in more detail into the various 'triplicities' (regularly spaced patterns of three signs), each of which was said to exert its influence for 240 years at a time – namely the *aquatique triplicité* (which would last until 1640, and during which the powers of the South would be victorious over those of the North); the 'fire triplicity' (which would last until 1880, and when the powers of the East would reign supreme); and the 'earth' and 'air' triplicities (when the powers of the West and North would rule the roost respectively). To the last of these he attributed the future Antichrist, who, he wrote, would have his temple near Nicopolis or Emmaus, from where he would march forth with a great army against Christendom. By way of offering suggestions as to the kind of things that might happen during these various periods, Roussat once again recalled previous times when the same triplicities had reigned, in line once again with the then-fashionable idea that history constantly repeated itself.

After discussing the anticipated Saturn/Jupiter conjunction of 1702 and the expected upheavals resulting from it, Roussat then went on to consider the circumstances likely to surround the End of the World, mentioning the Venerable Bede's celebrated prophecy that the rainbow would not be seen for forty years, and the idea that the heavenly bodies would eventually return to the celestial positions from which they had started and would thereafter no longer wander around.

On the basis of the writings of the Arab astrologer Albumasar, Roussat now went further into the already-mentioned 'ten revolutions of Saturn', which he called the *falcifer*, or 'scythe-bearer' (i.e. Old Father Time), listing various events that had coincided with its revolutions in the past. He also examined the anticipated major planetary conjunction of 1789 (the date, as we now know, of the French Revolution!), warning that there would be 'great, terrible and horrible changes' at this time, especially for religion and government. At that time, he warned, the Antichrist would come with 'his damnable faith and his miserable sect totally repugnant to Christians'.

At this point, however, Roussat broke off his argument to summarize the main points of a prophecy by the seventh-century Saint Methodius that was (as we saw earlier in connection with the *Mirabilis liber*) already hugely influential at this apocalyptically minded juncture. The Muslims, the latter had allegedly prophesied, would occupy the Holy Land until the time of the end; many people would abandon their faith, though the then ruler of Turkey would not have long to reign; the king of the Romans – i.e. the Pope – would rise against them with great fury in the Promised Land, and would subjugate them seven times more than they had ever been before; and then there would be a great peace and tranquility over all the world. Thereafter the Gates of the North would be opened and the people of Gog and Magog would spread across the earth. Following this, the Prince of the Romans (presumably the Pope again) would take up his abode in Jerusalem, at which point the Antichrist would appear 'with the aid of the false prophet and his pernicious and damnable sect'.

Finally, Roussat brought his distinctly disturbing book to a close with the ominous suggestion that the time of the Antichrist was something not for the remote future, but for there and then. 'Already', he wrote, 'the bark of Saint Peter is most disturbed and *periclitante* (tottering)', just as the prophecy of St Brigid had foreshadowed in the *Mirabilis liber*. As witnessed by various eclipses of the *grands luminaires* (the sun and the moon), to say nothing of the appearance of comets in various parts of the heavens, the End of the World was already Nigh, and knocking at the door...

All this was heady stuff. It inevitably gave a powerful jolt to Nostredame's prophetic nervous system, and reminded him of all those other gruesome prophecies that he had first encountered some 26 years earlier in the pages of the *Mirabilis liber*, then just as newly published as Roussat's book now was. Indeed, virtually all of it would subsequently resurface, barely disguised and sometimes almost word-for-word, in his own prophetic writings. But he needed time to digest it all first. And in the meantime there was the usual, inevitable problem of where the next crust was coming from.

Actually, of course, there was no immediate financial problem, at least where he was concerned. For the moment at least, his family treasure-chests were comfortably full. But he could hardly rest on his laurels. The question of a future income for himself and his family still needed to be addressed. And it cannot have escaped his attention that there might be a very good income to be gained from writing in the very area by which he was now increasingly enthralled.

Not that anybody was making a full-time occupation of it yet. But with the increasingly desperate climatic, economic, political and religious situation, people were prepared to pay good money for what they assumed were reliable guides to the future, and especially to next year's weather. The result was a positive rash of annual 'almanacs' – basically, glorified calendars containing added predictions and other useful information. First launched in 1470, two or three dozen of them were by now appearing each year in Europe, some of them written by the very doctors with whom Nostredame liked to associate himself.[8] Certain of them, indeed, claimed to be not merely annual, but perennial – so-called 'perpetual prophecies' that could be applied either cyclically or repeatedly on the basis of the positions of the planets, or the day of the week on which the New Year fell, or even simply on a recurring 'golden number' of years. Some were illustrated, some written in Latin, others in large letters and in the mother tongue, yet others in a mixture of the two, with the technical parts in Latin and the interpretations in German, or English, or French. Some were entirely in prose, while others included occasional verses. Many were divided into subject areas – lords and kings, kingdoms, peoples, wars, seasons, harvests, eclipses, health and diseases. Such, for example, would be the later 8-page 1554 *Prognostication* of the celebrated Toulouse doctor, Augier Ferrier (whom we have already encountered above), writing under the anagrammatical pseudonym of 'Frager Riviere'. And they were hawked freely in the streets at the annual November fairs throughout France, many of them virtually identical to each other, even though purportedly by different authors entirely.[8]

Not all of them were even serious. Unable to resist the obvious temptation, the irrepressible François Rabelais had satirized the genre as early as 1533 with a wonderful and oft-reprinted spoof almanac of his own ('certain, truthful and infallible for the *perpetual* year'), using his own outrageous anagrammatical pseudonym of 'Alcofribas Nasier' and his usual, racy style:[61]

> There is nothing to say about the Golden Number. I can't find any for this year, whatever calculations I have made. So let's move on...
>
> Considering the infinite abuses that have been perpetrated because of a whole lot of *Prognostications* coming out of Louvain under the influence of a glass of wine, I have presently calculated for you one of the surest

and most truthful ones that have ever been seen, as experience will reveal to you... Wishing therefore to satisfy the curiosity of all my good buddies, I have done the revolutions of all the Pantarchs in the heavens, calculated the quarters of the Moon, picked the brains of all the astrophiles ['star-lovers'], hypernephelists ['above-the-clouders'], Anemophilacs ['lovers of wind'], Uranopetes ['Uranus-farts'] and Ombrophores ['shadow-bearers'], and checked it all with Empedocles, who commends himself to your good grace. All this *tu autem* [palaver] I have drawn up in very few chapters, assuring you that I only say what I think, and only think what is, and that that this is none other in truth than what you will read at this time. What will be said, moreover, will be passed through a coarse sieve, hither and thither, and perhaps will happen, or perhaps won't... So blow your noses, little kiddies: and you old dreamers, polish your specs and weigh these words with reverence...

On the eclipses of this year:
This year there shall be so many eclipses of the sun and moon that I fear (and not without good reason) that our purses shall suffer from emptiness and [thus] our minds from perturbation. Saturn shall be retrograde. Venus direct. Mercury changeable. And a whole lot of other planets won't go where you want them to. As a result, this year crabs shall go sideways and rope-makers backwards, stools shall stand on benches, spits on fire-irons and bonnets on hats, pillows shall finish up at the bottom of the bed, men's balls shall hang down for lack of pouches, fleas shall be mainly black, fat shall give way to pease potage in Lent: the belly shall go forwards, the arse shall sit down first, nobody shall be able to find the bean in the Twelfth-cake [i.e. the sixpence in the Christmas pudding], there shan't be a single ace in your hand, the dice shall not say what you want them to (however nicely you speak to them), the luck you're looking for shall rarely come, animals shall speak all over the place...

On the maladies of this year:
This year the blind shan't see very much, the deaf shall be pretty hard of hearing, the dumb shan't speak a lot, the rich shall do a bit better than the poor, and the healthy better than the sick. A lot of sheep, cattle, pigs, goslings, chickens and ducks shall die, but there shan't be such cruel mortality among monkeys and dromedaries. Age shall be incurable this year as a result of the passing of the years... In view of the comet of last year and Saturn being retrograde, some old rogue shall die in hospital, all runny-nosed and scabby. On his death, there shall be awful ructions between cats and rats, between dogs and hares, between hawks and ducks, between monks and eggs...

On the state of certain people:
Holding it for a certainty, then, that the stars care just as little for Kings as they do for paupers, and for the rich as for rogues, I shall leave the other stupid prognosticators to talk about Kings and the rich, and shall speak about people of lowly estate. And first of all about people subject to Saturn, such as people lacking money, the jealous, dreamers, ill-thinkers, the suspicious, whorers, usurers, rent-men, riveters, tanners, tilers, bell-founders, loan merchants and melancholy people. They shan't get everything they want this year, they shall study themselves in the light of the Holy Cross, shan't throw their fat to the dogs and shall often scratch themselves where it's not itching...

On the state of various countries:
The noble kingdom of France shall prosper and triumph this year in all pleasures and delights, provided foreign nations are prepared to leave it alone... Little banquets, little revels, thousands of frolics shall take place that everybody shall enjoy, and never shall there have been seen so many wines or delicacies, lots of rape in Limousin, lots of chestnuts in Perigord and Dauphiné, lots of olives in Gotland, lots of sand at Olonne, lots of fish in the sea, lots of stars in the sky...

On the four seasons of the year – and first the spring:
During the whole of this year there shall only be one Moon, though it won't be a new one...

For the summer:
I don't know what wind will blow, but I know that it has to be hot, and the sea-breeze shall prevail...

Anyway, if things turn out otherwise, that's no reason to deny God. For he is wiser than we are. And he knows what we need much better than we do, I assure you on my honor. Despite what Haly and the others have said. The best thing will be to look on the bright side and drink plenty of wet stuff. Despite what some have said, there's nothing better for combating thirst. That's what I believe, anyway. Besides, *contaria contrariis curantur* ['opposites are cured by opposites']...

Rabelais had brilliantly hit the mark. His merciless spoof put its finger on exactly the kind of thing that was going on. Moreover, everybody was at it. Even though some of the authors claimed to be 'doctors', there was clearly no need even for any special qualifications. And so Nostredame decided to join the club. Even before he had finished reading Roussat, he was hard at work on his first *Almanach*. By 1550 it was published. Moreover, to encourage people to take him seriously, he had decided to add a touch of *gravitas* to the proceedings by adopting a Latin pseudonym of his own for the first time. From now on he was officially 'Michel Nostradam*us*'.

No copy of that first *Almanach* has survived, but his later secretary Jean de Chavigny took minute care to record eleven prophecies from it, mostly in fairly Latinate French:[13, 16]

> The bodies aloft threaten great bloodshed at the two extremities of Europe, in the east and in the west, and the center shall be in most uncertain fear.
>
> And changes of state shall be so great through the variation of fortune, that whoever shall manage to calculate it shall discover that the age of Sylla or Marius has returned, and that it has not yet reached its final period: and whoever shall be far from its blood [or, alternatively, 'far from his relations'!] shall be fortunate.
>
> Towards the Ligurian sea great secret preparations, pillage through unfaithfulness, internal upheavals. And the people who shall be injured shall not dare to undertake anything, *metuens Poenos Gallumque ferocem* ['fearing the Carthaginians and the ferocious Gaul'].
>
> Throughout Gaul [France] there shall be certain uprisings, which shall be appeased by stern counsel.
>
> The betrayal of a city, that was hidden in the spring, shall be discovered during the summer of this year 1550.
>
> In the autumn, heavy rains, which shall be the cause of many setbacks, shall even confound some very great enterprises.
>
> At this time, whether in wars or in illnesses, love, honor and fear shall be the reason why the people shall not be oppressed, but shall live in peace.
>
> At the same time there shall be a great change of condition, almost from top to bottom, and the opposite from bottom to top.
>
> The wild perturbation caused by the entry of Orion shall lend to war a certain tranquility in western parts: but in those of the south and east it shall nevertheless not cease.
>
> In the progressed chart for winter, some hardly durable agreement shall be negotiated between certain Princes: even though by some it shall be observed, the others shall arrange to corrupt the alliance once observed.

It was suitably vague and general – much more so than his perfectly clear account of the Aix plague outbreak, for example (see chapter 3). The notion of historical repetition made its expected appearance, too. None of it was specific enough to be proved wrong. It was a fairly safe bet that the various wars and conflicts would continue as usual. The riskiest prediction was that of the discovery of a plot against a city in the summer of 1550 – but he hadn't actually specified which one, and so if no such plot were discovered nobody would know about it while, if it was, everybody would.

Nostradamus, clearly, was learning his trade fast, and the royalties (whether fixed or *pro rata* – next to nothing is known about his financial arrangements with his publishers) were starting to roll in. So now he committed himself to something that almost nobody else had done so far – he decided to make an annual rigmarole of it. Starting in early spring each year, he would have the *Almanach* for the following year ready for October, so that the printer could publish it by around November.[8] Thus, he had to start work on the 1551 *Almanach* almost at once.

Unfortunately, no part of this has survived. The next *Almanach* whose predictions Chavigny was able to record was that for 1552.[13, 16] There were 37 such prophecies, most of them summed up by the very first of them:

> I see so many hard and bitter destructions that I dare not rightly sum up in so small a space the hundredth part of the afflictions and calamities that this miserable earthly shore must without doubt suffer, even in many places and lands of the kingdom of France.

The style was getting heavier and more obtuse all the time. And meanwhile, in hinting darkly at what he dare *not* say, Nostradamus had hit on a rich vein of alarmism that (as we shall see) he would exploit to even more dramatic effect as the years wore on.

Meanwhile there would allegedly be some 'portentous sign' in the general area of the Italian papal states, France would undergo plots and mutinies, great nobles and prelates of no great age would suffer sudden death. And both God and his own infallibility put in a first appearance:

> Would God Immortal that the war, famine, barrenness, sudden gales and the death of much livestock – which for sure shall occur – were not as is manifestly demonstrated [by the astrological chart]!

As for the summer, this would be unnaturally cold. There would be widespread calamity and misery; worrying signs and portents, uprisings for lack of grain, afflictions and diseases, and yet another failed pact between the Princes in the autumn, leading to renewed wars, internal seditions and plots in the winter. Some Princes and lords would be in danger, some of them being raised up, the others cast down. Despite the ministrations of Saturn, France would be well defended and even strengthened during the year, even though the people would be oppressed. Uprisings and killings would occur in Italy, Germany would be disturbed (with a rebellion in the west), a Swiss city would be in danger of attack, and Spain would suffer famine, while the Mediterranean coasts would be pillaged from the sea (as they regularly were at the time) by the Ottomans and by North African pirates. Olive oil would be in short supply, there would be great hailstorms, signs of plenty of wheat and wine, yet the harvest in danger, with little honey and even less wax. Flour would rot, wounds would abound, and there would be an earthquake. And in February, at the time of a lunar conjunction, some long-mourned personage would die.

This last prediction was almost worthy of Rabelais – while, surprisingly, the last few also appeared virtually word-for-word in another contemporary almanac by one Claude Fabri.[16] The technique of listing separate predictions for the various seasons of the year, as well as for particular countries – already the vogue in some other almanacs – was also starting to put in its appearance. Much of the rest, though, was not so very different from what he had written two years before.

There was a problem, however. Nostradamus was claiming to base his predictions on astrology. There can be no doubt that he was consulting the widely published ephemerides, or planetary charts – especially for the winter and summer solstices and the two equinoxes – as a guide to the temper, or tendency, of each succeeding season. He himself stated as much. Probably, too, he was noting the passage of the major planets from sign to sign as the year progressed, as well as the dates of the various lunar quarters. Certainly this is what he would do in his later *Almanachs*. Yet astrology, by definition, could predict only tendencies, not events. There was nothing infallible about the practical outcome of the planets' movements. What Nostradamus was saying was in fact largely intuitive, and not really astrological at all.

And so professional astrologers such as Laurent Videl, who actually taught the subject at Avignon and Lyon and was the co-author of almanacs with the already-mentioned Claude Fabri, would in due course lay into him quite unmercifully on the question. Regarding the last extract quoted above, Videl would pointedly later ask: 'Given that you say that it will happen for sure, why do you pray that it won't happen?'[70]

Clearly, then, with his *Almanachs* becoming ever more popular, Nostradamus had to find some way of establishing the infallibility of his predictions that didn't rely solely on the stars. He had a growing reputation to protect. It would be better if it didn't depend too much on verification in terms of actual events, either. Not much, after all, had happened to bear out his predictions so far. His best prediction had been for the strengthening and consolidation of France.

But war had not been unusually evident in 1550, whether on land or sea. In fact a peace had actually been signed with England, under the terms of which Boulogne was surrendered to the French, and militarily the year had been relatively quiet. If a plot had been discovered against any city, nobody seemed to know about it. The autumn rains had not been so heavy as to cause any great dislocation. And while some nobles had died (notably Claude duc de Guise and Jean, cardinal de Lorraine) and others had been 'raised up' to replace them, no obvious pacts or federations had been formed or torn apart. Even Chavigny, always determined to prove his master right, would later be unable to pinpoint any events that fulfilled the predictions either for 1550 or for 1552, even though this latter year did admittedly see the Treaty of Chambord signed between the German Protestant states and France, and war with the Empire resumed in the spring. However, this turned out to be somewhat to France's advantage, and scarcely impinged on French soil in the way that Nostradamus's predictions seemed to hint. Clearly, he would have to watch his step. Vagueness was of the essence. Some additional source of authority would also be welcome if only he could think of one, especially if it could be credited with the ability to change its mind if the actual outcome didn't fit...

6. *The Celebrity*

BUT THEN, IN 1552 NOSTRADAMUS HAD OTHER THINGS ON HIS MIND, TOO. It was not merely that the first child of his new marriage (Madeleine) had just been born. His proposed medical cookbook had likewise just come to the end of its long gestation, and was ready to be exposed to the light of day. Or at least, 1 April 1552 was when he completed its long *Proem*, or Foreword – a task that would normally be carried out after the main text of the book was finished. Perhaps, though, as an inexperienced author, he had actually *started* with the Foreword – which might explain why it would be 1555 before the work was actually published. Otherwise one can only assume that the publisher found his writing too indistinct to try setting the many technical terms in his prescriptions and recipes, given that to do so was to risk poisoning unsuspecting readers, so that Nostradamus had (not for the last time) to employ a professional secretary to copy it all out again legibly.

Either way, soon it was back to the next year's *Almanach* – or rather, this time, to *both* of them. For in 1553 not just one, but two of them appeared, each of them saying significantly different things. One of them would be heavily criticized (once again) by Laurent Videl (see Appendix E), while 90 predictions from the other would, as usual, be carefully recorded by Jean de Chavigny.[13, 16] And this time the ancient notion of historical repetition (the so-called 'Doctrine of the Eternal Return') was to be even more in evidence:

> This year is that which was at the time of Caesar and Pompey: and the end of the year the banishment which of Augustus, Mark Antony and Lepidus [*sic*].

Thanks to the omission of vital verbs and prepositions, the language was getting positively impenetrable too. He presumably meant a modern replay of the banishment by Augustus of the other two original members of the ruling Roman triumvirate, or junta, following the death of Julius Caesar.

Then, for the spring, an evidently garbled prediction that looks as if it was originally meant to read, albeit in notably stilted language:

> The great Hannibal on the matter is in danger of failing.

And again:

> A new Themistocles shall inflict a great and unhappy vexation on his own people.

In referring respectively to 'new incarnations' of the famous Carthaginian general and the great Athenian admiral and statesman in this way, Nostradamus was starting to become not just indecipherable, but positively gnomic – thus successfully contriving to conceal his true, intended meaning (assuming that he actually had one) not only from all but the most educated, but possibly from the most educated as well.

Once again, too, he played his devastating trump card of hinting at events that were allegedly too awful to describe:

> I would not know how to set down on so little paper the great calamity that poor humans shall suffer in divers ways, even the greatest Princes and Lords after the total oppression of the people.

So who was going to be oppressed – the Princes and Lords, or the people? The deliberate ambiguities were starting to widen the possibilities of his predictions to the point where they would cover almost any eventuality. Similarly:

> The divine power or some fatal disposition is bound to operate this year. In the event that this were not to be, a new age would have returned.

– which was as clear a case of trying to eat one's prophetic cake and have it too as anybody could wish to see.

For the rest, there was to be a risk of war and revolt throughout France, whether on land or sea, and whether of internal or external origin. There was much danger of bloodshed, too, whether caused by war or by disease. A prominent cleric would try to mediate in a conflict, but would retire under fire. The spring would see an impetus towards war on land and sea, with perils of doubtful and ambiguous type, but probably involving North African pirates (who were continually active at the time). Disease was as much to be feared as war, as part of the birth pangs of the coming new age. The summer would see a repetition of the age of Persia and of Zoroaster, with Europe steeped in blood. On the basis of what Nostradamus called his 'Egyptian doctrine' (a particular version of the system of astrological houses), the autumn would be marked by disputes, looting, covert activities and both a strengthening and a weakening of the kingdom (!!). An army would advance towards the Columns of Hercules (i.e. the straits of Gibraltar), some cities would expel subversives, but either Marseille or those within it would hold firm. War and disease would sweep all three Gauls (i.e. France and the Low Countries), despite attempted mediation by the Pope. Winter, however, would see war subside (as it usually did!), apart from certain ambushes and other activities in Italy, while severe frosts and rains would affect the north and west (as they rather tended to in winter!). There would be plots in Rome, and the Pope would be robbed of some treasure, while himself giving contradictory messages. A huge treasure would leave the country. Some would flee, some be killed or captured, some surprised by ambushes, revolts and treasons. The poor would get poorer and the rich richer (another fairly safe prediction, almost worthy of Rabelais!). Parts of Iberia would experience sudden joys, wars, fears, terrors, extreme drought, late rain, famine, barrenness, popular uprisings, pestilence and insubordination, encouraged by a comet. Sedition and mutiny would occur in Germany, and people would resist the North African pirates. Some of lower Germany, part-western and part-northern, would mutiny, and blood would flow knee deep. The Low Countries would acquire a new ruler and become like the Savoyards and Piedmontese. The Papal states, too, would change rulers, while towards the end of the year great bloodshed and violent injustice would result from the actions of Europe's rulers. Many wolves would be on the prowl in northern Italy as far as the French frontier, some prince would secretly leave both the court and his country, and 'some great Neptune' (i.e. an admiral, probably Ottoman) would die in the east, while a king who ruled over several countries would be attacked.

Clearly, not only were Nostradamus's predictions getting steadily vaguer and vaguer. They were getting increasingly repetitious and... well... predictable, too. And, even forty years later, his faithful latter-day secretary Chavigny was still unable to put his finger on any specific fulfillments, other than by making the lame excuse that he 'really meant some other year'. Indeed, as we have seen, 1552 actually saw France advancing into Imperial territory, rather than experiencing war on its own soil.

Things were getting worrying. Indeed, one might almost have thought that this sorry catalogue of failure – or at least of unpinpointable success – would have put off potential purchasers of Nostradamus's *Almanachs* for good. Not a bit of it, however. What happens, after all, when this year's almanac turns out to be wrong (even if you have noticed the fact)? The answer is clear. You still buy next year's, just in case...

And so Nostradamus, having dug himself into a hole, and never having heard of the now-familiar advice to stop digging, started work on his *Prognostication* for 1554. Indeed, so great was his appetite for digging by now that this time Chavigny would be able to record no fewer than 149 new prophecies, now arranged month by month (starting in January) and lunar quarter by lunar quarter.[13, 16] Most of them, though, were just as vague and ultimately unverifiable as before. The deaths of two Popes were predicted for February, for example – something which, curiously enough, would indeed occur, *but not until the following* year. However, a few of them, as it happened, did hit the nail squarely on the head, while others were to re-appear almost word-for-word in the later *Propheties* for which Nostradamus is much better known today. In particular, as re-applied at the latter's verse I.90,

> Between our area and the Durance shall occur a case as curious [either printed or recopied as 'furious'!] and strange as has been seen in living memory. It shall be around four or five leagues from Avignon, a truly portentous thing...

And again, in the predictions for April:

> At this new moon shall be born many monsters as much human as animal, which shall denote great ills, such that if they are well and learnedly interpreted it would be possible to work out what we are menaced with by the stars.

Now it may be that such 'monsters' (deformed births of infants or animals) occur all the time, but are simply concealed from our modern eyes by the politically correct procedures of modern medicine. Such dissimulation was much rarer in Nostradamus's day. Even so, as we shall see in the next chapter, these two predictions were indeed to be borne out, the first of them in January, the other a month-and-a-half later.[16, 37, 42]

However, yet another 'monster' was forecast, too, this time for May:

> The Adriatic sea shall see in this lunar quarter a great and horrible monster Nereid in the form of a fish.

So far as is known, this particular monstrosity failed to put in any appearance in the Adriatic, but it *would* duly show up (once again) in the first edition of Nostradamus's subsequent *Propheties* – at verse I.29[38, 52] – in the form of an omen (which is what such phenomena were generally taken to be at the time):

> When fish aquatic and terrestrial
> By mighty waves upon the beach is cast,
> In form horrific, sleek, fantastical.
> The seaborne foes the wall shall reach at last.

and again at III.21:[52]

> At Adriatic Crustumerium
> There shall appear a fish of fearful look
> That, fishy-tailed and human-faced, shall come
> And let itself be caught without a hook.

Moreover, it was something that had apparently *already happened* – in 1523 on the Illyrian (i.e. Yugoslavian) coast.[60] The *singulier duel* forecast shortly afterwards would likewise famously appear in his subsequent *Propheties* (at I.35[52]), while the 'fire in the sky' over Lyon predicted for August would later appear at verse VIII.6.[55] Clearly, there was nothing like milking an idea for all it was worth.

Once again, too, the old idea of historical repetition was duly aired:

> Diseases shall be so vehement that it shall be thought that the age of Artaxerces [*sic*], who was of the time of Hippocrates, has, as a result of the celestial revolutions, returned.

In other words, some at least of Artaxerxes of Persia's alleged stars – his horoscope, or at least a significant chart for his time – would have come around again, and so, therefore, might a new Artaxerxes himself. The principle is worth bearing in mind for future reference.

Most interesting of all, however – at least for modern readers who are so often tempted to read into Nostradamus's writings, and especially into his word *Hiſter*, what frankly isn't there – was the prediction for November that read:

> A very learned man in this last quarter [of the moon], while walking along the river Hister, also called Danube, the ground subsiding, in the said river shall be lost.

Even more interesting is the fact that this unfortunate mishap had been reported in almost exactly the same words by Nostradamus himself in the *Proem* to his medical cookbook of 1552 as (yet again) *having already befallen* one Gaspar Ursinus Vellius, a councilor of Vienna![57a]

Yet conspicuous success still seemed to elude him. True, both sales and royalties were looking healthy – despite the fact that he had had to take legal action in November the previous year to prevent his Lyon publisher Jean Brotot from selling any further copies of the 1554 *Prognostication* on the grounds of incompetent printing[42] – but events were still spinning out of control, obstinately refusing to fit what he had predicted. There was nothing for it, then, but to go for the jugular.

For a start, in his predictions for 1555, he would for the first time include regular summary-prophecies *in verse*, which would allow him to use even vaguer and more elliptical language than usual, while at the same time creating a notably 'oracular' effect. Many of the most ancient prophets had written in verse, after all. Then, in order to make sure that his prophetic net was cast wide enough to catch even the most fleeting fishes of actuality, he would once again write not just one *Almanach* for the year, *but two*, of 201 and 97 prophecies respectively. No wonder that the ever-persistent Brotot, when he received the manuscripts in September[16], was flabbergasted:

> Today, 19 September, eminent Doctor [he wrote in Latin], I received the two prognostications dutifully included in your post. To each was prefixed a dedication, one addressed to the Governor of Provence and the other to the Lord de Panisses, Provost of Cavaillon.
>
> I am astonished at all this verbose mish-mash, and the mind boggles not a little. To be honest, this should not surprise you: remember my feelings on the subject. I suspect that such verbosity may put off a lot of readers. Amid life's storms, my most learned Michel, they do appreciate the spirit of brevity. Everybody says: 'It is no use saying with more words what can be said with less.' But then it is not for me to play 'Minerva's pig' [i.e. an ignoramus criticizing a scholar], is it?
>
> In all honesty, I should like very much to be able to follow your orders. Of course, I wouldn't want to reduce the fruit of your vigils to nothing. But for heaven's sake open your eyes: how do you suppose that the average reader will accept two separate prognostications without raising

> his eyebrows, especially coming from one and the same source? Who wouldn't suspect you of trying to put two coats of whitewash on the same pot?[21c]

Who indeed? However, for Nostradamus, multiple whitewashing was now definitely the flavor of the month – or rather of the year – and so the pot was duly decorated twice.

On top of that, in the first of them, the *Prognostication nouvelle, & prediction portenteuse, pour l'An M.D.LV*, he would finally solve the problem of how to claim an unimpeachable authority for his predictions that could nevertheless be credited with the ability to change its mind.

He would claim to be divinely inspired!

Or rather, by using the word *divin* (from Latin *divinus*, which meant both 'of God' and just 'prophetic'), he would contrive to claim in his summary verse (often erroneously ascribed to his first *Almanach*) to be divinely inspired *and* to be merely prophetic both at once – a clever example of the precautionary double-speak that he would develop into such a fine art in his later verse-prophecies:

> By sprite divine, soul filled with prophecy;
> War, famine, plague, upheaval shall come by.
> Floods, droughts, while blood shall stain both land and sea;
> Peace, pacts; Prelates be born and Princes die.

The terms were still vague enough to permit those who didn't want to believe him, or who might be dangerously offended by the idea (of whom there were many in high places), to assume that he was not claiming to be divinely inspired at all. But for most readers the message was quite straightforward. His predictions were from God, and therefore if they didn't come true it was simply because God had changed His mind – as of course He was perfectly entitled to do. It was His universe, after all. The best that Nostradamus could claim to do was to read His mind at the time when he was writing any given *Almanach*. And so in future he would repeatedly rub the point in: *Dieu sur tout* ('God over everything')... *Dieu est sur tous les astres* ('God is above all the stars'). Thanks to this blessed let-out, even Nostradamus could now convince himself of the divinity of his divinations...

And so what was God thinking right now? In the *Prognostication* it was of Islam rampant, terrible consequences for Christendom, the worst war ever, huge losses in both north and south (i.e. against both the Holy Roman Empire and the Ottomans), failed peace talks, widespread plague, variable weather, refugees from war, an attack on Rome, murmurings of discontent because of taxes, Europe disturbed, Turkey hopeful, the return of a new Maximinus and Sylla to a war-torn France, the death of a prince, dangers at sea, an earthquake, bloodbaths, invading fleets, the demand of 'the blood of the just' for expiation, troubles for various cities and, in general, everything one might expect from a new 'Age of Iron' dominated by Saturn. And all that before the autumn, and without even mentioning full details of the impending troubles in Italy, Corsica and Burgundy!

Then would come great peril for the islands, unexpected storms at sea, worries for the King's health, initiatives by a 'great Neptune', extortion in the south, the welcome of somebody from far away at Court (not Nostradamus himself, surely?), a new-found tomb in Rome, letters discovered inside an animal's stomach, crimes, frauds, worrying news at Court and heavy losses at sea. And that was before even passing on to the monthly forecasts – of new monsters, uprisings throughout France, sieges in Spain, a mysterious 'Crocodile', two earthquakes at once, lightning bolts and stones from the sky, triumph for the Muslims, sudden changes of weather and estate and religion, lightning strikes on major buildings, squabbles at the top, fire from the sky, a new 'infallible' eruption of Vesuvius, deceptions, abandonment of the Mediterranean islands in the face of Muslim invaders, a new Hannibal, whirlwinds from the Mediterranean, damage to the wine crop, elephants in France, the sea covered with ships, deaths of kings and lords, flights of bishops, Avignon ('our Mesopotamia') flourishing, admirals on the rampage – but less warfare towards Christmas. And a whole cast of characters 'resurrected' from classical antiquity, from Hannibal, through Thrasybulus and Brennus, to Trajan and Nero.

And Nostradamus did not shrink, either, from trotting out the usual kind of contradiction in terms for which Videl was later to castigate him so roundly – though in this case a distinctly (because politically) disturbing one:

> Let us pray the good GOD that he may preserve the Prince from happening to him what shall infallibly happen to him, notwithstanding that the inclemency of the air, the change of treatment and of region shall deliver him.

But how did all this sit with what God was allegedly thinking at the time of the *second* 1555 *Almanach*? This time it was big trouble for

France, the Pope in two minds, one 'Neoclidas' wanted for superstition, either Lyon or Avignon subject to warring religious sects, maritime preparations, the south-western borders attacked, secret letters from the enemy, the Crocodile again, the failure of an Italian admiral and the return of another, the nearness of a new age in most of Europe, the arrival of Sylla and (once again) Marius, princes and kings with Midas ears, rulers incensed and at mortal war, continuing Muslim attacks on Christendom, the whole country prosperous under a King of true 'Trojan' blood who would turn out to be a new Augustus Caesar, the Spanish treasury exhausted, support from the south and from Scotland for the King, an alliance against the Muslims, the Pope in perfect safety all this year and for a long time to come, a classical revival in France, savage war in Italy, vast maritime invasions (yet again), German attempts to return to Catholicism, a doomed German invasion of Italy and, most worrying of all:

> The King shall beware of some one or many of his Court lest they seek to do what I dare not put in writing, as the stars, in accordance with occult philosophy, demonstrate.

Clearly, God was in something of two minds, though fairly decided about fleets, invasions, admirals, Marius and Crocodiles. He was also catastrophically wrong about the safety of His own Vicar on earth: in accordance with Nostradamus's prediction for the *previous* year, not only the current Pope Julius III, but his successor Marcellus II would in fact *die* during the next few months! And despite the two-pronged approach, still hardly any of the predictions listed in either work in fact came true. There was not a word, for example, about anything resembling the important Peace of Augsburg of October, still less the sudden abdication of Charles V shortly afterwards or the subsequent division of the Holy Roman Empire between his son Philip II and his brother Ferdinand.

But it was the prediction just quoted, using Nostradamus's most devastating and now well-honed technique of hinting at what he *dare not* write – together with the equivalent piece from the *Prognostication*, quoted previously – that really caused the furore. In fact, when this prediction appeared in November of 1554, it created an immediate sensation.

The incensed astrologer Laurent Videl, pursuing his vitriolic attack on Nostradamus of 1558,[70] would recall the exact circumstances. After giving details of the full moon of 7 January 1555 (he reminded Nostradamus),

> ... you say that you dare not declare what would happen that year: why did you resort to such ruses, if not so that you should be sent for from the Court? For later in the said year, for the month of July, you said: *The King shall beware of some one or many of his Court lest they seek to do what I dare not put in writing, as the stars, in accordance with occult philosophy, demonstrate.* You knew perfectly well that the King would want to know the truth.

Other aspects of the *Prognostication* and its twin had struck home, too. Alexandre de la Tourete, President of the Masters General of the Minters of France and author of an alchemical work on potable gold, enthusiastically bought several copies to send to his friends, including one Jean de Morel (whom we shall meet again later). In fact, his accompanying letter read, 'I am sending you some new almanacs, prognostications and marvelous presages by Nostradamus of three sorts.'[8] Evidently, then, the would-be seer had in fact – and not for the last time – produced not two, but *three* such publications for a single year. Gabriel Simeoni of Florence, one of the Queen's tame menagerie of prominent astrologers and magicians, made much of their references to monsters in a book of his own that Nostradamus's publisher Brotot was likewise about to bring out.[8] And perhaps it was he who, in the event, drew them to the attention of the Queen.

For what now happened was quite extraordinary. Nostradamus was suddenly sent for to attend the Court in Paris, as Videl would later recall and as the budding seer's own *Prognostication* for the autumn of 1555 had apparently predicted – just possibly with intent. Full details of the visit would be recounted nearly sixty years later still by Nostradamus's eldest son César.[42, 47] The budding seer, having received the Queen's summons via the Governor of Provence, left Salon on 14 July, arriving before the walls of Paris on 15 August – an extraordinarily rapid passage which some later accounts would put down to the fact that the royal posting service had been placed at his disposal, thus involving Nostradamus in only one month spent on horseback rather than the more usual two. Finding that the Court had already removed to its summer residence at St-Germain-en-Laye[P] for the summer, he put up for the night at (auspiciously) the sign of St Michael, from where he was fetched the next morning by none other than the Lord Constable,

Anne de Montmorency. On the orders of the King, he was lodged at the palatial residence of the Cardinal de Bourbon, Archbishop of Sens. Sent some 130 gold crowns in a velvet purse by the King and Queen to cover his expenses, and having no doubt rather over-indulged himself at the Cardinal Archbishop's expense, he was then stricken by the gout, which laid him low for nearly a fortnight, during which he carried out private consultations for all and sundry, no doubt for good money. No sooner had he recovered than he was packed off to the royal castle at Blois to examine the three young royal princes who would in due course become the Kings François II, Charles IX and Henri III of France.

So, at least, César would later claim. But César, as we now know, was a born romancer and an incorrigible embellisher of any story touching his famous father. In his account,[47] actual facts would always come a very poor second to the family's glory and reputation. In particular, the idea that the mere author and popular soothsayer Nostradamus had been fetched by the Lord Constable in person seems... well, distinctly *far*-fetched – especially as the latter (evidently no admirer of his) could read only with difficulty and write not at all. And the story of the visit to Blois seems to be based on a complete misunderstanding of a contemporary symbolic engraving by one Jan Wierix of the 'third age of life', showing a teacher (decidedly not Nostradamus) surrounded by his young charges and their parents at a castle or country house that is emphatically not Blois.

Yet some of the details do seem to gel with contemporary accounts. The contemporary *Chronique Lyonnaise*, for example, recounted of the period between 20 May and 27 July 1555 that

> at this time there was (and passed through this town) an astrologer named Michel de Nostredame, of Salon-de-Craux in Provence, a man most learned in chiromancy [divination by examination of the hand], mathematics and astrology, who said weighty things to several individuals as much about the past as about the future – even to the point of divining their thoughts, so they say; and he was on the way to the King's Court, whither he had been summoned, and feared greatly that harm would be done to him, for he said himself that he was in great danger of having his head cut off before the 25th day of August following.[8]

At this point, Laurent Videl would later take up the narrative, if admittedly in his own distinctly jaundiced way:

It irks me to recount the daylight robberies you committed on the way to the said Court, in Avignon as in Lyon and Valence and Vienne and other towns, such that I was ashamed to hear of them – and you were as shameful as a dog. Among other things, I saw a woman from Lyon to whom you had issued some worthless prescription, to the extent of stinging her for 10 crowns [a huge sum equivalent to about $900 today]. When you came out of the house of the late Lord Lieutenant Tignac she called after you 'Give me back my ten crowns, for your prescription is no good.' And like a shameless charlatan you said 'It's all right'. Even though she had realized that it was no good, you refused to give her back her ten crowns: *there's* an honest and honorable act for you – like so many others that you performed before you left Lyon as a known charlatan ignorant of all sound knowledge!

In addition, you confessed in the presence of Messieurs the Doctors of Medicine that you were not a physician, but had been previously, and that now you were working entirely in astrology, as if astrology stopped anyone being a physician or as if somebody had made you forget what you knew. And what response did you give Jacques Bassetin when he asked which type of domification [the division of the sky into houses] you found best? You answered his question just like (to quote the common saying) Magnificat at Matins [the Magnificat belongs in the evening service, not the morning one!]: for you just told him what fine things his epicycles were. O mighty ignorance! In short, you performed such noble, honest deeds at Lyon that on your way back from the Court you didn't dare to show yourself there, nor to let anybody know except Jean Brotot [Nostradamus's publisher], and him forbidden expressly to tell anybody you were coming, for fear that you might be forced to pay back what you had been clever enough to trick out of people. For certainly you did such things at Lyon as merited your being thrashed or burnt. Do you really think that if the King had been told about it you wouldn't have been?

Indeed, Videl hadn't finished with him yet:

I think that your only thought is to predict all the ills that come into your head, without any other source of information – for every year you predict pestilence, famine and war. Don't you see how often you have got it wrong? Even in that same year, when provisions were so abundant and cheap everywhere, you nevertheless said at the end of March that you doubted whether this age would be renewed. But first there must [clearly] come other prophets than you – for you also say 'my calculation is just and true.' How can it possibly be just and true, when you cannot cal-

> culate and don't understand the very principles of astrology, as anybody can see for themselves? You would do much better to refrain from ever talking about astrology, but if you insist on carrying on predicting as you have up to now, simply say that you have the spirit of prophecy and then just prophesy in your own newfangled way![70]

The contemporary Claude Haton, vicar of Provins, was much more objective and impartial. In his *Memoires* for the time he would write:

> At this time there was entering into great renown an astrologer mathematician of Salon de Craux in Provence named Master Michel Nostradamus, a doctor of medicine, maker of prophecies and almanacs, who in his said almanacs and prophecies was predicting many future events for Christianity, namely its desolation, and specifically in the countries of France and Germany, speaking now openly of the ills to come in these countries, now in covert terms, riddles and disguised speech; and principally of the future ills that would befall France following the decline of the French monarchy, the Church and the Catholic religion – things which even the most expert could not understand until they saw the fulfilment of the details of the said prediction... This Nostradamus had many emulators and contradictors who accused him (while saying whatever bad things they could about him) of being in communication with devils, and claimed that he was a sorcerer, soothsayer and magician because he was predicting future things to come [*sic*]. Others argued for him, saying that it was the experience he had in astrological science, in which he was the most expert in the land, that was revealing to him what he was writing, and also that it seemed he was writing and saying supernatural things that God was inspiring him to write through the Holy Spirit – things that he himself possibly did not understand – in the form of prophecies about ills that have since happened... While Nostradamus lived, no other astrologer has produced an almanac having renown or currency throughout the kingdom of France other than by doing so under the name of the said Nostradamus.[8]

And it was true. From this point on, in the wake of the commercial success of the 1555 *Almanachs*, numerous rank forgeries would start to appear, many of them bearing the name of Nostradamus, with the result that, rather like nineteenth-century American purveyors of patent medicines, he would often feel obliged to include in his text the facsimile of a handwritten, signed authentication.

Meanwhile Gabriel Simeoni himself, in his Latin letter to Nostradamus of 1 February the following year, would write:

> Last night our Brotot came to see me, whereupon he showed me your letter, in which you desired him to greet me in your name and asked him to inquire about my affairs. It would have been unreasonable of me not to want to hand the same Brotot a letter for you whereby you might know that I have constant hope of greater good or better fortunes.
>
> As soon as I arrived back unscathed from the war of Volpiano, I was delighted to learn that your business with the King, the Queen and other dignitaries had gone off as desired, even though the fact is quite commensurate with your great merits, your wisdom and the influence of favourable stars. Yet I know that, in all honesty, you will also attribute some of your success to my advice.[3, 21c]

Obviously, then, Simeoni had indeed had a hand in organizing the Paris visit.

But our final light on it comes from the already-mentioned Jean de Morel, a distinguished humanist, former secretary to Erasmus and gentleman of the Queen's household, who had, it seems, lent Nostradamus money to pay his hotel bill on the night he had arrived in the city, apparently penniless. Having since asked to be reimbursed, Morel had received no response from Nostradamus. A further complaint resulted in a letter from the would-be seer[21, 41] that, six years later, throws much light not only on the event itself, but on his typical style and habits of thought, and for that reason is worth citing *in toto*:

> This Saturday, 29 November 1561, I received your letter sent from Paris on 12th October of this present year. And it seems to me that, as far as I can see, your letters are full of bile, antagonism and indignation against me, who cannot make out the reason why.
>
> Now you complain that, I being in Paris and on my way to pay my respects to Her Majesty the Queen, you lent me two rose nobles and twelve crowns, which is just, equitable and true – and, in that, you showed what was and is patently obvious, I not knowing you nor you me, other than by hearsay. And you should understand, My Lord, that as soon as I had arrived at the court and had spoken a little to Her Majesty the Queen, I mentioned specifically to her your more than Caesar-like liberality in what you had lent me. And it was not just once that I told Her Majesty so, but be assured that it was reiterated by me more than four times. And I am grieved that you hold me in such estimation as to think I am not so ignorant as not to know [*sic*] *quod benefacta male locata male facta arbitror* [Latin: 'that benefits badly conferred are judged to be badly granted']. But I recognize that in your letter you are speaking out

of anger and indignation and, as it seems to me, without knowing too much about me.

And as for what you say you have written to me via some Captain or other in Aix, be assured, My Lord, that I have never received any letter from you other than this one, [and] that I was firmly of the view, regarding what I had said to Her Majesty the Queen, that you had been satisfied. *Sed de minimis* [Latin: 'But (the Master does not concern himself) with trifles'] regarding such matters. But to come to the point, since it is just and very reasonable that you should be satisfied, you should be assured that in this matter and all others I see myself as much a man of goodwill not only where you are concerned but in all other matters as you have shown yourself to be noble and heroic. And truly I thought that in going to the court I was summoned to go there. But also, contrariwise, I was countermanded by others not to go there at all, and this would not have been without asking you or fully satisfying you [Morel too, then, had evidently had a hand in arranging the Paris visit].

Recently, there was at the home of My Lord the Baron de la Garde a young gentleman page who professed to be your stepson, so that I often said and offered him the chance to advise me of your news to the effect that I had amply satisfied you in all respects. But he never spoke to me about it. Even though I mentioned it to him quite often. As regards what you wrote, that I left Paris *hospite insalutato* [Latin: 'without bidding farewell to my host'], be assured that, although you may be pleased to write thus, I was not thinking in that way, and that it is not in me nor in my nature: I do not know how to affront, nor to insult. Such imperfections I do not recognize within myself and they do not belong to me, but are quite alien to my nature, quality and condition. But I was ill: as a fine reward from the court, I became ill there, His Majesty the King paid me a hundred crowns. The Queen paid me thirty. And there's a fine sum for having come two hundred leagues! – having spent a hundred crowns, I made thirty.

But that is not the point. After I had arrived back in Paris from Saint-Germain, a very honorable great lady, whom I do not know, but who by her appearance showed that she was a very respectable and honorable lady, whoever she was, came to see me the evening I returned and spoke to me about this or that, I couldn't say what, and took her leave when it was almost night. And the next morning she came to see me, and after Her Grace had conversed with me as much about her personal affairs as about anything else, she finally told me that the Lords Justices of Paris were proposing to come and see me in order to ask me by means of what science I was predicting what I was predicting. I told her by way of reply that they need not take the trouble to come on such business, that I would cede place to them and that I had also determined to leave the next morning to return to Provence, which I did. And that it might be in order to frustrate you never even occurred to me. But then you can have as sinister an estimation of me as you like, I am certain that you will know [the truth] very shortly.

And if I am very displeasing [*sic*] that you did not write to me sooner so that you might have been given satisfaction sooner, and if I tell you that though I never saw you other than by letter, and if I do not know you, yet I know *conniventeis oculos* [Latin: 'when I shut my eyes'] your physiognomy, your singular honesty, goodness, faith, probity, learning and erudition. But you will think that with all these words I am making this out to be sufficient to satisfy you. Not so. I send you enclosed in this your letter two small [credit-]notes, the which please cash as soon as they are delivered to you. I am sure that your money will be handed over to you, and promptly, too. One is on the account of Mademoiselle de Saint-Rémy and the other of Monsieur de Fizes. And I beg you to be kind enough not to fail to hand them over to them. For afterwards I shall have word from them as to whether, having received them, there was any error. And there are many others in Paris and at the court who would not refuse me a much greater sum, and if in any way in the world I can be of service to you, I would beseech you most earnestly that it might please you to make use of me, whether it be for yourself or for various of your friends.

You may rest assured that you can rely on me as much as on any man in this world. And were it not for the disturbances that are happening daily on account of religion, I should have taken to the road [for Paris], and it would not be without my inquiring about you fully. I await your letters most anxiously, being sure that your reply that you will send that you are satisfied [*sic*]. I hope to go to court, as much to take my son Cesar Nostradamus to his studies [*sic*: César was 7 at the time!] as to satisfy several people who are begging me to go there; which I will do. However, I beg you to write to me with your news as soon as you please. And I will not fail to employ in your favor all the services of which I am capable, and you shall know more fully by my deeds how affectionately I commend myself, Monsieur de Morel, to your good grace.

Praying God that he may give you health, long life, increase of honor and the fulfilment of your noble and heroic virtues. From Salon de Craux in Provence, this last day of October [*sic* – see top of letter!], 1561, Your humble and obedient servant, ready to obey you,

M. NOSTRADAMUS

So *that* was why he had left Paris in such a hurry, and without paying, too! No doubt Morel had heard better excuses. 'Methinks,' he may well have thought, 'he doth protest too much.' *Far* too much, in fact – for the writer came across as an incorrigible flanneler who was never prepared to use one word when a hundred would do...

Whatever the subsequent ructions, though, Nostradamus did seemingly return home to Salon from the Court in triumph. According to César,[47] at least, he was welcomed and acclaimed by the townsfolk as 'the most famous prophet in all of France'. And rightly so. He had finally hit the jackpot, after all.

Yet it is worth noting that none of Nostradamus's critics or commentators – not the author of the *Chronique Lyonnaise*, not Videl, not Haton, not Simeoni – even bothered to mention a further little book of his that he had no doubt been carrying in his pocket all through his visit.

Which is odd, given that it would become far more famous after his death than all his *Almanachs* put together.

7. *The Researcher*

IT NEEDS TO BE STRESSED AT THE OUTSET THAT THE *PROPHETIES* were in no sense Nostradamus's life's work. In fact they were more of a one-off. At most their composition spanned some four years of his life, at an average rate of no more than one prediction per day. In effect, they were really just a natural extension of the *Almanachs*.

These latter publications had each so far been for a single year only. Their predictions were designed to cover either the year as a whole or particular seasons, months and lunar quarters within it. As such, they were highly valued by the public and sold like hot cakes – even though, as we have seen, they were far from reliable (and much less digestible, too!). But Roussat's truly seminal book of 1549/50[67] (see chapter 5) – to say nothing of the celebrated *Mirabilis liber* of 1522/3 (see Introduction) – had opened up much longer-term vistas of unknown events, in Roussat's case culminating far ahead in the year 2242. Could it really be that their detailed triumphs and disasters were unknowable? Or was it just possible that, by combining the known cycles of astrology with the notion of historical recurrence, these, too could be divined by anyone with the right equipment and know-how?

Certainly, mere intuition could not possibly hope to put its finger on every detail of what might happen in the interim, even if it were relabeled 'divine revelation'. Besides, even at a rate of only four prophecies for each intervening year – a general verse for each season, say – any attempt to predict what was going to occur between now and then would involve the writing of at least 2600 new prophecies. This would probably be altogether too tall an order. And even then, nothing very specific could be said. Dramatic events such as those outlined by both books rarely cover periods as long as three months apiece.

Nostradamus must have toyed with the idea for some time. Should he commit himself to a more long-term prophetic work such as this? If so, what form should it take? If mere intuitive prophecies such as those in his *Almanachs* were out of the question, could simple historical repetition fill the bill? By way of putting some flesh on the bones of the ancient prophecies, could he find enough ancient events to project into the future by calculating the relevant astrological cycles? Were his astrological equipment and know-how up to the task? Dare he attach definite dates to such prophecies? How many specific events would it take to fill nearly 700 years?

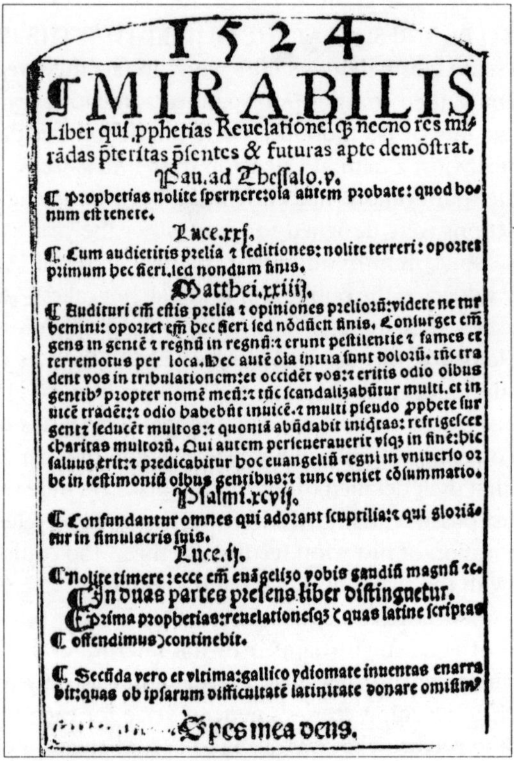
1524
MIRABILIS
Liber qui pphetias Reuelationesq3 necno res mirãdas pteritas psentes & futuras apte demõstrat.
Pau. ad Thessalo. v.
Prophetias nolite spernere: oia autem probate: quod bonum est tenere.
Luce. xxi.
Cum audieritis prelia & seditiones: nolite terreri: oportet primum hec fieri, sed nondum finis.
Matthei. xxiiii.
Audituri enim estis prelia & opiniones preliorũ: videte ne turbemini: oportet enim hec fieri sed nõdũ est finis. Consurget enim gens in gentẽ & regnũ in regnũ: & erunt pestilentie & fames et terremotus per loca. Hec autẽ oia initia sunt dolorũ. Tũc tradent vos in tribulationem: et occidẽt vos: & eritis odio oibus gentib⁹ propter nomẽ meũ: & tũc scandalizabũtur multi, et inuicẽ tradẽt: & odio habebũt inuicẽ. & multi pseudo pphete surgent & seducẽt multos: & quoniã abũdabit iniqtas: refrigescet charitas multorũ. Qui autem perseuerauerit vsq3 in finẽ: hic saluus erit: & predicabitur hoc euangeliũ regni in vniuerso orbe in testimoniũ oibus gentibus: & tunc veniet cõsummatio.
Psalmi. xcvij.
Confundantur omnes qui adorant sculptilia: & qui gloriantur in simulacris suis.
Luce. ij.
Nolite timere: ecce enim euãgelizo vobis gaudiũ magnũ &c.
In duas partes presens liber distinguetur.
Prima prophetias: reuelationesq3 (quas latine scriptas offendimus) continebit.
Secũda vero et vltima: gallico ydiomate inuentas enarrabit: quas ob ipsarum difficultatẽ latinitate donare omisim⁹.
Spes mea deus.

Title page of the Mirabilis liber

More to the point, would people even want to know? Most of them, after all, were far more concerned about where their next meal was coming from. On the basis of recent gruesome events, a good many of them actually expected the End of the World to come within their own lifetimes, no matter how many other events the great prophetic sources catalogued by Roussat and the *Mirabilis liber* insisted must happen first. For them the distant future was thus a pretty dubious idea in the first place – and even if there *were* one it was more than welcome to look after itself. For Nostradamus, though, there might admittedly be a consolation, namely that both he and his immediate readers would be dead long before anybody could check up on whether most of his long-term predictions had been right or wrong.

In the event, it seems to have been a constellation of three dramatic occurrences that eventually spurred him into action. Two of them would subsequently be recounted by his son César in his *Histoire et chronique de Provence* of 1614:[9, 47a]

> The 54th year [of the century], as a result of all kinds of unhappy and bad contingencies, began and continued hideously with deformed and ominous creatures. Hardly had January come to an end than a monstrous child was found alive and kicking at Sénas with two heads, which the eye could scarcely behold without some kind of horror. It had been foretold some time beforehand by those who have knowledge of the course of future events, in so far as their randomness permits [see previous chapter!]. It was brought to my father, and seen by many people, who found it a strange and unhappy encounter.
>
> One month and fifteen days later, another was brought in from a place called Aurons, a league from our walls – of a different species, but with the same deformity. It was a black and white kid, the front part black and the back part as white as cotton, truly a marvelously hideous beast, having a single body but a double head just like a kid's, with the two muzzles suitably separate, with two eyes, one throat, one tongue and two ears to each head without blemish or default, but on top, around the spot where the horns grow, the division and roots of the two heads. The two ears of the right and left parts were [suitably] double, and in addition so nicely separated that both had their natural, proportionate breadth and length. In short, both heads were so perfect and alike on a single neck that if it were permitted to compare brute monsters to humans, it was quite like the little child from Sénas, given that all the rest was that of a true and perfect kid, apart from having the back legs of unusual length and somewhat deformed.
>
> At that time Palamedes Marc, Lord of Châteauneuf, was governing Salon as first Consul – one of the most splendid and honorable gentlemen of our town, a special friend of my father (into whose hands the kid, as also the child, had been delivered out of express curiosity) who, following his advice and that of the most noble and prominent

> Citizens, thought good to show it to the Governor of Provence, who, with the Baron de la Garde and the Commandeur de Beynes, as well as many other Barons and Gentlemen who happened to find themselves at Salon, was on his way to attend a baptism for the Lord of Granville at St-Rémy.
>
> This was duly put into effect, and the monster brought that very evening, carefully inspected and assessed with such wonderment that during almost the whole of supper nothing was discussed other than these hideous monsters and the disasters and divisions that they always seem to foreshadow without fail, and notably the bloody schism and Wars of Religion that followed shortly afterwards, given that they always happen contrary to the order and ways of nature – not, certainly, as causes, but as true signs and extraordinary and certain presages of dark and baleful events.

César, admittedly, was more than a little woolly about his dates, apparently placing the first occurrence at the end of January and the second on 17 April – which was hardly the same as the month-and-a-half's interval that he claimed – but then, given that he himself was only born at about this time, he can only have got the account at second hand anyway. Nevertheless, the two events were more than enough to convince a man of Nostradamus's proclivities that Something Was Up – something big, overwhelming, perhaps even epoch-making. When, therefore, a falling meteorite likewise scared the living daylights out of the local citizens in February of the same year, his prophetic antennae must have started twitching uncontrollably. Such ominous things, after all, are always supposed to occur in threes.

So disturbed was he, in fact, that he fired off a special letter about it to his friend and protector, the already mentioned Claude de Tende, Governor of Provence (1607-66), who was his almost exact contemporary. Moreover, his text was subsequently taken up by the printer Joachim Heller of Nuremberg and duly published in German for all to see – albeit in an almost inscrutably Gothic German font, that the vagaries of contemporary printing technology didn't make any easier to read either:[18]

> TO THE ILLUSTRIOUS, HIGHBORN AND ALMIGHTY LORD CLAUDE, DUKE OF TENDE, Knight of the order of Regents and of the King and Honorary Citizen of Provence, Michael de Nostre Dame, his humble and obedient Servant bids greeting and good fortune.

Gracious Lord
According to reports received, on the first day of February in this year of 1554, a most terrifying and horrible sight was seen here at Salon at [...] towards evening, apparently between 7 and 8, which I am told was seen as far as Marseille. Then it was also seen at nearby St-Chamas by the sea, such that near the moon (which at that time was near its first quarter) a great fire did come from the East and make its way towards the West. This fire, being very great, did by all accounts look like a great burning staff or torch, gave out from itself a wondrous brightness, and flames did spurt from it like a glowing iron being worked by a smith. And such fire did sparkle greatly, glowing aloft like silver over an immense distance like St James's Road in the sky, known as the *Galaxy* [Milky Way], and raced overhead very fast like an arrow with a great roaring and crackling which the poets call *immensum fragorem* [a thunderous din] and as though it were being blown hither and thither by the [raging and roaring] of a mighty wind. Then slowly, over the course of 20 minutes, it turned until we saw it passing over the region of Arles via what we call the *stony road* [i.e. the Crau]. Then it turned towards the South, high over the sea, and the fiery stream that it created retained its fiery color for a long time, and cast fiery sparks all around it, like rain falling from heaven. This sight was much more terrifying than human tongue could say or describe. And I thought that it might have come from a mountain near [...] called St Welcome [?]. But on the 14th of this month I was sent for to go to [...], where I asked diligently of many people whether they also had seen it, but not all of them had experienced it. But it did appear only seven miles from there, and the Lord of that same place had seen it, and desired that I should be his witness that he had seen and wished to record it. Two days after the fire had been seen, the Prefect [?] of St-Chamas came to me and indicated that he and other townspeople had seen the same thing, and that it had taken the shape of a half-[rain]bow stretching as far as the Spanish Main. And if it had been low down rather than high up, it would have burnt up everything and reduced it to ashes as it went by. They also said that its breadth in the sky was around a Pisan running-distance or stadium [about 200 yards], from which the fire sprayed and fell. And so far as I can judge in the circumstances, it is [...] and very strange to hear, and it would be much better had it not appeared. For this apparition or comet gives certain indication that this Ruler of Provence and other stretches by the sea shall encounter unexpected and unforeseen calamity through war, fire, famine, pestilence or other strange diseases, or otherwise shall be attacked and subjugated by foreign nations. This omen was seen by more than a thousand people, and I have been bidden to confirm this and write to your Eminence about it, insofar as I have in my

> own estimation seen and heard how it happened. And I pray Jesus Our Lord that he may grant Your High Eminence long life, and that he may richly multiply and extend your good fortune.
>
> Given in France, at Salon-de-Provence, this 19th of March in the year 1554.
>
> Your Eminence's most humble and obedient servant
> Michael de Nostre Dame.

Doubtless the delicious irony of being threatened with war, fire, famine, pestilence, foreign attacks and subjugation, and then, almost in the same breath, being wished long life and good fortune, was not lost on the good Governor. But the point had nevertheless been made. Dire events were afoot – as equally witnessed by a widely reported rash of similar omens elsewhere in Europe.[8] Now more than ever, therefore, it was the job of would-be prophets such as Nostradamus to give his fellow-countrymen (and countrywomen too, though at the time these were for the most part blithely left out of the equation) due warning of what now awaited them at the hand of God if they did not quickly and drastically mend their ways.

But what awaited them would of course not necessarily happen either this year or next. It would therefore hardly fall within the remit of the usual annual *Almanachs*. There was nothing for it, then, but to embark on the adumbrated set of much longer-term prophecies. And already his ideas were getting clearer as to the form they should take. For a start, they must inevitably take as their basic framework the eschatological timetable of events laid down by the *Mirabilis liber*,[45] and especially by 'Bishop Bemechobus' (i.e. Pseudo-Methodius). That much was a *sine qua non*.

But then more detail would have to be offered, and this, it was evident, would have to be based on the notion that past events tended to recur in time with the revolutions of the planets, as vaguely floated by Roussat.[67] For, given the certainty (as it was seen at the time, at least) of the mechanism of historical recurrence, it was in such past events – historical events, that is, that vaguely matched those prophesied – that the true nature of those future events was necessarily to be found. In the Latin words that Nostradamus would later borrow directly from chapter 6 of the *Mirabilis liber* of 1523 for his *Almanach* for 1565: *certitudo praeteritorum & praesentium fidem facit futurorum* [the certainty of things past and present gives us confidence in things to come] – a statement of prophetic principle to which, highly significantly, he himself would add the three words: *eventum certa indicia* [as definite indications of events].

But this basic principle in turn inevitably meant that the proposed prophecies would by their very nature be *repeating*, or cyclic predictions – which of course meant that they would take the form of what were known at the time as 'perpetual prophecies'. And that being so, the problem of how to fill the 700 years was solved at a stroke. The cyclic nature of the prophecies would see to that. Indeed, it could be relied on to cope even if Roussat was right and the cosmic framework turned out to extend into a fourth cycle lasting until the year 4368. And of course no specific datings would be necessary.

And so, in his eventual *Preface* (in which he dedicated the book to his new son César, apparently as a first birthday present that he hoped to be spared to read and explain to him later), Nostradamus would come right out with it: *sont perpetuelles vaticinations*, he would write, *pour d'ici à l'an 3797* – or 'they are perpetual prophecies from now until the year 3797'. Which seems a strange and rather surprising terminal date to pick, until one realizes that he had simply taken the date when he had written the *Preface* (1555) and added it (apparently rather confusedly) to Roussat's initial date for the end of the world (2242).

The rest of the *Preface* was basically an exposition (without acknowledgement) of well-known ideas on the nature of prophecy originally propounded by Marsilio Ficino (1433-99), the distinguished Florentine philosopher, theologian, linguist and translator who had been one of the founding fathers of the Renaissance in the previous century, and to whom Nostradamus had already compared Scaliger in the *Proem* to his medical cookbook, warmly commending him for his mastery of Platonic philosophy.[57a]

In 1477 Ficino had written, but not published at the time, a work entitled *Disputatio contra iudicium astrologorum*, or 'An Argument against the Opinions of the Astrologers'. Its ideas – basically, an attack on the credulous, fatalistic crudities of astrology as commonly practiced – would subsequently resurface in his more famous third *Liber de Vita* of 1489. Divination of the future, he had concluded, could indeed work, but only by means of a fusion of three basic principles – divine inspiration achieved through pseudo-magical resonance with the heavens, a suitably 'melancholic', or introspective temperament, and what he had called 'the observation of heavenly patterns'. In 1463 Ficino had also translated into Latin the so-called *Corpus Hermeticum* of the semi-legendary Hermes Trismegistus, a manual of spiritual initiation whose 'secret doctrine' of intellectual endeavor combined with religious devotion it traced through Orpheus, Pythagoras and Philolaus to the 'divine Plato', and thence through Plotinus, Porphyry and Iamblichus (whom, in the very first two of his new prophecies, Nostradamus would directly paraphrase) to the fifth-century Proclus, the last of the Neoplatonist Greek philosophers. In particular, Hermes had allegedly told the healer Asclepius:

> This, then, is eternity, which can neither begin nor cease to be, which turns around and around in everlasting motion according to the fixed and unchanging law of its cycle, its individual parts rising and falling time and time again so that, as the times change, the same parts that had once fallen arise anew.

It was, of course, a perfect description of the philosophical basis of all 'perpetual prophecies'.

Unsurprisingly, then, virtually all of these ideas would resurface again in Nostradamus's *Preface*. Freely plagiarizing whole passages from various other authors (once again without acknowledgement), he would explain how prophecy is dependent on a combination of (a) divine revelation through semi-magical practices, (b) a natural prophetic gift and (c) astrology, which he made quite clear involved the projection of the past into the future with the aid of the known planetary cycles – though he would sternly warn his young son off all except the last:

> But as for the conclusions that can be attained by means of astrological exegesis, that is what I should like to reveal to you. It is by this means that one has knowledge of things to come, while rejecting out of hand all imaginary fantasies – and can through divine supernatural inspiration determine precise places in accordance with the celestial patterns. [Indeed, not only] places, [but] to some extent times, by occult means, through the virtue of the divine power and intelligence, in the presence of which all three [dimensions of] time[s] are included for eternity, holding circuit with past, present and future causes.

Elsewhere in the *Preface* he would again state that his prophecies concerned future events 'about which the Divine Being has granted me knowledge by means of astronomical cycles.' These in turn were determined by the Eighth Heaven, which is

> at the altitude where God eternal shall accomplish the turn of the cycle during which the celestial patterns shall return to exert themselves.

Indeed, as he would later claim, he had

> reckoned and calculated the present prophecies entirely according to the order of the chain that contains its revolution [i.e. periodical recurrence], entirely according to Astronomical teaching and to my [own] natural instinct.

Nevertheless, he seems to have admitted in his original manuscript (just as he would later admit in his private letters of 9 September 1561 and 4 February 1562) that:

> *Possum errare, falli, decipi* ('I can err, fail, be deceived'): I am a bigger sinner than anyone in the world, subject to all human afflictions.

While perhaps uncharacteristically frank, the two clauses of this admission (if that is how it was originally worded) would have been perfectly consistent with each other, and would have made perfect sense. Curiously, though, the intrusive word *non* would somehow manage to creep into the printed Latin – possibly at the behest of his publisher, who may have felt that it hardly became his tame prophet publicly to admit his own fallibility. Either the compositor's Latin or his attention to detail was evidently not good enough to insert the word in the right place, however, and so, instead of *Non possum errare...* ('I cannot err...'), he would print it as *Possum non errare...* ('I am able not to err...') – which would give the unfortunate impression that the would-be seer *could* get it right when he put his mind to it, but was unfortunately too beset with human failings to manage it reliably...

But then Nostradamus would also make it perfectly clear (insofar as he ever made anything perfectly clear, that is) that the underlying prophecies were in any case *not his*. 'Even though, my son, I have used the word *prophet*,' he would write, 'I have no wish to attribute to myself a title of such lofty sublimity at present [i.e. in the present work]'; and a little later, 'Not that I would attribute to myself either the name or the function of a prophet.' Whatever his own original astrological input, he would in due course hint pretty strongly (as we shall see) that the ultimate source of his ideas lay not in first-hand personal inspiration, but rather in second-hand texts such as the *Mirabilis liber* – that massive collection of prophecies written by Christian saints and divines who *could* be regarded as having been divinely inspired to the extent that they in turn had relied directly on the Bible.

Finally, after a brief and rather confused summary of parts of the 'doctrine of planetary ages' as expounded by Roussat, Nostradamus would conclude his *Preface* by warning his son to expect the deadliest of wars in the immediate future, but no End of the World until his prophecies had all been fulfilled and their meaning had become clear – which of course matched perfectly the expectations proclaimed by the *Mirabilis liber*.

Such at least, then, were the theories underlying it all. But how would they turn out to be reflected in the prophecies to which the eventual *Preface* was designed to be appended – and exactly what form were these to take?

Here the Lyon publisher Macé Bonhomme, to whom Nostradamus now turned, seems to have taken a direct hand in proceedings. Printing at Lyon had for some time been flourishing as nowhere else in France apart from Paris, where strict control by the Sorbonne's theological faculty made publishing anything unorthodox a risky business. By Nostradamus's day there were several hundred different printers and publishers within the city. Indeed, printing was, with the silk trade, virtually its prime industry. Bonhomme was admittedly not one of its most prominent publishers, even though he was possibly related to Pascal Bonhomme, who had printed the very first book in French during the previous century. Instead, he tended to specialize in comparatively 'popular' works. Nevertheless, in 1552 he had published *Les Considerations des quatres mondes; divin, angelique, celeste et sensible*, by Guillaume de la Perrière of Toulouse – a philosophical and religious work that had consisted of four *centuries*, or books of 100 verses.

Given, then, that Nostradamus had just started for the first time to include a selection of similar quatrains, or four-line verses, in his *Almanachs*, why not do something of the kind for his proposed new prophecy book, too? How about a book of 500 of them, or 600, or perhaps a thousand? If he were to write just one verse a day, even a project on this scale shouldn't take more than about three years, all things being equal. Ficino himself, after all, had suggested that ordinary prose was insufficient for expressing inspiration, and 'poetic fury' (i.e. poetic inspiration) and 'prophetic fury' (i.e. prophetic inspiration) had been thought of as intimately linked ever since the time of Plato. Meanwhile the verse-form would allow the would-be seer all his beloved vaguenesses and imprecisions, cloaked in a mantle of poetic ellipses, unconnected phrases and free-floating words. It would be rather like Isaiah or the Sibylline oracle all over again.

And so, instead of being expressed, as hitherto, in a Latin that was almost totally impenetrable (at least as far as the bulk of the population were concerned), the ancient prophecies could now be re-expressed and elaborated in *semi*-impenetrable *French*. This may seem strange – but, as is so often the case when ancient, almost ritual texts are newly translated into 'a language understanded of the people', there was evidently an uncomfortable suspicion that making them too clear might be tantamount to a kind of sacrilege. It was still felt to be important not to give the game away *too* much...

Clearly the idea appealed – and all the more so when the would-be seer realized that he could achieve that near-impenetrability by directly imitating his favorite Roman poet Virgil, in accordance with the principles already so resoundingly enunciated by Du Bellay in his seminal linguistic treatise of 1549 (at least as Nostradamus understood it). Virgil, after all (who had himself come to be regarded as something of a prophet), was prone to scatter the words of his verses freely about the line for poetic effect, relying entirely on their endings to tell the reader which word went with which. But French, which was, at basis, merely a degenerate kind of Latin creole (whence, of course, all the contemporary attempts to 'reform' it), now lacked most of those word-endings. And so, if he were to fling the words about largely as Virgil did, determinedly refusing to replace those missing endings with the pronouns and prepositions to which they nowadays corresponded, the result would be a series of virtual riddles, solvable only by readers who already knew Virgil and were aware of what his latter-day imitator was up to.

And so it was that all the pieces gradually fell into place. The stage was set. The nature and basis of the proposed book of long-term prophecies had been identified. Its form and style had been decided. It now only remained for the prophet to show his hand.

8 The Prophet

IT WAS A FASCINATING PROSPECT, AND NOSTRADAMUS SEEMS TO HAVE been inspired to get on with the project straight away. True, he first wrote a couple of verses freely paraphrasing Iamblichus's well-known account of the divinatory techniques that had been practiced at the ancient Greek oracles of Delphi and Branchidai, just so as to remind his readers of the awesome prophetic status that he hoped they would associate with him in turn. Later, too, he would include at verses 24-5 and 28-33 of his fourth *centurie* half-a-dozen or so verses in decidedly 'alchemical' language – possibly in order to describe in veiled terms some domestic incident of which all record has now been lost, while impressing readers with his occult credentials.

But then it was down to the nitty-gritty – the elaboration of a kind of poetic 'theme and variations' on the *Mirabilis liber*'s dramatic, over-arching scenario for the future, as sketched out initially by the ancient prophecy of Pseudo-Methodius and then further developed on the basis of such luminaries as the Tiburtine Sibyl, St Brigid of Sweden, Johann Lichtenberger and the immensely influential Joachim da Fiore, to say nothing of Richard Roussat's much more recent contribution.[67]

Unsurprisingly, then, large numbers of the resulting verses would duly reflect its major themes almost exactly in what would come across as a kind of chaotic prophetic kaleidoscope. Verse after verse would warn in general terms of war and death to come – well over fifty of them, in fact. Many quatrains would sketch out, however obliquely, specific incidents during a looming invasion of Europe from the east and south by massive Muslim forces (verses I.9, I.18, I.20, I.53, I.71, I.72, I.73, I.83, II.24, II.29, II.74, II.78, II.81, II.90, II.94, II.100, III.10, III.20, III.62, III.79, III.84, III.88, III.90, IV.4) via the Mediterranean islands (I.9, II.100) under a future bloodthirsty Antichrist (II.29):

L'oriental sortira de son siege,
Passer les monts Apennins, voir la Gaule:
Transpercera du ciel les eaux & neige:
Et un chascun frapera de sa gaule.

or, in translation:

Forth from his seat the Easterner shall go:
He'll cross the Apennines, he'll see fair Gaul.
Onward he'll press through heaven's rains and snow
And with his rod he'll strike both one and all.

Other prophecies would foreshadow the associated persecution and destruction of the Church (I.4, I.15, I.96, III.84), bloody oppressions (III.20, III.68), religious persecutions and the hounding to death of priests and religious (IV.24, IV.43), the rape of virgins (III.84), the murder of infants (I.67), the arrival of swarms of locusts or grasshoppers (III.82), famine (I.16, I.67, II.6, II.37, II.46, II.62, II.96, III.19, III.71) and pestilence (I.16, II.6, II.46, III.19, III.84). As though all this were not enough, there would be conflagrations (I.11, I.87, II.46, II.81, II.93, III.84), earthquakes (I.20, I.46, I.87, I.93, II.3, II.52, II.86), comets (II.15, II.43, II.62), droughts (II.62, III.19) and the virtual boiling alive of fish in the rivers and seas (II.3). The monasteries would decay (I.44, II.12), holy sanctuaries would be desecrated and destroyed (I.96, III.84), and the Pope would be forced to flee Rome (II.41, II.97).

Precisely the major events and developments, in fact, that had long since been foretold in the *Mirabilis liber*, as outlined in our Introduction.

Then would come an almost equally bloody counter-invasion under a future French *Grand Monarque*, extending as far as the Middle East (I.4, I.50, I.74, II.16, II.22, II.60, II.69, II.79, III.38, III.47, III.99, IV.3, IV.5, IV.23, IV.34, IV.36, IV.37, IV.39, IV.50). In a whole range of other verses, powerful players symbolized by eagle, wolf, lion, griffon, dragon, scorpion, ship and lily would fight to the death across an ever-darkening world-stage, just as they had in the words of the *Mirabilis liber*'s St Brigid and Hermit Reynard particularly.

Moreover, the current signs were that such things were almost catastrophically imminent. That they could be included in a purported book of *cyclic* prophecies, though, was due to the fact that many of them had already happened – many times over. And so Nostradamus could take as his model the past invasions of Europe by the Persians, the Goths, the Vandals, the Huns, the Saracens, the Moors and the Ottomans, and base his prophecies of attempts to reverse the trend on the efforts of Kings and Emperors as varied and as celebrated as Louis IX, Frederick Barbarossa, Charles VIII of France and the Holy Roman Emperor Charles V, together with all the inevitable grisly side-effects that these had entailed. Very little *Almanach*-type guesswork was necessary.

Yet in all this the overall model was clear. This whole series of developments directly reflected the sequence of events long ago laid down by generations of ancient prophets and reproduced in the celebrated *Mirabilis liber* of 1522/3, and were certainly not Nostradamus's copyright. Only in the matter of detail – of the who and where and when – was his own hand evident, and then only to the extent that he had carefully selected a whole series of known historical events to project on to that baleful future canvas by way of highlighting its various individual (and possibly repeating) aspects.

That – and, of course, his working of it all into memorable, if fairly impenetrable French verse.

Interestingly, though, the book was unexpectedly silent on one or two further themes that had been freely enough aired by the prophecies' original authors (most of them, of course, high clerics) – namely official corruption, priestly immorality and a range of sexual depravities. Possibly this was because Nostradamus knew only too well which side his bread was buttered on, and was consequently extremely careful not to offend his chief patrons and dedicatees, nearly all of whom were prominent clergy and high officers of state...

As for the Apocalypse itself, this could of course occur only once, and so was not quite as suitable for inclusion in a book of 'perpetual prophecies'. Consequently Nostradamus would mention the characteristic phenomena currently associated with it – the Venerable Bede's forty years without a rainbow (I.17), a star or comet from heaven (II.46), universal war and famine (I.91, I.63), a premonitory bird or eagle (II.75), the disappearance of sun and moon (III.4, III.5), man's attainment of immortality in the final kingdom of heaven (II.13), the final achievement of the alchemists' dreams (III.2), the return of the planets to their original positions (I.56), the coming of the Messiah (II.13) – in only a handful of verses. And he would mention the End of the World not at all.

The detailed content of the verses with which he chose to illustrate and supplement all these developments was meanwhile largely as expected. As we have already noted, the vast majority of them were simple projections into the future of known past events. A good many of them were lifted directly (and often almost verbatim) from classical histories – at I.9 and II.30 the campaigns of the great Carthaginian general Hannibal, as reported by Livy in particular; at I.100, II.23 and II.44 various bird-omens said to have accompanied the death of Julius Caesar, as reported by Suetonius; at I.27 the embezzlement of the captured treasure of Toulouse by the consul Quintus Servilius Caepio as reported by Strabo; at I.84 the assassination of Caesar as reported by Plutarch; at I.86 the siege of Rome by Tarquin and Porsenna and the escape of one of their female hostages across a river in the nude as reported by Livy; at I.96 an ancient Gallic picture of Ogmius, the Gallic version of Hercules, as described by Lucian; at II.41 the star that allegedly burned for seven days following the assassination of Caesar as reported by Julius Obsequens; at II.43 the prodigies surrounding the quarrels between the triumvirs Mark Antony, Octavian and Lepidus, once again as reported by Julius Obsequens; at II.91 an omen of 91 BC presaging the Roman civil war, as again reported by Julius Obsequens; at III.8 the invasion of Rome by the Teutons and the Cymbri, defeated (as Nostradamus had already repeatedly recalled in his 1555 *Almanachs*) by Marius in 102 BC, as well as the latter hiding himself in a marsh at I.19, as reported by Plutarch; at III.26 the activities of the classical oracles as described by Livy; at III.33 the entry of wolves into Rome in 104 BC, as once again reported by Julius Obsequens; at III.73 a crisis in the Spartan royal succession in 398 BC as recounted by Plutarch; at III.91 the alleged spontaneous breaking into leaf of an old oak on the arrival of Augustus on Capri as described by Suetonius; at IV.41 the tricking by Roman female hostages of their enemy guards as reported by Plutarch and others; and at IV.48 the masking of the sun by locusts as reported by Pliny the Elder.[9, 17]

And all that was just in the first 353 verses.

However, Nostradamus would evidently find suitable classical back-references harder to think of as time went on, and so an increasing number of his prophesied events would be drawn from the well-known medieval chronicles instead, such as Villehardouin's *Histoire de l'empire de Constantinople* (1209-13), Froissart's celebrated *Chroniques* (1358 onwards, first printed 1504), Commynes' *Memoires* (1489-98), D'Auton's *Chroniques de Louis XII* (1499-1508), the *Rozier historial de*

France (1522), and Joinville's *Histoire de Saint-Louis* – 'a chronicle in French prose, providing a supreme account of the Seventh Crusade' – (1270-1309), first printed in 1547.[60] In his *Significations de l'Eclipse* of 1558/9, Nostradamus would later admit to having consulted Froissart in particular.

Thus, he would base verse I.34 (on the analysis of Prévost,[60] at least) on the famous episode of the 'Sicilian Vespers' in 1282; I.37 and I.38 on the final days and death of the crusading Emperor Frederick II von Hohenstaufen; I.71 on the triple captures of Marseille – in 735 by the Saracens, in 1252 by Charles of Anjou, in 1423 by the Spaniards under Alphonso V of Aragon. I.81 and II.51 would be based on the famous *affaire des Templiers* of 1304-14, specifying (partly in terms of ancient Greek *gematria*) the exact numbers of the Templars who were (a) spared in England and (b) burnt in France in 1310. And at I.35 Nostradamus would project into the future the deposition of the old Byzantine emperor Isaac II Angelus and his son Alexius IV by the younger Alexius V Ducas Murtzuphlus in 1204, just as the Crusader and Venetian fleets were allying themselves to attack the city:

Le lyon jeune le vieux surmontera,
En champ bellique par singulier duelle,
Dans caige d'or les yeux luy crevera:
Deux classes une, puis mourir, mort cruelle.

Or, in translation:

The younger lion shall surmount the old
On martial battlefield in single duel.
His eyes he'll put out in a cage of gold –
Two forces joined – and then a death most cruel.[38b]

But even this was not enough. And so Nostradamus now turned to the events of his own lifetime for inspiration – some of them well known, others known only locally. Classical treasures and antiquities would be dug up, ancient tombs be rediscovered. Bishops would die, lords be stabbed, poisoned or starved to death, kings deceived, armies be defeated, fleets sunk. As ever, virgins would be violated, children killed, monks persecuted. The Vatican would be sacked all over again, just as it had already been by the forces of Charles V in 1527. And Charles's famous and triumphant expedition to Tunis of June 1535 would be projected into the future in no fewer than three different verses (I.74,

II.22, II.79), albeit with a carefully calculated geographical displacement.[35]

Then there were all those omens – births of deformed animals and children, strange phenomena at sea, strandings of sea-monsters, triple images of the sun ('parhelion'), reported battles in the clouds, fire from the sky – all of them just as liberally sprinkled across the classical archives[58] as across contemporary printed anthologies of unusual natural phemonena and plain urban myths,[23, 24, 59] and possibly even more relevant to certain predictions than the medieval chronicles adduced by Prévost (above).

The material, then, was ready and available – huge amounts of it. No special divinatory skills were necessary – though it is not impossible that Nostradamus occasionally indulged in a bit of nocturnal theurgy and scrying in an attempt to flesh out some of the details, as described in his own words in my Appendix E. Dating, too, was for the most part unnecessary, given that the events were bound to come around again anyway. However, he did later claim to be able to undertake this if asked, and even included a handful of dated verses just to prove it, plus a range of others that indicated just how. Basically, this involved looking up the positions of the planets at the time of the former, historical events – or at least, establishing which signs they were currently in – and then calculating when similar patterns would recur again in the future with the aid of the available ephemerides, or planetary tables. Comparing the two solar noon declinations would even make it possible to hazard a guess at the new, adjusted latitude of the future event.

There was absolutely no problem with any of this. The so-called *Alphonsine Tables*, drawn up by Jean de Murs, had been available ever since the fourteenth century – as had the *De magnis coniunctibus* of the ninth-century Albumasar, so often quoted by Nostradamus. Indeed, the *Alphonsine Tables* had only recently been republished as *Canones antiqui* (1545) by Scaliger's own former Italian mentor Luca Gaurico, who had also published his own book of *Praedictiones* in 1539. In addition, in 1540 Petrus Apianus (alias Peter Bienewitz), chief astrologer to the Emperor Charles V, had published his huge and lavish *Astronomicum Caesareum*, or 'Astronomy of the Caesars'. This was the last great work on astronomy/astrology to be published before the onset of the Copernican age, and thus represented, as it were, the summit of the Ptolemaic doctrine that all astrologers and astrophiles espoused at the time. More to the point, it was furnished not only with tables permitting the reader to look up the positions of Saturn, Jupiter and Mars at intervals of a hundred years all the way from (the theoretically non-existent) 7000 BC to (the theoretically impossible) AD 7000, but also with a set of little disc-type paper computers designed to make the job even easier.[P]

Using such tools, then, Nostradamus was able without difficulty to pinpoint a handful of actual dates (though only a couple in his first instalment, namely 1700 and 1727 respectively) when most of the major planets would simultaneously be in the same signs as previously, and when the events in question thus had a good chance of being repeated (though in fact they weren't). On a rather greater number of occasions, however (around ten in his first installment), he simply stated what those planetary positions had been originally, and left readers to work out the future timings for themselves – not least because most of them involved significant positions of the more 'difficult' inner planets as well.

Work proceeded apace. By the beginning of April 1554, on its own internal evidence, he had already reached verse I.42. On 1st March the following year he finished his Preface, dedicated to the infant César. By the end of April – having evidently managed to write around one verse a day as planned – he had the first 353 verses printed, ready for publication and approved by the authorities. And on 4 May the first installment of *Les Propheties de M. Michel Nostradamus* finally saw the light of day.

Granted, that was all it was. The little pocket book represented only a third of the planned opus. Moreover, given that it would have to be transported nation-wide on the backs of packhorses, it was distributed unbound to save both weight and volume. It would be for either retailers or customers to bind it in any way they pleased – or even to wait for the ensuing installments before binding them all together – in the case of the aristocracy, possibly, decorating the cover for good measure with their family coats of arms.

Nevertheless, it was a delight to the eye. Replete with decorative woodcuts, it positively invited readers to plunge in. Yet when they did, what looked so simple and inviting at first glance turned out to be well nigh incomprehensible to the untrained reader. Partly this was due to Nostradamus's constant resort to pseudo-Virgilian telegrammese, partly to his refusal to name dates or identify his future protagonists, partly to his frequent use of unfamiliar classical place names, partly to his deliberate failure to identify or explain his historical or mythical back-references – but mainly to the positively kaleidoscopic nature of the whole work.

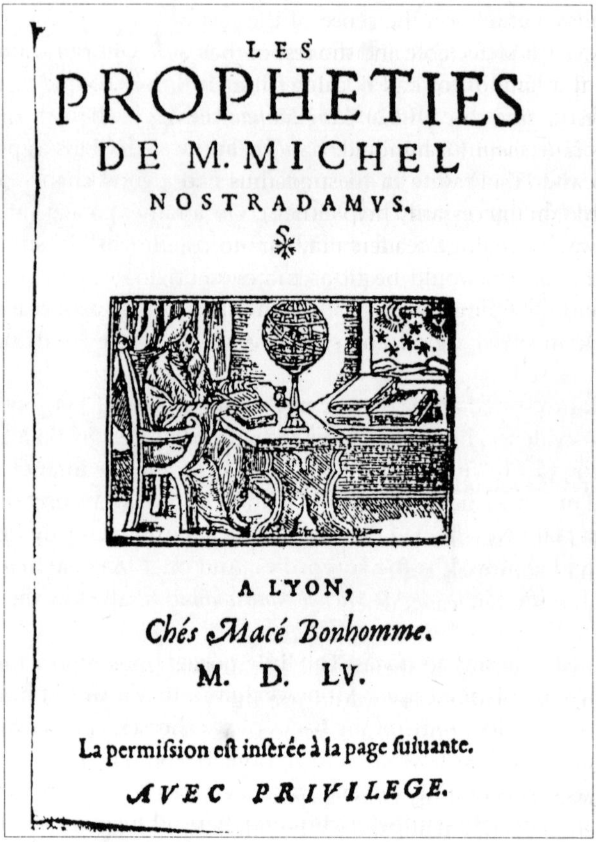

LES PROPHETIES DE M. MICHEL NOSTRADAMVS.

A LYON, Chés Macé Bonhomme. M. D. LV.

La permiſsion eſt inſérée à la page ſuiuante.

AVEC PRIVILEGE.

Les Propheties: title page of the original 1555 edition *(courtesy of Michel Chomarat, Bibliothèque Municipale de Lyon)*

All this was baffling enough in itself. The trouble was, though, that it had evidently baffled the printer, too. At the time, compositors usually set their type by dictation from a second compositor, or even from an apprentice – who in Nostradamus's case may well not have found his writing any too easy to decipher in the first place (his later correspondents were always complaining about it).[3, 8, 21] Everything therefore depended first on each word having been correctly identified by the person doing the dictating, and then on the sound of each word having been successfully identified by the compositor and married to the surrounding syntax. Whether it was *dame* or *d'ame*, or *deux* or *d'eux*, depended entirely on the sense of the rest of the sentence. But if the syntax was undetectable and the rest of the sentence therefore made no sense, the compositor had nothing to guide him. The result was chaos. In one extreme case (II.62), *sang humain* ('human blood') even came out as *cent, main* ('a hundred, hand'). The fact that two of the verses (IV.26 and IV.44) were in Nostradamus's native Provençal instead of French didn't necessarily help either.

By way of analogy, readers may care to consider just how confident they themselves would be of accurately taking down from dictation (unseen) the following few lines from Dylan Thomas's *A Prospect of the Sea* (Dent, 1954):

> After the funeral, mule praises, brays,
> Windshake of sailshaped ear, muffle-toed tap
> Tap happily of one peg in the thick
> Grave's foot, blinds down the lids, the teeth in black...

Besides, there was no set system of spelling at the time. Printers were quite happy to spell a word in three different ways on the same page. Only in those rare cases where, evidently doubting the printer's ability to decipher some particularly strange word that he had written, Nostradamus actually spelt it out in capitals, could he be reasonably sure that the compositor would use the same spelling – but then in such cases the compositor, as compositors will, simply took him at his word and *printed* it in capitals, too. On top of that, Nostradamus had (on the evidence of his *Orus Apollo*[50]) declined either to punctuate or to accent his script at all, and so the printer (who, it is quite clear from his work, was used to much more straightforward texts, and had not the slightest idea of the meaning of much that he was setting) had to punctuate it in any way he could – which was not necessarily the way intended. Authors, after all, were not welcome in the printing house, and unless they lived close by (as Nostradamus didn't) they were not even offered a chance to check the proofs for accuracy. As for accents, it is only fortunate that not too many of them were used at the time anyway.

Worse still, a process of 'continuous correction' in the printing-house was the norm. The type was constantly tinkered with between manual impressions. Sometimes, too, letters would get displaced, or fall out of their frames. All this meant that normally no two copies of any given edition would turn out to be textually the same. Consequently the two surviving copies of this initial edition (the one at Albi, the other in the State Library at Vienna) differ considerably to this day in matters of small detail.[9] There could thus not even be a single, authoritative text for readers and would-be exegetes to work and argue from.

One might have expected the would-be prophet to tear his hair out over all this. Not so, however. There is little, if any, evidence of subsequent authorial corrections in later editions. Quite the opposite seems to have happened. The fact that the text as printed was even more obscure than his original had been actually suited him down to the ground. The meanings were consequently muddied even further, the prophetic possibilities extended almost *ad infinitum*.

This would suit much later would-be interpreters down to the ground too, of course – but it wouldn't necessarily lead to any clearer comprehension of what the original prophecies had been about.

Curiously, the book seems not to have caused much of a stir at the time. Given that Nostradamus was by now becoming famous for his annual *Almanachs*, which were quite precise in their datings, predictions as to what might happen to unspecified future people at unspecified future times and often in unspecified future places were not of too much interest. Virtually nobody even bothered to comment on them in print.

Nevertheless, Nostradamus was not to be discouraged, and got on resolutely with the next instalment. Granted, his 1555 visit to Paris put back the timetable somewhat. It meant scrapping any ideas for having a 1556 *Almanach* ready in time, too. After all, the royal visit was not the only thing that had happened that year. It had also seen the publication not merely of the first edition of *Les Propheties*, but also of no fewer than three *Almanachs* and (at last) of his long-awaited medical cookbook. For Nostradamus, it had been a veritable *annus mirabilis*.

And so it was 6 September 1557 before his second instalment of 289 verses saw the light of day.[53] However, given that he had in the meantime transferred his Lyon custom to the publisher Antoine du Rosne, who evidently was not enamored of the idea of starting a new book in the middle, it appeared bound in with a reprint of the original installment, to which it rather grandly claimed to add no fewer than *300* (!!) verses that had never before been printed.

And, unsurprisingly, it was largely a case of the mixture as before. Once again, verse after verse would warn in general terms of war and death to come – a further nineteen of them, in fact. Further quatrains would sketch out specific incidents during what was again evidently a looming invasion of Europe from the east and south by massive Muslim forces (verses V.62, V.70, V.81, VI.56, VI.62, VI.64, and especially VII.6, VII.7 and VII.8) via the Mediterranean islands (VII.6) under a future bloodthirsty Antichrist (V.27, V.54, V.55, V.84). Except that this time the invasion was on three occasions described specifically in what were evidently intended as summary -verses. Re-arranged in logical order, these were VI.80, V.68 and VII.34:

De Fez le regne parviendra à ceux d'Europe,
Feu leur cité & lame tranchera:
Le grand d'Asie terre & mer à grand troupe,
Que bleux, pers, croix, à mort deschassera.

Dans le Dannube & du Rin viendra boire,
Le grand Chameau ne s'en repentira:
Trembler du Rosne & plus fort ceulx de loire
Et pres des Alpes coq le ruïnera.

En grand regret sera la gent Gauloise,
Coeur vain, legier, croira temerité:
Pain, sel, ne vin, eaue, venim ne cervoise,
Plus grand captif, faim, froit, necessité.

Or, in translation:

From Fez shall rulership to Europe spread,
Firing their cities, slashing with the sword.
O'er land and sea, by Asia's Great One led,
Christians, blues greens, dying, shall flee his horde.

He'll come to drink by Rhine's and Danube's shore
That mighty Camel no remorse shall show.
The folk of Rhône shall quake, of Loire e'en more.
Yet near the Alps the Cock shall lay him low.

In grief the folk of France shall mope and pine,
Light-heartedness be foolishness decreed.
No bread, salt, water, beer, nor drugs, nor wine:

Their noblest captive: hunger, cold and need.

Once again, too, other prophecies would foreshadow the associated persecution and destruction of the Church (V.43), the arrival of swarms of locusts or grasshoppers (V.85), famine (V.63, VI.10) and pestilence (V.63, V.90, VI.10, VII.6). Once again there would be conflagrations (V.100, VI.10, VI.97), comets (VI.6), droughts (V.98) and the virtual boiling alive of fish in the rivers and seas (V.98). Once again the church would decay (VI.25), holy sanctuaries would be desecrated and destroyed (V.73, VI.9), and the Pope would be forced to flee Rome, or at least be captured while away from it (V.15).

Once again, in other words, precisely the major events and developments that had long since been foretold in the *Mirabilis liber*.

Then, as before, there would come an almost equally bloody counter-invasion under a future European *Grand Monarque*, extending as far as the Middle East (IV.77, V.42, V.50, V.51, V.68, V.74, V.79, V.80, VI.21, VI.42, VI.70, VI.79, VI.85, VII.4, VII.10, VII.31, VII.36). Except that this time the campaign would be signaled by a further, quite explicit summary verse (V.13) referring to the actions of a future Holy Roman Emperor of the stamp of Charles V of Ghent:

Par grand fureur le roy Romain Belgique,
Vexer vouldra par phalange barbare:
Fureur grinsseant chassera gent lybique,
Despuis Pannons jusques Hercules la hare.

or, in translation:

The Roman Belgian king in fury black
Shall wish to harry the Barbarian host:
With fury grim he'll chase the Libyans back
From Hungary to stern Gibraltar's coast.

Once again, equally, Nostradamus happily drew his historical antecedents for all this from medieval sources and from classical history and mythology (including, at V.6 and V.75, Livy's description of the coronation of the semi-mythical King Numa of Rome and, at IV.93, Suetonius's account of the birth-legend of Augustus), as well as from more recent events. Indeed, these were, if anything, more prominent than before. A new King François I would come to the throne, just as in 1515 (IV.54); a new pirate Barbarossa, landing in search of water, would carry off and marry a new Doña Maria, just as in 1543 (IV.58);

a new rascally Chancellor Antoine Duprat would die of horrible diseases, just as the original one had in 1535 (IV.88); floods would once again destroy the San Angelo bridge in Rome, just as they had done in 1530 (V.31); new resistance would be offered near St-Rémy to new Imperial invaders from Italy, as it had been in 1536 (V.57); a new Constantinople would be invaded by a new Mehmed II, as it had been in 1453 (V.70); a new Emperor Charles V would repulse the Muslim pirate forces of a new Barbarossa, just as the original one had done in 1535 (V.74)... There was also a strange quatrain in dubious Latin at the end of the sixth *centurie,* freely plagiarized from a verse attacking lawyers by Petrus Critinus in his book *De honesta disciplina* of 1504 (republished in Lyon in 1543). In Nostradamus's case, though, he had changed a word or two to turn it into an attack on the professional *astrologers* who were by then starting seriously to lay into him for his obvious astrological incompetence.

But of course none of this was happening in a historical vacuum. For two years now, John Calvin had been sending Protestant missionaries into France and winning thousands of Catholic converts, to the alarm of Catholics everywhere. On the other side of the sectarian fence, the Vatican had issued the first edition of its notorious *Index Librorum Prohibitorum,* sternly forbidding Catholics to read anti-Catholic authors, especially Martin Luther (a series in which, interestingly, Nostradamus himself was never to appear). Religious sectarianism, in other words, was becoming even more rampant than previously.

Meanwhile, after a relative military lull, Henri II, egged on by the new Pope Paul IV, had decided that he was strong enough to go on the attack again. Charles V's highly religious successor Philip II of Spain likewise went on the rampage. Not content with arranging for his new wife, the Catholic Queen Mary of England, to declare war on France, in August he arranged for his brilliant general Emmanuel Philibert of Savoy to stage a surprise attack on the French holed up at St-Quentin at the head of a huge army. By the end of the month the town had fallen to the Spaniards, with 3000 French dead and 6000 taken prisoner, including the increasingly incompetent Lord Constable Montmorency and his four sons. It was a national disaster of the first order, even eclipsing Pavia in 1525. With the whole of northern France now open before the enemy, panic swept the country.

It seems to have been this almost 'End of the World' climate that encouraged somebody unnamed to publish a further, pirated version of Nostradamus's 1557 edition in Lyon in November.[54] Crude, virtually undecorated and littered with further errors, however – purely gratuitous this time – as well as missing both the new Latin verse and the two final ones, it was not a patch on its predecessor, even though it still claimed to have been published by Antoine du Rosne.

However, news took time to travel, and so the publishers of it (whoever they really were) were evidently unaware that Emmanuel Philibert had in the meantime discovered that he was fast running out of funds and supplies, and so it had suited both sides to sign a hasty truce. By early 1559, indeed, Duke François de Guise, newly returned from Italy, had launched a brilliant campaign to push the enemy back again, culminating in the immensely significant Treaty of Cateau-Cambrésis of April 1559, under which various territories changed hands and two dynastic marriages were arranged. Under the terms of them, Duke Emmanuel Philibert would marry Henri's sister Marguerite, while the newly widowed Philip II would marry the French king's daughter Elisabeth. The fact that huge numbers of troops, untrained for anything except killing, would also be put out of a job on both sides, thus freeing them to swell the numbers of belligerents in the impending Wars of Religion, was not foreseen by the politicians, however. They were not prophets, after all.

In the meantime Nostradamus, who *was* supposed to be one, had been hard at work. Not only had he published three *Almanachs* for 1557 and a further two for 1558. He had finally completed his prophetic opus, too. However, its new publisher, apparently the eminent Jean de Tournes of Lyon, not wishing, any more than Du Rosne had, to start a book in the middle of a *centurie* – and not wishing, either, to publish the previous material for a second or third time – evidently decided to forget the left-overs of the seventh *centurie* and make a fresh start with the eighth (I say 'evidently' because, alas, no copy of this reported edition has come down to us). And so the book (later to be incorporated into the posthumous 1568 edition) consisted of only the last three *centuries*, plus a dedicatory letter to King Henri II (no less!) variously dated 14 March 1557 (in the body of it) and 27 June 1558 (at the end). The prophecies were, of course, of exactly the same type as before. They were still based squarely on the earlier prophecies and illustrated with earlier (sometimes much earlier) events – including, at X.89, a memorable evocation of the Emperor Augustus's celebrated retrospective comment on the 57 years of his own Augustan age (as reported by Suetonius) to the effect that he had 'found Rome of brick and left it of marble' – an evocation that possibly also made the gentlest of references to Craponne's canal project:

> *De brique en marbre seront les murs reduits*
> *Sept & cinquante annees pacifiques,*
> *Joie aux humans renoué Laqueduict,*
> *Santé, grandz fruict joye & temps melifique.*

Or, in translation:

> In marble they shall brick walls reconstruct:
> Of peace seven years and fifty they shall see.
> For humans, joy; renewed each aqueduct;
> Health, honeyed times, joy, rich fecundity.

Being subject to exactly the same printing practices as their predecessors, though, the latest prophecies were (as the verse just quoted exemplifies) still full of obviously misidentified words, dubious spellings and fanciful punctuation. As previously, too, some of them presented the original astrological data so as to permit readers to identify potential future occasions when the base events might occur anew, while a few of them once again offered actual dates.

Perhaps the most famous of these last came just before the end of the book, at verse X.72, where Nostradamus, perhaps reminded by the disaster of St-Quentin, returned for his inspiration to one of the most striking national military disasters of his own earlier days – namely the slaughter of the cream of French chivalry and the capture of King François himself at the battle of Pavia in 1525, followed by the latter's imprisonment in Madrid. With the aid of the *Alphonsine Tables* and/or Apianus's little computers, he had looked up the astrological configuration that had marked the almost miraculous resuscitation of the evidently dying French King in August following an unexpected visit from Charles V to his gloomy prison, and had found that Jupiter had been in Taurus, Mars in Scorpio, Venus in Virgo, Mercury in Leo and the moon *de passage* between Cancer and Scorpio. Then, using the same technical aids, he had discovered that the self-same planets would all be occupying the self-same signs once again in July of 1999. Given that the date had a suitably apocalyptic ring to it, he had therefore felt it worth penning the quatrain that would have half the world hanging on his every word just 441 years later:

L'an mil neuf cens nonante neuf sept mois
Du ciel viendra un grand Roy deffraieur
Resusciter le grand Roy d'Angolmois;
Avant apres Mars regner par bon heur.

There are one or two imponderables in the last line, but a reasonable translation would be:

When 1999 is seven months o'er
Shall a great King and host – on heaven's part, he –
Restore the King from Angoumois once more,
Ere, after March, he'll reign propitiously.

In the process, however, many of his future readers, and especially his Anglophone ones who would for the most part (quite understandably) be untrained either in French or in Nostradamus's idiosyncratic use of it, would succeed in reading all kinds of horrors into the seer's simple message about an analogue of the former Holy Roman Emperor resuscitating his equally analogous captive from the house of Angoulême – horrors that ranged from Chinese invasions, through disastrous cometary impacts, to the dreaded coming of the Antichrist. And this was not helped by later printers' substitution of the suggestive phrase *d'effrayeur* ('of terror') for Nostradamus's original word *deffraieur* ('host, provider'). But then Nostradamus would probably have been perfectly content with that, too...

As for the covering letter to the King, this was a long, rambling screed full of exactly the sort of thing that we should by now expect. Even though the current edition of *Les Propheties* did not include the last 58 verses of the seventh *centurie*, Nostradamus had, he claimed, indeed completed the full thousand. And so, after the customary ritual groveling, he commended his latest offering to His Majesty, on the grounds that he had once again applied the familiar techniques of meditative introspection, divine inspiration and astrological calculation to predict the recurrence of ancient events:

> And the whole of it... by calculating almost as many of the events of future times as of ages past, including the present, and of whatever can be ascertained about future events in all regions as time rolls by...

Naturally (he predicted) he would be criticized, slandered and libeled, and so he had deliberately clothed his predictions in obscure language (well, that was *one* excuse!). While he could reveal all of their dates if asked, he would reveal them only if required by the King to do so (and that was another!). His prophecies, indeed, would be much more appreciated after his death than before it.

At least these last two personal forecasts were original – and, as it happens, more or less correct. This is more than can be said for most of the rest of the letter. Most of it was a confused cobbling together of various well-known existing apocalyptic prophecies from sources such as Roussat[67] and the *Mirabilis liber*[45] that had little or nothing to do with the predictions in the body of the book that it was apparently purporting to summarize – possibly because these were essentially cyclic, while apocalyptic prophecies can by definition be fulfilled once only. It looked almost like a blatant attempt to out-rival the earlier Pseudo-Methodius, or Joachim, or Telesphorus – many of whose prophecies had, similarly, been little more than cobbled-together plagiarizations of pre-existing prophecies. And indeed, Nostradamus was careful to stress – though not so clearly as to detract from his own astrological role – that he did not claim to be a prophet himself. If his prophecies were divinely inspired, it was because they were based on, and not merely (as he wrote) akin to

> the utterances of the thousand and two prophets that have been since the creation of the world, together with the summary and purple account of Joel, *Effundam spiritum meum super omnem carnem at prophetabunt filii vestri, et filiae vestrae* ['I will pour out my spirit upon all flesh and your sons and your daughters shall prophesy' – Joel 2:28]. For such prophecies [indeed] proceeded from the mouth of the Holy Spirit, who was the sovereign eternal power, together with the celestial one, [and were] conferred upon various of that number who predicted great and wondrous things to come [note the possibly unconscious reference to the *Mirabilis liber* or 'Marvellous Book', whose subtitle described it as 'A book that aptly reveals Prophecies, Revelations and many wondrous past, present and future things']. But personally I do not here [i.e. in the present work] attribute to myself such a title. Please God, I fully confess that all of it comes from God [i.e. from the presumably divinely inspired prophecies of such saints and divines as those in the *Mirabilis liber*]...

And so he had recorded the prophecies, he said, 'exactly as written, without adding anything superfluous', even though 'there are many who attribute to me what is no more mine than anything at all.'

Particularly did this reliance upon scriptural and post-scriptural precedent apply to Abbot Joachim, whose striking idea that future ages would inevitably follow the chronology of the Old Testament on a cyclic basis Nostradamus took up with enthusiasm, while reworking it on a new chronological basis of his own and veiling it with his customary mystifying verbiage after the manner of the *Almanachs*. He also included a long astrological rigmarole listing the positions of the planets for the year 1606 (a year that he clearly felt would be especially significant), evidently designed to give the impression that it had all been carefully calculated and worked out by himself from scratch.

In all three editions, meanwhile, Nostradamus's borrowings from his primary sources had often been quite specific, if sometimes characteristically garbled. (Many of these will be found listed for reference in Appendix D.) No doubt this was why all his various publishers entitled the book not just *Propheties*, but *Les Propheties*, even though they were cunning enough to set out their title-pages so that they read

LES PROPHETIES
DE M. MICHEL NOSTRADAMUS

– which could, of course, as easily mean 'The Prophecies *of* M. Michel Nostradamus' as 'The Prophecies, *by* M. Michel Nostradamus'.

Then, disaster... At the double royal marriage-celebrations of June 1559, arranged under the terms of the Treaty of Cateau-Cambrésis, the King decided to participate in a triple joust with the Captain of his Scottish Guard, Gabriel de Lorge, Comte de Montgomery, despite a specific written warning from Luca Gaurico only three years before that he should avoid all single combat in an enclosed space during his forty-first year. During the third encounter the Count's lance splintered and entered the King's eye, penetrating his brain. The doctors could do nothing. He died in agony ten days later, on 10 July.

At once the kingdom was thrown into confusion. Despite the prolonged and valiant efforts of the widowed Queen Catherine de Médicis, the only figure strong and capable enough to hold the kingdom together and the warring religious factions apart was gone. All hell was about to be let loose.

Yet Nostradamus had totally failed to predict this huge calamity. In his Letter he had even addressed Henri as 'Most Invincible'. Worse, in neither of his known *Almanachs* for 1559 (including the one that was translated into English at the time) had there been any mention of anything untoward happening to the King, whether in June/July or at any other time, despite his confident assertion that 'no affliction, calamity or misery comes into this world but that the stars make it apparent beforehand.' True, Nostradamus had announced for June that 'Some great Prince, Lord and sovereign ruler shall die, others fail and yet others greatly fall,' but then he had added in the very next breath (and still for June) that 'France shall greatly grow, triumph, be magnified, and much more so its Monarch.'[16] And, for July, nothing about the King at all.

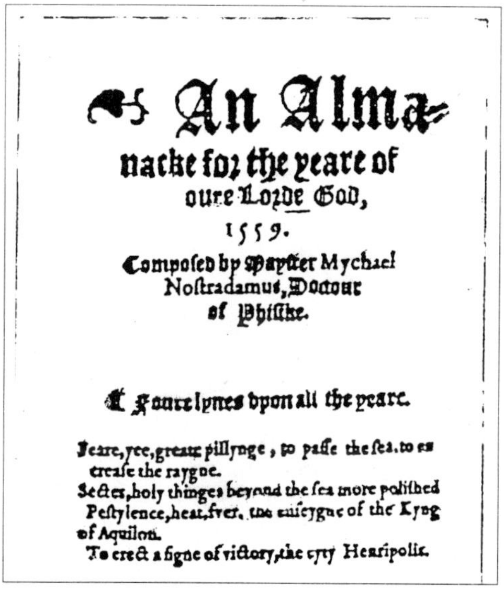
An Almanacke for the yeare of oure Lorde God, 1559.
Composed by Mayster Mychael Nostradamus, Doctour of Physike.

Foure lynes upon all the yeare.

Feare, yee, greate pillynge, to passe the sea, to encrease the raygne.
Sectes, holy thinges beyond the sea more polished
Pestylence, heat, fyer, the enseygne of the Kyng of Aquilon.
To erect a signe of victory, the cyty Henripolis.

Title page of the English translation of the 1559 Almanach

Granted, in an open letter to the cleric Jean de Vauzelles published with his *Almanach* for 1562, Nostradamus would later claim that he had indeed predicted the disaster. In verse III.55 of the *Propheties* (he insisted, while characteristically misquoting it) he had specifically described how

> The year when One-Eye power in France shall gain
> The Court shall undergo vexatious trouble:
> By Lorge of Blois his bosom-friend is slain,
> The kingdom placed in doubt and trouble double.

The *real* trouble, though, was that the verse as printed had not said 'By *Lorge* of Blois' at all, but 'By *Lord* of Blois (or, in the original French, not *grain,* as Nostradamus claimed, [given that *l'orge* meant 'barley'] but *grand* [the normal term for a lord]).[8]

It was no good. No amount of 'retrodiction' could retrieve the situation. It looked like the end of the road for France. And it was certainly the end of the road for Nostradamus's public career as a long-term prophet.

9. The Mage

NEVERTHELESS, NOSTRADAMUS HAD A CONSIDERABLE REPUTATION by now for writing best-selling annual *Almanachs,* counseling the great, interpreting personal horoscopes and allegedly having privileged access to arcane knowledge denied to most ordinary folk. Indeed, he had managed to draw around himself a dark aura of mystery and the occult that had the more credulous even of the nobility all but cowering before him in awe. When the young François II followed his father to an early grave in December 1560, as apparently predicted in that year's *Almanach,* foreign ambassadors were soon reporting home that it was virtually impossible to do sensible, rational business with anybody there, so stricken was everybody with raging Nostradamania. His *Les significations de l'eclipse qui sera le 16 Septembre...* published both in French and in English during 1559 and predicting dire consequences for the same year, simply added to his prestige as an interpreter of signs, whether celestial or otherwise.

His reputation still persisted in the medical sphere, too. In 1557 Antoine du Rosne had published not only the second edition of his *Propheties,* but his *Paraphrase de C Galien, sus l'exhortation de Menodote, aux estudes des bonnes Artz, mesmement medecine.*[51] This was, as its title suggested, a paraphrase – or rather an extremely free French version of a Latin translation of Galen's Greek re-working – of Menodotus of Alexandria's original Greek text recommending the serious study of the arts and sciences, and one wonders quite why he had chosen to publish it now, especially as Erasmus had already published a much more accurate and elegant Latin version. One almost has the impression that it was an old manuscript that he had dug out, written during his days as a rather factious apothecary, and designed to prove that Galen had (as we suggested earlier) not been nearly as *Galenesque* as the current medical establishment liked to make out. What he seems to have been doing, in short, was using his now established position as a recognized author finally to make the manuscript public. Its theme, after all, was that people should not merely accept, animal-like, what was imposed upon them, but use their own higher faculties – a suggestion that might not be too welcome to most doctors of the day, with their authoritarian dogmas blindly accepted from antiquity. Certainly it was not merely about medicine, as Nostradamus's title slyly proposed, but rather a diatribe against crude athletics. Possibly his purpose was simply to thumb his nose at the established medical profession by showing that even Galen himself didn't agree with the way in which they were applying Galen.

And so Nostradamus was able to permit himself the delicious irony of putting *himself* forward as the true representative of Galen. Rubbing the point home, he claimed actually to have consulted the original Greek, and to have got a number of celebrated scholars – including his own brother Jehan – to check and approve his version, listing them in his preface. Even more ironically, he preceded all of this with a verse-eulogy of Galen himself, likewise allegedly translated from the Greek:

> Time was when Earth one mortal man infused
> With Galen's science and brought him forth to birth;
> When savage healing arts, till then confused,
> He did o'erturn as things of little worth.
> Still did Earth bear immortals in those days
> When his great fame the gates did burst apart
> Of damnèd Hell, thanks to his healing ways,
> His much-praised doctrine and physician's art.

And, to make sure of at least some financial reward, he dedicated the whole thing to his old cronies, the Baron de la Garde and the Commandeur de Beynes, whom we last encountered at Salon at the time of the celebrated 1554 omens.

The book was reprinted in 1558, and again in 1559. Then, a few weeks after the king's death (and almost certainly before he even heard about the tragedy), Nostradamus suddenly embarked on a trip to the south west, partly at the behest of the 36-year-old Bishop of Béziers, Cardinal Lorenzo Strozzi, who was suffering terribly from gout. After the consultation, he left his most reverend patient with the following prescription, which I have not attempted to make any more grammatical or clear-minded than it actually is:

Monsignor
Having calculated the affair of your illness, harmonizing it via a triple method, by the method of medicine together with surgery, the agreements of judicial and natural astrology, and having not omitted any other secret methods of any merit, and first of all, in order to get to the end and conclusion of what you wish, which is the total cure of your illness, it is necessary that first of all on Sunday, at one o'clock of the afternoon, having dined at your accustomed hour, that a burning knob be applied to you on the spot that I showed you and touched with my finger. And let the knob be as follows, and let it not be pushed in any further than the rim of the knob.

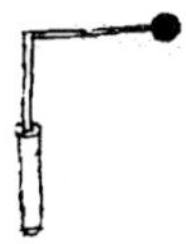

After the burning cauterization has been carried out, let the digestive [?] be in the form of the yoke of an egg, rose-juice oil and fresh butter. Once the scar – which is the burn made by the fire – has fallen off, push in a silver bead made half of copper and half of silver, and push it into the hole until it is right in. Then take one or two leaves of *hedera paretis* [climbing ivy], the broadest and freshest, and lay them on it, and bind it up with a small bandage, and bathe it once every 24 hours, either in the morning or in the evening. However, the evening, when you are going to bed, will be best. And wear it continually for the space of about seven months. But be assured, Monsignor, you will not have borne the openings in your two legs more than seven or eight days before you will suddenly experience major relief, and most of that inner cold will disappear. And this will not only benefit the illness of which you are complaining, but also as long as you bear the said open, discharging wounds, you will feel neither headaches, brain-aches, nor any fever nor pain in the shoulders, stomach or legs, nor any part of the body, for there is no medicine in the world that approaches this one. I will not harangue you any further about the virtues and effects, since you yourself will soon have further evidence of the truth. Also do not fail to use the distillation that I am prescribing for you, which you will find a sovereign remedy if morning and evening you rub it into the back of the neck and all the vertebrae of your back right down to the base, as well as some of the joints. Praying God, Monsignor, that you obtain what you desire. Given at Béziers, on my way from Provence to Narbonne, this 20th October 1559.
[Concluding note in what appears to be Nostradamus's hand:]
Faciebat [Latin: written by] M. Nostradamus. Béziers, 20th October 1559. Your humble servant. M. de Nostre-Dame.

The treatment described, which must have been excruciating, was of course designed primarily to allow the 'bad humors' to flow out. Needless to say, though, poor Strozzi was still suffering cruelly from the gout ten years later, to the point of being virtually crippled at age 46.[8, 47]

Long before that, however, Nostradamus was back home again. Possibly he left as soon as he heard the awful news from Paris – which he had clearly not anticipated, or he would never have left his 'power-base' for the south west in the first place. Certainly he was back by December of the same year. For in that month the late King's sister, the Princess Marguerite, called at Salon on her way back from the royal funeral to her new home in Savoy in the wake of her husband Duke Philibert (who had already passed through while Nostradamus was still away and out of touch), accompanied by the usual huge royal retinue. Nostradamus's first-born son César was only five at the time, having in the meantime been joined by Charles (3), André (2) and Anne (1) (one could of course ask what the supposed prophet was doing bringing so many children into the world at a time that he knew was going to be so ghastly!). But he was later to describe the visit in vivid terms:

> That excellent Princess, her Barons and her Ladies-in-Waiting, the litters and horses, the pack-animals and baggage-mules, the carts, the luggage and its awnings, the pages and lackeys, the officers and servants... in their black and funereal livery... drew from the eyes of the onlookers tears and pitiable laments rather than laughter and shouts of joy... The magistrates of our town received the Duchess right properly from a dais of violet and crimson damask... and accompanied her, with the marks of their responsibilities on their shoulders, from the gates of the town all the way to the gate of the castle beneath various arcades, erected at intervals, decorated with fresh, green branches of box and crowned with coats of arms.[42, 47]

Nostradamus, as the town *savant*, was inevitably called upon to supply a suitable address in verse, and addressed the Princess in the words

> Daughter of Trojan blood and Trojan stock
> And Cypris Queen...

Then he reportedly had a long talk with her on the subject of the royal virtues that she had allegedly inherited from Great King François.[47] As for the 'Trojan' reference, this went back to a fashionably classical myth then current – much celebrated by both Nostradamus and Ronsard – that the French royal family could trace its ancestry all the way back to Francus, son of Hector of Troy, whose own ancestor had been Cypris, goddess of love...

All of this could only enhance Nostradamus's reputation even further, of course. Certainly by now he was in lively Latin correspondence with people all over western Europe to whose ears his acquired fame as a mage had come.[3, 21] By and large, they were after readings of their astrological birth-charts, 'progressed' to indicate their likely fortunes for the current year – charts which, as often as not, Nostradamus expected *them* to supply, as drawn up by prominent astrologers such as Leowitz. Given that, of his own horoscopes, every one was to contain at least one significant error, and about half would contain whole rafts of them,[8] this was a wise precaution. But the fact itself is not too surprising, since we now know, thanks to the detailed researches of Pierre Brind'Amour,[8] that he merely took his figures from other people's tables for noon at wherever they were based (generally Ulm in Germany) and applied them 'cold', without any attempt to adjust either for his clients' time or place of birth. It was not just that he was incapable of drawing up his own tables: he clearly had no idea even of how to interpolate from other people's. As the astrologer Videl, declining to pull his punches, had put it the previous year in his widely-sold pamphlet unashamedly entitled *Declaration des abus, ignorances et seditions de Michel Nostradamus*:[70]

> I can say with complete confidence that of true astrology you understand less than nothing, as is evident not merely to the learned, but to learners in astrology too, as your works amply demonstrate, you who cannot calculate the least movement of any heavenly body whatever: and no more than knowing the movements do you understand how to use your tables... And it is no use covering yourself with astrology, either, for it teaches us no such fantasies, not to fool around with going out at night to look at the stars. I realize that for those who wish to learn astrology it is necessary to observe the sky in order to recognize the fixed stars, the planets and their courses. But to say that you have to go and look at them to write Almanachs is pure deception [Nostradamus would later claim to have written part of the 1566 *Almanach* atop the tower of Salon's castle]. Besides, as far as doing so in order to calculate their movements is concerned, you know nothing about it. If you knew even the basics of astrology, you would know that there is no need for you to leave your study to write Almanachs. For in our own time there are plenty of learned and educated people who have already calculated for us the movements of the eight heavens. But these matters are too obscure for your brain, for it is certain that you know how to calculate neither by the heavens nor by any tables whatsoever.

But then, given that Nostradamus's readings had much more to do with native intuition than with actual astrological indications, possibly his evident astrological incompetence was not too important anyway.

His clients were many, various and often distinguished. He is known to have supplied horoscopes for the lawyer Jean Suffren, sometime consul of Salon and an eventual witness to his Will; for Queen Catherine de Médicis on behalf of her eldest son, the future King François II, at the time when he was still Dauphin; for his successor the young King Charles IX; for the Imperial Crown Prince Rudolph Maximilian in Vienna; for Duke Emmanuel Philibert of Savoy on behalf of his new-born son Charles-Emmanuel; and for the Canons of Orange when in 1562 they asked for his help in tracing their stolen church treasures and identifying the thieves.[8]

There were admiring letters from the young man who from around 1561 would become his secretary, Jean de Chavigny, as well as both to and from François Bérard, lawyer and Procurator Fiscal to the Papal Legation at Avignon – a keen alchemist and, latterly, would-be disciple and assistant – concerning the reading of his birth-chart and a 'psychic reading' of his allegedly magic ring. Regarding the latter, Nostradamus's initial response elicited from him the following rather pointed comment:

> I have read what you wrote back to me about the ring but truly I was unable to divine in the slightest what it may have meant, and unless, as they say, you write it less learnedly – i.e. more clearly and openly – I can hardly hope to understand it: for it is truly ambiguous.[21c]

On a later occasion Nostradamus would have another go at it – and this time came up with the intriguing letter reproduced in translation in Appendix D, which reveals some of his 'psychic methodology'.

There were exchanges with Bishop Pierre de Forlivio of Apt, former regent of the university of Avignon and secretary to the papal Legation there; with Sigismund Woysell of Breslau, sometime lawyer in Avignon; with Olrias de Cadenet, also a former regent at Avignon; with Jerome Purpurat of Turin; with the Italian Petrus Martyr Carbo; with Jacobus Securivagus; with Johannes Lobbetius of Augsburg on behalf of the Emperor Maximilian and his family, and with a variety of others both lay and religious, all requesting either birth-charts or readings of them. There was also a brief correspondence with a couple of seekers of buried treasure suggesting where they might find it, and an even briefer one with a monk who was absolutely desperate to escape his monastery.[3, 21]

By way of example – and a particularly revealing one, at that – there was a particularly long Latin exchange with the important German mine-owner Johannes Rosenberger of Augsburg (a Renaissance gentleman with a great thirst for learning), either directly or via his agent Lorenz Tubbe of Pomerania – who would no doubt have preferred to deal with their local mage Paracelsus instead had the latter not apparently been murdered at Salzburg in 1541. This correspondence began in 1559 and continued on and off until 1562, with the intermissions due largely to non-existent postal services, the varying availability of suitable travelers to act as messengers and huge social disruption resulting from the ever-spreading Wars of Religion. Its main subject was Nostradamus's astrological predictions for the likely health, fortunes and prospects of Rosenberger and his two sons as year succeeded year, particularly in connection with his failing lead and silver mines – work for which Tubbe proposed to pay with business recommendations, and his master mainly with gilded silverware from his mines, using as intermediaries a German merchant called Kraft, a French doctor called Liparin and Nostradamus's Lyon publisher Jean Brotot.

All was not plain sailing, however. Some items got mislaid. Others got misdirected. Then there was Nostradamus's own writing and choice of language. As Tubbe wrote to him on 16 March 1560:

> You should not doubt my promise that you will be suitably rewarded for your most learned and diligent work. I would have already started to pay off my debt if, alas, I had not been delayed by your writing and the language that you used in the commentary on the birth-chart. I implore you, counting on your indulgence, not to be annoyed. I devoted enormous study and diligence to reading your explanations, and I engaged several French readers to help me because I have not yet learned the French language; but they all complained about how difficult it was to read. If it had been possible simply to read it, I would have arranged for your text to be translated into Latin and then would have sent to Germany both the translation and your manuscript. Being unable to do anything else, therefore, I transcribed the birth-chart, your calculations, and the titles of the chapters, which are forty-two in number. I have dispatched the whole thing, with a copy of your own letter, to my master in Germany. I promised to send him as soon as possible the study of his birth-chart written in Latin – because he more or less understands Latin, but he does not

> know French. Thus, I implore you, most illustrious Nostradamus, Your Excellency – do not blame me, I pray, for imposing so much work on you, for I do not doubt that the many things that take up your time could prevent you from accommodating my request. However, I return this thesis to you with confidence, so that you may transcribe it from French into Latin and have it written in letters that are a little larger, like the size of those in the inscription that was on the covering sheet in which your memorandum was wrapped. There is no point in creating purple prose: just explain it simply and clearly. Besides, your Latin prose style, to judge by your recent letters, is elegant, which is rare among astrologers. I am not unaware how annoyed a scholar such as yourself must be when the whole work and labor than you had thought finished comes back home to roost. But, as God loves me, I do not see any other remedy, so I find myself reluctantly compelled to return this manuscript to you. I have discussed the matter with my great friend Doctor Liparin and he saw it the same way. I beseech you, therefore, as well for my patron, to add this great task to your labors. It is simply a question of dictating in Latin this French text to one of your secretaries who writes clearly, and of sending it back to me.[21c]

The complaint, alas (which Tubbe had to repeat on 20 September before finally receiving a reply at the beginning of December), was not untypical. Even then, the requested Latin version was not forthcoming. However, Tubbe refused to be discouraged. Not only did he now send Nostradamus yet more information on Rosenberger – full details of his name, as well as of his mother's, to say nothing of descriptions of the mines themselves – but a request for details of *his own* prospects, too. And meanwhile he decided to make the best of a bad job and try to translate it himself, first into Latin and then into German. Thus it was that, four months later, he was able to write back:

> By 1st January, illustrious Nostradamus, I came to the end of my translation of your text; but only with great difficulty and incredible labor. It contains more hidden depths than it promises at first sight and, for the most part, what you wrote was clearly designed to be read not by a Davus [a proverbially dense Roman slave], but by an Oedipus [i.e. a solver of the Sphinx's riddles]. Therefore it has been difficult for me to put it into Latin. I was helped somewhat by some French people, but they are ignorant in matters of astrology, as is nearly everybody here.[21c]

However, Rosenberger himself was so delighted that he now replied in person:

I became aware of the celebrity of your name, especially in what I had heard of your doctrine, a long time ago. Your reputation was universally widespread – a judgment which I, too, had always strongly held. But now that I hold in my hands the present birth-chart, now that I have perused it, I recognize by it, as one might a lion by its claws, your perfect judgment of things astrological, as though consecrated by the Delphic oracle.[21c]

Evidently Rosenberger was a truly satisfied customer. Anxious to learn even more about himself and his prospects, he went on:

I note how very true many of the events are that have already happened to me, many of which, with the stars currently being adverse, are now threatening me with losses, as much in connection with my mines as with other things that are wont to touch mankind. However, I will not lose all hope of better fortunes, and I will not abandon my projects, even if they lose me money; but I will try to act according to your most wise counsels. I will let a little time pass and, as you sincerely advise, try to overcome through patience, while bearing the blows of misfortune. 'GOOD FORTUNE SHALL ARRIVE AT AN UNHOPED-FOR HOUR' [Horace]...

I am sending to you, my dear, most kind and erudite Nostradamus, my image. Although you cannot really know me face to face, you will recognize me, far away from you though I am, on this present medallion, which expresses me to the life. On the back of this my image, you can see an image and diagram of one of my mines. On the edge, you will see inscribed in Latin letters but in the German language the goal and target towards which I direct all my actions and my intentions, namely that I pray to God, and that in giving thanks to Him, I give on His behalf to the deserving poor what is owing to them. While thus acting for the glory of God, I am confident that I shall obtain His favors one day by the intermediary of his stars...

If you would work out the birth-charts of my sons, and would carry them out with all diligence in order to send them to me, there will be a far different fee commensurate with the man, and I will remunerate you in a fashion worthy of so much labor. I nevertheless commend you for your virtue, kindness and knowledge. My son Karl was born in 1534, on Friday, April 24 at night, at a quarter past one. My other son, Johannes, was born in 1544, on Saturday, February 2, in the evening, at a quarter to five.

You learned, I believe, from my dear Lorenz of Pomerania the first name of my late mother. If, however, you still require the first name so

> as to complete the revolution [progressed chart], her first name was Clara, and her surname Ehinger; I was her eldest son. My wife's first name is Kunigunde, and her surname is Pimlin. All this will be conducive to your completion of the progressed chart and to informing your wise judgment. You will [thus] be able to take account all the more easily of the soul whose nature I am drawing to your attention.
>
> I do not quite know how to finish this letter, but I think the following is worth adding: given that the subject is prophecy, I am neither quick nor experienced as a reader of esoteric texts, but much more of those concerning thoughts to do with politics. Therefore, I would be extremely grateful to you if you would accommodate whatever you write to me subsequently about birth-charts or revolutions just a little to my intelligence, which is slight, (to the extent that it is worthy of it) by writing in Latin – which, as a common language, I understand, while I do not understand French, even though I respect it for its elegance and richness. Please write in clear, unmutilated letters, without abbreviations, so that I can read what you write without help from others.[21c]

The point was gently put, but it was the usual old point for all that. French had not yet acquired the international reputation that it has today thanks largely to the efforts of Nostradamus's contemporaries such as Du Bellay and Ronsard, and it was of absolutely no use for Nostradamus to persist in writing in it. And meanwhile Rosenberger's likeness on the medallion and the details of his family names were all supposed to help the French mage by virtue of the special forms of divination that were supposed to apply to such things.

Three months later, having received no reply, Rosenberger was still repeating his request for birth-charts for his sons. The man was clearly obsessed with his astrological prospects, and attached great importance to them. Come June that year, Tubbe was hastily sending off to Nostradamus a promised goblet in anticipation – presumably lest the Frenchman lose interest – and wondering whether the letters had perhaps been intercepted. Shortly afterwards, Rosenberger himself was repeating his request yet again and hoping that the medallion and goblet had duly arrived.

Finally, on 15 July 1561, Nostradamus replied, thanking Tubbe for the medallion and goblet, promising to undertake the astrological work for Rosenberger's sons and guaranteeing clarity this time:

> Regarding the birth-charts for Karl and Johannes, I will work on them promptly. I hope to have finished this work before the Lyon Fair, which

> generally takes place after November 1. I cannot do them more quickly. Before completing them, however, I would like to have in my hands the birth-charts previously calculated by Cyprian Leowitz. Could our friend send them to me, if, as I believe, he still has them? Please be kind enough to do all that you can to ensure that these documents wing their way to me as quickly as possible. Otherwise, I shall operate according to my own method. Your master need have no fears about ambiguities, enigmatic meanings or equivocations. All of my forecasts are clearer than day itself. None of them will be [obscure]: I shall hide nothing.[21c]

Chance (one feels tempted to add) would be a fine thing!

By 9 August 1561 Tubbe was acknowledging receipt of the requested work, but regretting that he did not have Leowitz's charts to hand in Bourges, and a month later Nostradamus was replying to Rosenberger in person to thank him for the silverware and assure him that the requested work had not only been performed, but transcribed to make it readable by 'a young Frenchman' who was almost certainly his new secretary and amanuensis Jean de Chavigny. The German mine-owner would, he assured him, shortly run into new, rich veins of silver, *provided that he continued with what he had begun*. He was to stress this principle on several occasions – and perfectly reasonably so, given that, if Rosenberger *failed* to continue, he would assuredly *not* run into such veins! (Certainly, there was nothing particularly astrological about the principle: it was simply part of Nostradamus's genius for making the commonplace seem extraordinary.)

By October, Nostradamus was writing to Tubbe with the final pieces of work and telling him that he was not, after all, going to be able to go the Court in Paris that year as he had hoped, nor, consequently, to meet him there, because he still had the birth-chart of the new King Charles IX to finish (Charles's elder brother François II had just died suddenly at age 16, and his almost equally young wife, Mary Queen of Scots, had been smartly packed off home to Scotland again). Besides, winter was coming on. Also, he should no longer send his letters via the publisher Jean Brotot, as the latter had died and his son Pierre was not necessarily as reliable. As for himself, he would in future seal his letters securely, just in case anybody should try and open them. At the same time, he also wrote again to Rosenberger directly, assuring him that, for him, the good times were about to begin.

In return, a month later, Tubbe was writing from Antwerp to advise Nostradamus that, for France, they certainly weren't. Civil war was about to break out between Catholics and Protestants in France, with disorder already breaking out in the Low Countries. Ever since the Conspiracy of Amboise of 1560, when the Protestants had tried to kidnap the King and the Catholic Guises had brutally repressed the incipient coup, things had been going from bad to worse. There had been riots, public burnings, threatened massacres, emergency meetings at the top. And indeed, five letters and six months later Nostradamus was telling Tubbe at great length (as was his wont) how the troubles had finally reached Salon and how, amid all the anti-Protestant threats and the chaos, he and his family had been forced to rent a safe house in Avignon for the duration – not, presumably, because they were Protestants, but because Nostradamus was perceived to be 'different' and therefore suspect, as well as having pronounced reformist sympathies that made him even more so.

Meanwhile, other things were happening, too. It was not just that the Nostradamuses' sixth and last child, Diane, was born in September. The annual *Almanachs* were still demanding to be written and published, and taking up ever greater amounts of the seer's time as they became ever longer and more complex. Not everybody was happy with them, though. True, the late King Henri II had apparently been addicted, and had made a habit of consulting them daily.[8] But when Nostradamus published his 1562 *Almanach* in late 1561 without bothering to get the *imprimatur* of a bishop, as was newly demanded by the law in the light of the currently explosive religious and political situation, he was promptly arrested and flung into prison at the castle of Marignane (which overlooks today's Marseille airport) by none other than his old friend the Governor of Provence, Claude duc de Tende. As the latter reported to the King on 18 December:

> As to Nostradamus, I have had him arrested and he is with me, who have forbidden him to make any further almanacs or prognostications, which he has promised me. Be pleased to command me what you would that I should do with him.[8]

Article 26 of the Edict of Orleans of 31 January 1561, after all, had been rather vague about it:

> And against whoever shall have made or composed the said Almanachs [it said] our Judges shall proceed extraordinarily, and by corporal punishment.

Upon the answer, therefore, much depended...

10. *The Controversialist*

IN THE EVENT, NO ANSWER AT ALL SEEMS TO HAVE BEEN FORTHCOMING from the Court. Perhaps the young King was reluctant to prosecute the seer, given that he had only recently requested and received from him his own birth-chart and commentary. True, it would have taken at least a couple of months for his jailor the Duc de Tende to be sure, given that that was how long even the relatively fast royal posting service would have taken to convey the messages both ways. But at the end of that time – and given that Tende *was* his friend – Nostradamus was smartly freed again and, despite his alleged promise not to, continuing work on his *Almanachs* as if nothing had happened.

But the world into which he was released in early 1562 was no longer as friendly as it used to be, either on the political or on the literary front. Ever since he had achieved fame in 1555, in fact, he had started (no doubt for that very reason) to become the butt of an increasingly virulent campaign of public abuse, nearly all of it relating to his *Almanachs*. In those for 1557, consequently, he was already attempting to counter such attacks, prefacing all three with the impressively prescient inscription:

> Against those who have so often wished me dead:
> *Immortal, I, alive; more, having died:*
> *When I am dead my name shall live world-wide.*

Indeed, even in his *Significations de l'eclipse...* of 1559 he had mounted a further vigorous counter-attack that may even have been the real object of the publication. His detractors, he had claimed, were 'stupid, ignorant asses' and 'barking dogs vomiting their rage against me'. Motivated by the Devil, they were trying to steal his feathers in order to adorn themselves. In the *Almanach* for 1561 he had taken it further: 'It is easier to blame than to imitate,' he had quoted in Latin, vigorously defending his highly dubious practice of drawing concrete predictions from astrology against 'slanderers who never stop disgorging their poison and anger towards me... '[8]

His protestations were evidently heartfelt – and understandably, too. After all, in 1557 an anonymous author calling himself 'The French Lord Hercules' (a presumed reference to Nostradamus's own frequent use of the term 'the Gallic Ogmion', or 'French Hercules') had published an outspoken critique of him provocatively entitled *La Premiere Invective du Seigneur Hercules le François, contre Monstradamus...*[25] (*sic* – reproduced in translation in Appendix E), accusing him of being, among other things, a '24-carat liar'. This had been closely followed in November by Videl's already encountered and widely sold tirade entitled *Declaration des abus ignorances et seditions de Michel Nostradamus,*[70] which roundly berated him in the most damning terms for his sheer astrological incompetence (translated extracts of this are likewise to be found in Appendix E).

But these two pamphlets had merely opened the floodgates. In 1558 one 'Jean de la Daguenière' had published another attack anagrammatically entitled *Le monstre d'abus,*[19] which was rude about its easily identifiable subject's Jewish origins and remarked, of his visit to the court in 1555:

> Do you not recall how much your arrival at Court gave authority to the reputation of your works? Yet I who was there at the time know perfectly well that there was nobody there who was not convinced that you had come there expressly in order to receive by way of reward all the mockery that all your poor little treatises and fantastic statements richly deserved. Even you must be fully aware of how many times you were nearly handed over to the pages' clutches and whims for having so impudently and clumsily been sparing with the truth by tarting up and disguising your language... What do you suppose it means, what these disguised words are trying to say? [*sic*] I say [all this] again by way of accusing [the French has 'excusing'!] the fault, error and imperfection of your argument, in which one can find, however hard one looks, neither sense, nor reason, nor continuity, nor any good, intelligible order; and there is no adequate and competent grammarian capable of honorably construing (to use their own term) a piece of writing so badly put together and where all good order and substance are lacking...

The words 'black', 'kettle' and 'pot' do rather spring to mind – and not necessarily in that order.

In 1560, similarly, the future Chancellor Michel de l'Hospital, recalling in Latin verse his visit with Princess Marguerite of Savoy to Salon in late 1559, had included the lines:

> Appeared afar off stony Salon's roofs:
> Here gave to those who asked crooked response
> The lying Nostradamus. O what folly!
> Already by his words he ruled the minds
> And hearts of kings and lords alike. This wisdom
> Comes not from God, who mortals doth forbid
> What things shall hap by mortals to be seen.

By 1562 Conrad Badius, a member of the Protestant faction in Geneva, was joining in the fray, apparently referring almost uniquely in his *Les vertus de nostre maistre Nostradamus* to Nostradamus's *Propheties*, rather than to his *Almanachs*:

> Ere I forget, or further forage,
> He writes his verse like stirring porridge.
> And for a mumbler of the Mass
> He mangles endings like an ass.
> Of stirrup-straps his lines remind,
> Too short in front, too long behind,
> Born beneath such a sign and season
> As to have neither rhyme nor reason.

At some point, too, a poisonous little Latin two-liner started going the rounds. In Latin it read:

> *Nostra damus cum verba damus, quia fallere Nostrum est,*
> *Et cum verba damus nil nisi Nostra-damus.*[8]

Such intricate plays on words – in this case based on the would-be prophet Nostradamus's evident failure to foresee that, in medieval Latin, *Nostra damus* might be taken to mean 'We dispense nostrums, or quackeries' – are not easy to render into comparable English, but a very rough counterpart indeed might read something like:

> Nostrums be damned! Such words we speak
> When nostrums fail, for we are weak.
> And when such words we choose to mutter
> We 'Nostra damn us!' merely utter.

The growing controversy about Nostradamus was not confined to France. In England in March 1559, Dr Matthew Parker, who had been proposed as Archbishop of Canterbury, wrote to his patron Sir Nicholas Bacon, Lord Keeper of the Great Seal (and father of Francis), rejecting the offer, but hurriedly added at the same time that this was assuredly not because of anything that Nostradamus had written:

> I pray you think not that the prognostication of Mr Michael Nostre Dame reigneth in my head. I esteem that fantastical hotchpotch not so well as I credit Lucian's book, *De veris narrationibus;* nor yet all other vain prophecies of such more than I regard Sir Thomas Morys' book of 'Fortune's Answers upon the chance of three dice casting'.[8]

In August the same year Sir Thomas Challoner, English ambassador to the Low Countries, reported to Queen Elizabeth's Secretary of State William Cecil:

> On Friday last the King [Philip II] embarked with his whole fleet towards Spain, with an easterly wind, very small, next to a calm, but such as most gladly he embraced... This foolish Nostradamus, with his threats of tempests and shipwrecks this month, did put these sailors in a great fear.[8]

In January 1560, Sir Thomas Randolph wrote from Glasgow to Sir Ralph Sadleyr and Sir James Craft with news of a newly captured prisoner of his called La Marque, *valet de chambre* to the French royal family:

> He brought 3 books with him – one as papistical as ever was written, the other of love, to recreate his troubled spirits: the third was 'the prognostication of the venerable personage Nostredamus, of this yere'. I would have sent it to you, but there are too many here that give credit to such follies.[8]

Extracts from yet further English commentaries of the time will be found in Appendix E.

In Switzerland, meanwhile, the Protestant leader Théodore de Bèze (Calvin's successor) reported in 1563 that in Toulouse

> On the fifteenth of February in the said year, the town came very close to being ruined by another sedition, and all because of a letter sent to Toulouse by that fine Astrologer Nostradamus, who had written to various people that they should be on their guard, as the town was in danger of being captured that day... So much for putting one's faith in such a rabble of prognosticators and soothsayers...[8]

The Catholic Ronsard, though, was much more enthusiastic. In his

Elegie à Guillaume des Autels... sur les miseres de ce temps of 1560, which bemoaned at considerable length the dire times that France was then passing through, the leading court poet (and canon of the Church) included the lines:

> France, all these ills from your own folly flow:
> A thousand times God's voice has told you so...
> Too little do you value their good name:
> Well should your face about it blush for shame.
> You even mock those seers whom God doth raise
> Among your children, so that in these days
> From out your bosom they may spring and say
> What ills shall come. Laughing, you turn away.
> Be it Great God beyond all space and time
> Roused Nostradamus' rapture into rhyme;
> Be he by daemon good or evil stirred,
> Or gifted with a soul that like some bird
> Soars up to heavens no mortal man may know
> To bring back auguries for us below;
> Be his a mind so gloomy, dark and dim,
> Crammed with gross humors, as to cozen him –
> Whate'er he is, he is: yet none the less
> Through the vague portents that his words express
> Like some old oracle he has foretold
> For many a year what fate for us shall hold.
> I'd doubt him, did not heaven, that to men
> Imparts both good and evil, guide his pen.

But the Protestants were not going to let him get away with that. In 1563 an anonymous pamphlet entitled *Les Palinodies de Pierre de Ronsard* appeared by way of a riposte – a pretended and not very subtle 'recantation' that, after quoting the first eight lines of the above verbatim, satirized the rest in the words:

> But if by chance some Julian should appear,
> Some fraud like Postel, some mad, magic seer,
> Some dreamer or some Devil, then at once
> You'll hear and trust, you superstitious dunce,
> Though stinks his ignorance, that the eternal
> Roused Nostradamus' rapture quite infernal.
> Not God but th' Evil One doth take him in
> When he believes he has a soul within

That soars to heavens no mortal man may know
To bring back auguries for us below.
His is a spirit gloomy dark and dim,
Stuffed with gross humours, fit to cozen him.
In short, they're worse than Satan or the Plague,
Those who with lying tongues and portents vague
Like some old oracle have long foretold
For many a year what fate for us shall hold.
Don't trust a single word: heaven does not share
Both good and ill to men – that's from elsewhere!

In the same year a further Protestant pamphlet continued the argument, this time appealing to Queen Catherine de Médicis in person. The *Remonstrance a la Royne mere du Roy sur le discours de Pierre de Ronsard des miseres de ce temps*, published in Lyon in 1563, included the lines:

Ronsard, you fool, how dare you take to heart
This damnèd Nostradamus and his art,
Calling him true, and for a maniac's word
Betray the revelation of the Lord!

However, the Queen, who was in any case not a Protestant but a faithful Catholic, was not to be swayed. For her, as for her adolescent son King Charles IX, Nostradamus was by now the pre-eminent prophet and sage of France. And so, when in 1564, the two of them set out on a two-year progress through the kingdom to try and cool tempers and spread the spirit of peace and reconciliation, they took care to see that their route southwards took them and their 20,000 courtiers through Salon itself.

> Passing through Salon [she later wrote to Montmorency], we saw Nostradamus, who promised all kinds of good things to the King my son, and that he will live as long as you, who, he says, shall reach the age of ninety before dying.[8]

(Needless to say, Charles would die only ten years later at the tender age of 24, while Montmorency would only reach the age of 75.)

César (then still only ten) would later recall the occasion.[47] After a false alarm about the sudden arrival of the Plague, the King duly appeared:

> Simple arcades of box-branches had been erected all the way from the Avignon gate to the gates of the castle, that magnificent and pontifical

> residence. The cobbles of the streets had been covered with sand and sprinkled with rosemary, which gave off a most pleasant smell of flowers. The King was seated on an African horse with a gray caparison trimmed with black velvet, with broad bands and edges of gold. He himself was dressed in a crimson Phoenician outfit, commonly called 'violet', adorned with silver cords, with matching hat and feathers.

The King was suitably welcomed by that year's three town consuls and leading citizens under a violet and white damask awning, their speeches no doubt written for them once again by Nostradamus the town savant. Apparently he had even quoted the Latin line 'Great man of war, second to none in piety' – which may have sounded good, but was hardly appropriate to the 14-year-old King. According to one admittedly apocryphal account, however, the young monarch waved all that aside, protesting that he had 'only come to see Nostradamus'. And so the sage was duly produced, and accompanied the King through the little town on foot

> always side by side, with his velvet hat in one hand and a big and very fine Indian cane with a silver handle... to lean on *en route*, because he was sometimes tormented by that troublesome pain in the feet that is commonly called gout...[47]

Climbing the long hill, they arrived at the castle (overleaf), where both the King and the Queen Mother, who was his Regent, entertained the seer and his family, the Queen cooing particularly (as César recalled with especial delight) over three-year-old Diane.

During the visit, various sources recount how Nostradamus asked to examine the 14-year-old Henri, Prince de Béarn, as he got out of bed in the nude in his lodgings at the house of the seer's own future kinsman Pierre Tronc du Coudoulet, in order to assess his future prospects – and pronounced, on the basis of the moles on his body, that he would not only become king, but reign for a long time.[P] This was something of a relief to the Prince, who was naturally afraid that the old man was going to beat him with his stick. After he had indeed become the later King Henri IV of France, he would, it is said, endlessly recall the occasion with some amusement.[42]

The royal progress then continued via Aix, Marseille and the sacred grotto of La Sainte Baume in the mountains north of the city (the legendary final retreat of Mary Magdalene), then back to Marseille and finally on to Arles, where, to fill a long delay caused by that year's

Rhône floods, Nostradamus was sent for once more. Quite how he got there along the old Roman road across the Craux nobody knows. Possibly he was still fit enough to ride a horse. At all events, he duly underwent further royal questioning at his neighbor the Bishop's palace, during the course of which he was invited to support the suggestion that a proposal of marriage be sent on the young King Charles's behalf to the determinedly virginal Queen Elizabeth of England, who was twice his age. Evidently Nostradamus agreed, as he clearly had no choice but to do. As the then Spanish ambassador, Don Francès de Alava, would tell his master Philip II, 'The first day that the king and queen saw Nostradamus, he assured them that the king shall marry the

The cour d'honneur *and main tower of Salon's Château de l'Empéri*

said Queen.' Indeed, this would be only one of several such initiatives on behalf of the royal princes. And so the proposal was duly sent, together with a copy of the birth-chart and commentary that Nostradamus had already prepared for him. Queen Elizabeth, on receiving it, is said to have protested that 'My Lord is too great for me, and yet too small', and her inevitable rejection arrived back in February. But this was too late to prevent Nostradamus being appointed Privy Councilor and Physician in Ordinary to the King and awarded a grant and a pension to match.

Three months later, Don Francès was reporting to King Philip full details of the royal visit – as was, of course, his duty:

> So that Your Majesty may see the lunacy of what is going on here, I have to report that the Queen, when she passed through the place where Nostradamus lives, had him summoned and made him a grant of two hundred crowns. She ordered him to draw up the horoscope of the King, and another of the said Queen. Since he has all the guile in the world, and only ever says what is pleasing to whomever it may be, he resolved in the said two horoscopes to flatter the King and the Queen, in such wise that they commanded him to follow their Court, treating him right royally until they tired of him and left him at Arles. The Queen said to me today... : 'Do you know,' she said, 'Nostradamus assured me that in 1566 a general peace would reign across the world, and that the kingdom of France would be most peaceful and that the situation would settle down.' And while saying that, she had an air as earnest as if somebody had been quoting St John or St Luke at her.[8]

Less than a year later, on 13 December 1565 (the day before his sixty-second birthday), Nostradamus, increasingly ill now, was writing to one Johannes Lobbetius, who was acting as go-between for the Imperial Court:

> Through I know not what fate, most eminent Doctor Lobbetius, the day after I was visited by Gaspar Flechhaimer, a citizen and patrician of Augsburg, I was seized by such an attack of gout to the hands that I was unable to calculate or explain his birth-chart by the time I had promised. Thereafter the illness got worse and worse, and the agony too. The severe pain that had attacked my hands moved to my right knee, then to my foot. I was so ill that I went for 21 days without being able to sleep. Now the pain is decreasing somewhat and I am beginning to breathe again.

Nevertheless, he was evidently still just as keen on the prophetic omens as ever:

But alas, be it known to you that I see, as in a mirror, what disasters are threatening our unhappy France, as well as all of Italy. Danger lurks ahead for us, eminent Doctor, and it is great (unless some god protects us), even assuming that the insurrections, the upheavals, in a word the wars of religion do not resume. The two parties are both seething with such ardor that it is not at all certain whether it will be possible to calm them down again without bloodshed.

At Arles recently, a fiery arrow was seen – a kind of falling star. The same phenomenon occurred, according to reports, at Lyon and in the Dauphiné: all this presages many and varied woes that shall befall our land. An alien people is preparing to invade us, and there shall be great dryness of the air. The trees and nearly all the harvest shall dry up, and in many places there shall be no water in the wells and springs, and even the watercourses shall start to run dry – whence the danger of famine. This is what I said in my prognostications for the year 1564, where I declared: 'Civil war shall visit France, accompanied by dishonor.'[21d]

Just over a week later, in almost his last known piece of written work, he was addressing to the Queen an official letter (unusually short and to the point this time), evidently with the idea of catching her on her eventual return to Paris.[56] Presumably he felt that he ought to do *something* at least to justify his position as Privy Councilor. And in it he said substantially the same thing as he had apparently told her previously – though it was surprisingly, if not worryingly, different in tone from what he had just told Lobbetius:

Madame, having heard that the Council of your kingdom is shortly to be summoned, even though your Majesty may be advised of the fact by various others, nevertheless according to the knowledge that God has given me, and by way of doing my duty by my King, as a most obedient servant and subject, and added to the burden of my position that Your Majesty gave me, namely that if by the Stars it might be possible to know and understand the future, I should advise Your Majesty accordingly... I find by various celestial patterns drawn up in this place some brief extension of time and place, and that all shall be in peace, love, union and concord, without dissimulation or concealment, even though there shall be some great contradictions and differences. But in the end everybody shall return content of mouth and heart... This assembly shall be the cause of a great peace and contentment throughout your Kingdom... May it also please Your Majesty to send me the celestial Astronomical chart for the 17th year of the most Christian King your son, so that I may draw up the

> explanation of it in full detail... but exactly calculated, so that I may compare it with my own.

Evidently Nostradamus had lost none of his old skills, somehow managing to forecast both concord and discord at once, while at the same time still basing his predictions on others' horoscopes rather than his own. And indeed, he continued to apply them right to the end. The *Almanach* for 1566, already on sale, turned out to be his biggest and most comprehensive yet, combining three different sorts of almanac in one (see Appendix C). Moreover, in the light of what had transpired at Arles, its predictions for August actually contained what purported to be the King's wedding announcement, which 'I am assured that in this month shall be proclaimed everywhere'. Translated from the Latin, this read (in Nostradamus's best tautological style):

> CHARLES IX OF THE FRENCH THE MOST INVINCIBLE AND PUISSANT KING, AS HE HAS SPEEDILY CONQUERED THE KINGDOM, SO HE HAS BEHELD THE PEOPLE. AND AFTER MY HAPPY RETURN TO GAUL I SHALL CELEBRATE MY WEDDING AND MUTUAL CONJUGAL MARRIAGE-FEAST.

Needless to say, it didn't happen. Charles did not marry until 1570, and four years later he was dead.

Nostradamus completed his last *Almanach* – for 1567 – only a fortnight before he himself died in July 1566, including in its dedication the by-now familiar line 'Not that I am foolish enough to pretend to be a prophet...', claiming nevertheless to be privy to 'the augury and prediction that Heaven reveals and manifests by certain signs to those whose minds are apt to touch and participate in the eternal essence,' and complaining, as he usually did, about the constant 'calumniators and mischief-makers' who

> are quick to blame and to speak ill of me and say that such pronouncements come from a familiar demon... Which is a thing assuredly as alien to the truth as they themselves are for certain far from reason or good judgment, having their minds deranged by envy and ignorance.

Also included was the verse for November 1567 that Chavigny would later 'edit' to make it refer to his death:

> Th'ambassadors, returned, repaid shall be,
> The King in honor of his life be shorn:

> His friends, his kin, shall lack posterity,
> Blood-brothers too, as I do truly warn.

Clearly, though, the verse was much more appropriate to the young King Charles (if somewhat previous) than ever it was to Nostradamus.

Still suffering terribly from the gout, as well as from arthritis and dropsy (oedema), the old seer hung on until the end of June, then summoned his lawyer, Maître Joseph Roche, to prepare his Will. In it, apart from a few small bequests to the local Franciscans, he left virtually everything (including a considerable fortune in cash equivalent to some $300,000 today) to his wife to enjoy pending her remarriage, in trust for their sons pending their twenty-fifth birthdays and for their daughters pending their marriage. Signed by him, it was witnessed and

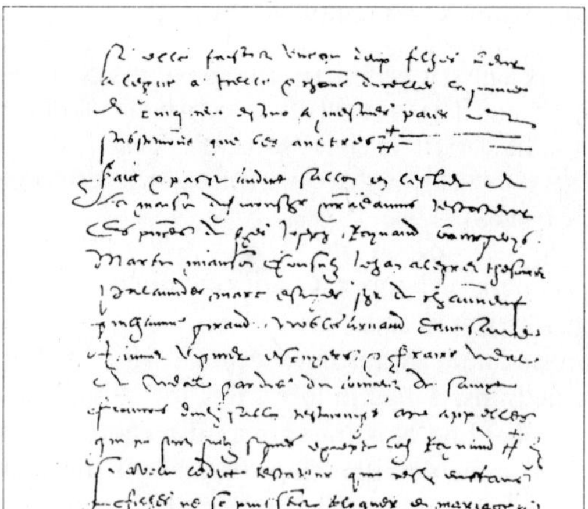

Last page of lawyer's copy of Nostradamus's Will (courtesy of Michel Chomarat, Bibliothèque Municipale de Lyon)

countersigned by eight witnesses (except for one of them, who could not write). Three days later, a codicil was added, leaving his astrolabe and cornelian-inset gold ring to César, and his two walnut chests and their contents to his eldest child Madeleine. This in turn was witnessed by two of the former signatories, plus his doctor, his apothecary and his surgeon – a detail that hints fairly gruesomely at what was being attempted at the time (César, too, would much later suffer from the dropsy, and have to undergo a life-saving operation to drain excess fluid from his body). By the end of June, virtually unable to breathe, he was writing on his copy of Johannes Stadius's *Ephemerides* for 1564 the ominous Latin phrase *Hic prope mors est*, or 'Death is close at hand'. On the evening of 1 July he warned Chavigny, 'You shall not find me still alive at sunrise.'

Just for once, Nostradamus had got a prediction right. In the morning they duly found his body, barely cold, lying between his bed and the bench that had been provided to help him climb into and out of it. And so it was that Chavigny felt moved to alter what was almost the last thing his revered Master had written, to read:

> Once back from embassy, and garnered in
> The royal gift, all's done: to God he's sped.
> The dearest of his friends, his closest kin
> Beside the bed and bench shall find him dead.

The mere fact that the original verse had been for November 1567 was neither here nor there. The long tradition of twisting Nostradamus's words to make them say what people wanted them to say had started out on its long and dishonorable passage through history...

The dead sage was duly buried with full civic honors in the nearby Franciscan chapel (part of which has now been incorporated into the restaurant *La Brocherie* in the rue Hozier). The tomb was set not in the floor, but against the left-hand wall of the chapel, so that people should not walk on him – which seems to have been a particular dread of his. Sixteen years later his faithful wife would join him. As for César, he would become a distinguished local historian, poet, First Consul of Salon (twice) and, in his old age, amateur painter. César's younger brother Charles, too, would become a poet and 'Captain of the town of Salon'. The youngest brother André would become a courtier at Aix but, after killing a man in a duel, would be forced to spend the rest of his life as a Capuchin friar. Madeleine and Anne would both marry, but

Diane, rather like her aunt Delphine, would remain determinedly and contrarily single.* Since none of the sons had sons, while only the daughters did, the name 'Nostradamus' was not handed on any further.

At the French Revolution, the old chapel, now abandoned, would be looted, and Nostradamus's remains taken away as keepsakes by the local citizenry. The then Mayor David appealed for their return, on the grounds that the prophet had allegedly predicted the Revolution itself, and some bones – whether entirely Nostradamus's may be doubted – were subsequently re-entombed in the wall of the rather grander church of St-Laurent, where Craponne, too, had hoped to be buried. To start with, the side chapel in question was known as that of St Roch, appropriately the patron saint of plague-sufferers. Subsequently, though, it was rededicated to Our Lady, with the result that the remains of Nostradamus (the sole burial in the church in question) are now to be found opposite the south door in the chapel of... *Notre Dame.*[P]

As for the epitaph on his tombstone,[P] this was allegedly drawn up by his wife Anne and translated into slightly dubious Latin by the then 12-year-old César. It was reinscribed on the new tombstone in the Collégiale St-Laurent in 1813. In English it reads:

> THE REMAINS OF MICHEL NOSTRADAMUS WERE TRANSFERRED TO THIS CHAPEL AFTER THE YEAR 1789. HIS EPITAPH WAS RESTORED IN THE MONTH OF JULY IN THE YEAR 1813.
>
> D O M
>
> THE BONES OF THE MOST ILLUSTRIOUS MICHEL DE NOSTREDAME, ALONE IN THE JUDGMENT OF ALL MORTALS WORTHY TO DESCRIBE WITH NEAR-DIVINE PEN THE FUTURE EVENTS OT THE WHOLE WORLD UNDER THE INFLUENCE OF THE STARS. HE LIVED 62 YEARS, 6 MONTHS, 10 DAYS AND DIED AT SALON IN THE YEAR 1566. BEGRUDGE HIM NOT HIS REST, YOU WHO COME AFTER. ANNE PONSARDE, THE TWIN, OF SALON WISHES HER HUSBAND TRUE FELICITY.

The claimed birthplace of Michel de Nostredame in the Rue Hoche at St-Rémy-de-Provence, as recently renovated.

The former priory of St-Paul-de-Mausole at St-Rémy

Glanum: the recently excavated site, overlooked by the Mont Gaussier

Jaume seals and signs off a legal deed

Glanum: the city gate and mausoleum of the Julii   Inset: The Latin inscription over the north arch of the mausoleum

Glanum: view out of one of the subterranean galleries in the former stone quarry

Glanum: the 'Pyramide' in the former Roman stone quarry

Altars to Hercules from Glanum (Hôtel de Sade, St-Rémy)

The stony Crau today

Avignon: the papal palace

Montpellier: the modern Medical Faculty and cathedral of St Peter

François Rabelais in doctor's robes

The old harbor, Marseille: entrance and Fort St-Jean

Marseille: ruins of ancient Greek harbor

The Fontaine de Craponne at Salon

The gigantic Roman Pont du Gard aqueduct north of Nîmes

Working aqueduct at St-Chamas, just south of Salon

The original rock citadel of Salon, just east of the modern town

Salon's medieval castle dominates the town from atop the Rocher du Puech

The Roman Pons Flavianus carries the ancient Via Domitia across the river Touloubre

Craponne's memorial bust presides over his distribution pool at Lamanon

Craponne's fast-flowing canal in mid-Crau

Craponne's canal arrives at Arles

The royal castle of Saint-Germain-en-Laye

One of Apianus's volvelles, or astrological computers

Nostradamus 'discovers' the future Henri IV at Salon, 1564. Detail from painting by L Denis Valverane in the Musée de Salon et de la Crau, Salon

Salon: the Collégiale St-Laurent, Nostradamus's last resting place

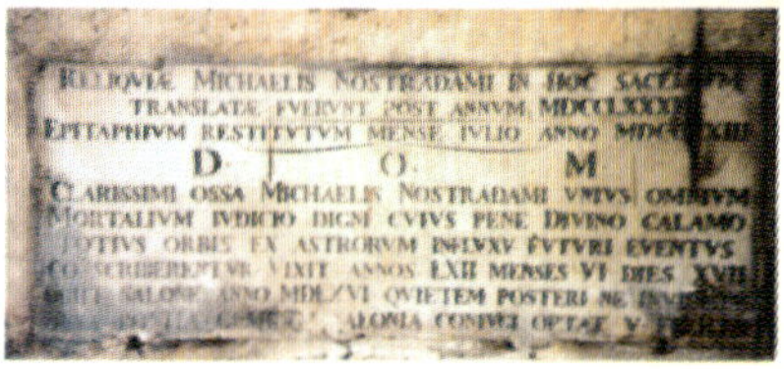

Nostradamus's tomb at Salon

Nostradamus's house at Salon today

Story of a legend: Nostradamus as he may have looked (Salon)

Story of a legend: Nostradamus as other-worldly entity (Salon)

Story of a legend: Nostradamus as disem-bodied idea ('Spirit of Nostradamus', Salon)

11. The Legacy

WITH NOSTRADAMUS GONE, IT WAS ONLY EIGHTEEN MONTHS OR SO before all interest in his annual *Almanachs* faded virtually to zero with the expiry at the end of 1567 of the final publication in the series. Only his faithful secretary Chavigny, who had religiously collected all but one of them (he had been unable to get hold of the *Almanach* for 1551) subsequently attempted to resurrect their memory by suggesting in his own much later books that their prophecies might, after all, apply to much later dates than those specified.[11, 12, 13]

At the same time he attempted to preserve in a now-famous pen-portrait the memory of his beloved Master himself, whom he had known during the last five or six years of his life, at least as he remembered him – evidently through somewhat rose-tinted glasses – from thirty years before:

> He was of somewhat less than average height, physically robust, lively and vigorous. He had a broad, open brow, a straight, even nose and gray eyes whose gaze was gentle, but which blazed when he was angry. His countenance was both severe and smiling, so that his severity was seen to be tempered with great humanity. His cheeks were crimson, even in extreme old age, his beard was long and thick, and except in old age he was hale and hearty, with all his senses acute and quite unimpaired.
>
> As for his mind, this was lively and sound, and easily able to understand anything it cared to. His judgment was acute, his memory admirable and reliable. He was taciturn by nature, thought much and spoke little, yet discoursed perfectly well as time and place demanded.
>
> For the rest, he was alert, subject to sudden, instant rages, yet a patient worker. He slept only four or five hours a night. He praised and valued liberty of speech, and was light-hearted by nature, as well as facetious, biting and derisive.
>
> He approved the Ceremonies of the Roman Church and remained faithful to the Catholic faith and religion, holding that outside it there was no salvation. He gravely reproved those who, having withdrawn

> from its embrace, were prepared to let themselves be fed and watered by the easy-going freedoms of damnable foreign doctrines [i.e. Lutheranism in particular]. Their end, he asserted, would be evil and nasty.
>
> Nor should I forget to mention that he was a keen practitioner of fasts, prayers, almsgiving and austerities. He abhorred vice and castigated it severely. Indeed, I recall that when giving to the poor, to whom he was most generous and charitable, these words from Holy Scripture were constantly on his lips: 'Make friends for yourself with the riches of unrighteousness' [a strange Vulgate translation of the Greek of Luke 16:9 which, in the original, actually meant 'Use your worldly wealth to make friends for yourself'].

This last reported comment, if genuine, sounds more facetious and self-deprecating that it does truly religious.

But with both Nostradamus himself and his dated *Almanachs* removed from the equation, the much less well-known *Propheties,* which were for the most part *un*dated, could at last come into their own. And so appeared the first omnibus edition of 1568, apparently organized by Chavigny himself – presumably because nobody had thought it worthwhile to bring out such an edition previously. Published by Benoist Rigaud of Lyon, it naturally consisted simply of reprints of the second and third editions bound together, each retaining its own title page and page numbering. The royal dedication of 1558 still preceded the section corresponding to the third edition only – and the last 58 verses of the seventh *centurie* were still missing.[55]

The result was almost a case of *Après moi le déluge.*

The point was, of course, that Nostradamus had deliberately designed his *Propheties* to refer to almost any incident at almost any time. They were generic rather than particular, 'perpetual' rather than time-specific, telegrammatic (*à la* Virgil) rather than written out at length – still less written out *ad nauseam,* as had been Nostradamus's preferred style in the *Almanachs* (see Appendix C). They were therefore open to interpretation, re-application, deliberate twisting and, ultimately, the grossest kinds of exegetical abuse. Worse, as this was realized, editors of later editions would increasingly attempt to 'make sense' (*their* sense, of course) of Nostradamus's deliberate obfuscations by adjusting, changing and eventually shamelessly altering the very words themselves so as to make Nostradamus say what they wanted him to say.

But then, of course, prophecies have always been treated in this way, as Nostradamus's own prophetic sources in the *Mirabilis liber*[45] demonstrate perfectly clearly.

This tendency would already start to become apparent in the very next edition – that of 1605 – for example.[6, 18] Moreover, the latter would also add a surprise series of *Sixains*, or six-line verses (curiously, just 58 in number!) to the official canon, plus some two dozen 'extra' quatrains – some of whose numbers duplicated those of verses already published, while others claimed to belong to two additional *centuries* that nobody had hitherto heard of. We do not have to assume, however, that the 'extra' quatrains in particular were necessarily forgeries. Indeed, computer-analysis of them suggests quite the contrary. The answer to the conundrum is probably that they were simply rough drafts that Chavigny had found lying around amid the chaos of his Master's workroom after his death – mere discarded drafts that had not been intended for publication. Whence, presumably, the duplicate verse numbers.

The result, at all events, was an increasingly flourishing Nostradamus industry dedicated to imposing the most lurid kinds of interpretations even on his more harmless predictions, especially at times of perceived world crisis. In this, scant regard was usually paid to what the original words had actually said, let alone to what the seer had presumably intended them to mean in the light of the clear historical antecedents and other known sources on which most of them had been based. But then history had disappeared from the picture in other ways, too. The *Propheties* were now being read and interpreted quite independently of the historical, cultural and linguistic context in which Nostradamus had originally written them, which was increasingly a *terra incognita*. Indeed, so *incognita* was it that people were soon inventing their own pseudo-histories to fit the man whom they now supposed him to have been.

At which point, of course, it was increasingly a case of 'anything goes'. Unsurprisingly, therefore, anything now did.

It had all started with Chavigny's former Paris mentor, the distinguished classical scholar Jean Dorat (or D'Aurat). Much respected as a decoder of literary mysteries, especially classical ones, he was already being eulogized as an interpreter of Nostradamus by the Lord of La Croix du Maine as early as 1584:

> Not all learned men lack esteem for the prophecies of the said

> Nostradamus, among whom I shall name M. d'Aurat, Poet to the King, so highly esteemed in his day, who is such a happy interpreter or faithful exegete of the quatrains & prophecies of the said *Nostradamus* that it seems as if he were the very genius of the said author...[8]

As Dorat's star pupil Pierre de Ronsard would write of him in his eulogy *A Jean d'Aurat, son precepteur, et poëte royal*:

> Thy learning's high and mighty fame
> To this our age reveals the same –
> How thou destroyest Ignorance
> And art renowned throughout all France
> As 'twere an oracle of God
> For straight untying for the wise
> Each knotted phrase that sense defies
> In labored books arcane and odd.[8]

In fact it was the very oddity and laboriousness of Nostradamus's verse, much of it based on classical syntax and classical allusion, that Dorat seems to have found so alluring in the first place – especially given that he himself was reputed to be a dab hand at interpreting dreams and omens. As Chavigny would later write of him:

> He interprets dreams, visions, prodigies and monsters of whatever kind so diligently and with such dexterity – and not only that, but also oracles, and anything that is predicted and sung in a [poetic] frenzy wherein the voice and will of God seems to be the most veiled and hidden from men – that the effect of it surpasses all renown and praise.[8]

It was only natural, then, that Dorat's enthusiasm for Nostradamus should have moved him to send his own pupil Chavigny to Salon in 1560 or so to become the seer's disciple and secretary. Unfortunately, though, Chavigny was not gifted in quite the same way as Dorat was. Granted, as the seer's secretary and amanuensis, he came to know the tricks of Nostradamus's linguistic trade better than anyone, as he himself did not fail to point out. But when it came to discovering hidden, alternative meanings in the *Propheties* that even Nostradamus himself had possibly not thought of, it was a different matter. Whereas Dorat's exegetics had been based on the shrewd application of philology – and especially classical philology – Chavigny's expertise lay far more in comparative literature, philosophy and religion. As a result, his methods of interpretation turned out to be somewhat banal and crude by comparison. Often the best he could suggest was that Nostradamus had been writing about some date, place or person other than the one specified, or even that he had 'really meant the opposite'. And if the worst came to the worst, he was quite prepared actually to alter the odd word here and there in order to prove his late Master 'right'.

This was a bad precedent. Once Chavigny had done it – and especially once he had allowed the principle to spill over into his books on Nostradamus published at around the end of the century[11, 12] – it suddenly became legitimate for everybody else to do it too. Editors would increasingly try to make sense of Nostradamus's more puzzling words – whether based on Latin, or Greek, or even pure fantasy – by substituting the nearest French words they could think of, or even words that had the additional merit of making the verse refer to whatever they wanted it to refer to, whether in the political, religious historical or even personal sphere.

Moreover, given that it would be a long time before printing would become anything like reliable or accurate (not least because of the principle of 'typesetting from dictation' mentioned earlier) and that later copies tended to be made from earlier ones, rather than from the originals, the whole thing tended increasingly to turn into a game of Chinese Whispers (or *téléphone arabe*, as the French prefer to put it). This situation was further complicated by the fact that because of the policy of 'continuous correction' already referred to, no two copies were the same. And so it came about that Nostradamus became, of all authors, possibly the most misrepresented by his published texts. Later editions would become so corrupt and mangled, indeed, as to present those trying to make honest sense of them with a virtually impenetrable mish-mash, while those who were merely in search of the lurid (even where it had not originally been present) were presented with an almost infinite chance of finding versions that more than satisfied their desires.

Indeed, the water would be muddied even further by the seventeenth-century Lyon publisher Pierre Rigaud, son and successor of Benoist, who published a whole series of editions (admittedly based on his father's 1568 edition) bearing the fanciful date '1566', apparently in an effort to suggest their authenticity.[6, 18] The publisher Vincent Sève of Beaucaire (possibly a relation of Nostradamus) did much the same. The fact may be a useful, if curious, piece of evidence that Nostradamian authenticity was already recognized as a problem, but in practice the fact that a supposedly 'original' edition was already showing a range of misprints that in reality only appeared somewhat later would merely serve further to bewilder and mislead the already constitutionally confused of later times.

But that was merely *in French*. As soon as the native English-speaking commentators muscled in on the act, especially during the popular Nostradamus boom of the late twentieth century, all hell was let loose. Now millions of readers of the world's leading language were presented with an incredible hotch-potch of translated (or rather, for the most part, *mis*translated) versions by people many of whom either didn't know sixteenth-century French or (in some cases) didn't know French at all – and who were certainly unfamiliar with Nostradamus's idiosyncratic use of it. Their knowledge of the contemporary French historical and cultural context was often equally non-existent, and many of them showed little sign even of knowing what translation itself was about, apparently imagining that it merely involved rendering each French word literally into English – an approach which, it has to be said, has never been known to work with any other author. And their publishers, who were (for perfectly natural reasons) in most cases no more knowledgeable about Nostradamus than *they* were, had no option but to assume that they knew what they were talking about – even though the prospect of droves of English-speaking commentators writing about a Nostradamus whose language most of them evidently hardly knew ought to have seemed to them about as sensible as having a convention of monoglot Frenchmen decide on the meaning of Shakespeare with the aid of nothing more than a pocket English-French dictionary – or, for that matter, pronouncing on the finer points of cricket purely on the basis of having procured a copy of *Wisden*.

It would be incredible were it not true. Through a mixture of accidental misprinting, deliberate falsification, plain old-fashioned ignorance and the simple vagaries of 'translation' by non-translators, Nostradamus had been turned, from a riddle, successively into a mystery and then into an enigma. And the more enigmatic he became, the more it naturally became permissible to read anything into him that you liked. Increasingly, writers simply took the prophecies hostage and tortured them until they said what they wanted them to say. And what they particularly wanted them to say was *whatever had just happened*.

The phenomenon still jumps out repeatedly from popular books on the seer, and spreads itself world-wide via the Internet. No sooner had the French Revolution occurred than he was found (as we have seen) to have prophesied the French Revolution. Napoleon, Hitler, both World Wars, the atom bomb, the mysterious death of Pope John Paul I, the attempted assassination of Pope John Paul II, the successful assassination of President J F Kennedy, the *Apollo* moon landings, the *Challenger* space-shuttle disaster, the death of Diana Princess of Wales – whatever it was, as soon as it happened Nostradamus was immediately supposed to have predicted it. Which is odd, given that virtually nobody ever seems to have claimed as much beforehand – with the honorable exception of Vlaicu Ionescu who, on the basis of Nostradamus's covering letter to Henri II, did successfully manage to pinpoint the collapse of the Soviet Union well in advance.[31]

And so, when two airliners were deliberately crashed by Muslim terrorists into New York's World Trade Center, and a third into the Pentagon, on 11 September 2001, killing literally thousands of Americans and others at a stroke and completely destroying the complex's celebrated twin towers, rumors immediately started to circulate world-wide that Nostradamus had predicted the catastrophe. Within a week, the Internet Newsgroup *alt.prophecies.nostradamus* had received over 8000 queries and comments on the topic; Nostradamus Websites were overwhelmed with hits that ran into the hundreds of thousands. The expression most sought after by the world's search-engines was suddenly not 'New York', nor 'World Trade Center', nor 'Osama bin Laden', nor even 'sex' ... but 'Nostradamus'. Authors of books on Nostradamus discovered, to their mixed delight and horror, that all their books had sold out – thus proving, alas, the old adage that 'It's an ill wind that blows nobody any good.'

Moreover, like certain previous catastrophes, it had happened just a year or so after a major planetary line-up – that of May 2000 (compare the end of chapter 2 above).

Yet Nostradamus had never written any such prediction. He had never mentioned New York, and had referred to America only once, if at all (in quatrain X.66). He had stated specifically, in his covering letter to King Henri II, that his prophecies were mainly about Europe, North Africa and Asia Minor. Only two of his other place names ('Carmania' and 'Tartarie') fell outside that area. The 'New City' at 45° latitude that he had threatened with fire from the sky at VI.97 could not have been New York, given that the latter lies all of 300 miles south of that, and is in fact much more likely to have been Villeneuve-sur-Lot in south-western France – which *does* lie at roughly at 45° North

('Villeneuve', like 'Naples', *means* 'new city'). The subsequent widespread assertion that Nostradamus's *Cinq & quarante degrés* ('Five-and-forty degrees') really meant '40.5 degrees' ignored totally the fact that the decimal point system had not yet been adopted in the Europe of Nostradamus's day – even given that the true figure for New York would in any case be nearer 40.6 or 40.7, and that French has never expressed decimal places in this way. Even when these sobering facts were duly pointed out, though, the usual response was, 'Ah, but he was a *prophet!*'

It made no difference that the alleged 'Nostradamus prophecies' that now started to flood into people's mailboxes all across the world were virtually all *in English*, and either (a) based on very late and corrupt French editions, (b) hopeless mistranslations, deliberately twisted to fit the events, or (c) pure inventions, and not by Nostradamus at all. The wave of credulity simply continued. One such alleged prophecy (a frankly admitted spoof) was blithely dated 'Nostradamus 1654' – when he would, of course, have been just 150 years old (!). Neither fact seemed to register with the public at large, though. For added verisimilitude, another offering preceded several lines of its own with yet further lines stitched together from quite different quatrains that were indeed by Nostradamus: in vain did I point out in response that you could do much the same even with the Bible... 'And he went and hanged himself (Matthew 27:5). Go, and do thou likewise (Luke 10:37).' And even pointing people towards Websites such as *http://run.to/nostradamus*, where they could see actual facsimiles of the original predictions and check them for themselves, proved less than effective, not least because they were already jammed with enquirers...

If seekers for justifications of Nostradamus's prophecies in the immediate past (presumably in order to try and give some kind of larger meaning to the present) are apt to let their common sense desert them in this quite staggering way, much the same goes for people's even more dramatic expectations about the future, and especially their religious ones. Almost anybody with a crazy theory to propound nowadays hijacks Nostradamus to justify it. If the financial share index falls, Nostradamus predicted a crash. If a comet appears, Nostradamus predicted that it would hit the earth. If a Middle Eastern leader makes a belligerent speech, the world is about to succumb to the Antichrist. If war flares up in the Balkans, or in Central Asia, or in the Far East, Armageddon is at hand.

And always the rationale is that Nostradamus's prophecies are pure gobbledygook, and that you are therefore entitled to make of them whatever you like. In some cases this involves translating them word-for-word as though they were legal documents rather than poems, but then applying to them all your cryptic crossword-solving skills so as (paradoxically) to falsify them. In others, the would-be translator is entitled to rope in any alternative meanings he or she can find in the French dictionary while totally ignoring not only the more usual ones, but the verse's grammar and overall syntax, too – or, failing that, to look up the same words, or even individual parts of them, in other languages entirely. Fortunately, the results of such linguistic acrobatics are generally even more unreadable than the originals, thus ensuring that nobody is likely to understand them, let alone take them seriously.

Sometimes, though, the initial supposition is subtly modified: Nostradamus's prophecies are pure gobbledygook, certainly – but since it is unthinkable that anything so crazy could have been printed by accident, it has to have been intentional (which means, of course, that Nostradamus is somehow supposed to have stood over the Lyon printer throughout, even while he was typesetting the *posthumous* 1568 edition [!], in order to ensure that the 'sillies' were printed exactly as such – notwithstanding the fact that, in the case of the original 1555 edition, he presumably had simultaneously to stand over the Avignon one as well!). On this model, the whole thing is then treated as though it were in some fiendishly clever code – as if Nostradamus's literary and intellectual capacity had not already been fully stretched merely by the demands of writing four lines of ordinary verse! In some versions, decoding it involves mapping the letters extracted from each verse (often in one of the late, corrupt editions) on to a grid and reading off the results according to a predetermined template: the Italians and French seem to be especially adept at this particular kind of pseudo-scientific rigmarole. Or alternatively, each verse has to be treated as if it were an extended anagram, and the would-be interpreter then has to work out the message that emerges when certain (often extraordinarily flexible) rules are applied – a message that, curiously enough, often turns out to be in bad French, and never in its sixteenth-century form. Often, indeed, the result turns out to mention the name of the commentator himself or herself, thus duly confirming his or her role as Nostradamus's appointed interpreter. Needless to say, there are as many alleged 'appointed interpreters' as there are claimants, and so such claims may usually be taken as an index not so much of Nostradamus's intentions as of the extent of the claimants' self-delusion.

Especially since, as we saw at the outset, the whole purpose of Nostradamus's initiative was not to put the ancient prophecies *into* code at all (they were, after all, already 'in code' to the extent of being in medieval Latin and printed in an almost impenetrable Gothic script that was full of scholarly abbreviations), but to take them *out of* it and make them, almost for the first time, readily accessible to all in the French of the day.

But then such arcane and far-fetched theories as the above are usually only a means to an end anyway. Sometimes the aim is to prove that Nostradamus was infallible and that (by implication) the commentator's interpretations therefore are, too – a mind-numbingly credulous, if strangely widespread thesis to which textual authenticity, historical fact and academic research inevitably have to be sacrificed lest they undermine it. In particular, none of Nostradamus's writings must be considered other than his *Propheties* – rather as if all academic debate about Shakespeare had to be restricted to a narrow discussion of *Hamlet*, uninformed by any of his other writings. Sometimes the aim is to prove that the seer was a Rosicrucian, or a Cabbalist, or a leading member of the ancient Prieuré de Sion of 'Rennes-le-Château' fame (so ancient that it was in fact founded in the 1950s), whose occult meanings only the writer in question is therefore in a position to decode. So far, however, those who propose such notions on the Internet have not shown too much enthusiasm for my alternative suggestion that Nostradamus was really an alien from Alpha Centauri...

And virtually none of the operators concerned ever shrinks for a moment (to quote the admittedly constitutionally skeptical James Randi's immortal words[62]) from using the theory they are trying to prove, to prove the theory they are trying to prove.

In an attempt finally to give the lie to all these preposterous fantasies, a number of respected French academics and scholars have of recent years done their best to draw people's attention back to the actual facts of the case that are so often hidden beneath all the clouds of mystical smoke and drowned out by all the accompanying mumbo jumbo, especially in Anglo-Saxon countries. As early as the 1940s Dr Edgar Leroy, a psychiatrist at the Clinique van Gogh at St-Paul-de-Mausole, St-Rémy (see chapter 1), was diligently unearthing the real

Nostradamus and his family from the local archives.[42] By the 1980s Michel Chomarat was establishing his huge and unrivalled collection of Nostradamia at the Bibliothèque Municipale de Lyon and, with Dr Jean-Paul Laroche (another psychiatrist) publishing the first full Nostradamian bibliography,[18] which Robert Benazra would follow with a further, even more extensive one of his own in 1990.[6] Benazra had meanwhile ferreted out one of the two long-lost surviving copies of the original 1555 edition from the municipal library at Albi, and Chomarat the one in the Vienna State Library. Having duly published the former in facsimile, Chomarat followed this up with facsimiles of the November 1557[54] and 1568[55] editions, as well as of Nostradamus's letter to the Queen of December 1565[56] – to say nothing of a whole range of reproductions drawn from various of his letters, *Almanachs* and other documents. Jean Dupèbe had meanwhile published virtually all of Nostradamus's surviving correspondence,[21] and the late Pierre Brind'Amour, of the Department of Ancient Studies at the University of Ottawa, had published his own far-reaching critical analyses both of the 1555 edition[9] and of Nostradamus's astrology,[8] incorporating various of his horoscopes, letters and a huge amount of supporting archival material for which I have been particularly grateful in preparing this book. On top of all this, 1999 saw the publication by Bernard Chevignard, Professor of Language and Communication at the University of Burgundy at Dijon, of the first four books of Chavigny's massive manuscript minutely recording all Nostradamus's 3668 prophecies outside the *centuries*,[13, 16] and by the Paris historian and classicist Roger Prévost of his ground-breaking research into the seer's historical sources.[60]

This was all very well, of course – but unfortunately it was all *in French* (when it wasn't in Latin, that is). This meant that the very people who most needed to read it were, by very definition, for the most part totally incapable of doing so. And so, for them, it was almost as if none of it had ever been published. Blithely ignoring all the work mentioned above, the Nostradamian fantasies of the Anglo-Saxon world simply continued unabated until, in 1997, I at last published some of it in English in my own *Nostradamus Encyclopedia*[37] in collaboration with Michel Chomarat – since when I have to say that the frequency with which such idiocies are published seems to have declined considerably, even though those who are keenest on them (especially on the Internet) still tend to refuse point-blank to read either the original texts or the research on them lest their delusions be fatally undermined, characteristically calling the scholars 'liars' and/or 'frauds' and presumably hoping that this will make the facts go away.

And so where does this leave Nostradamus today? Does his propensity to write now as a walking thesaurus, now as a drunken telegram clerk, destroy his reputation as an author? Does the fact that he turns out, perfectly understandably, to have had feet of clay invalidate him as a scholar, translator or writer of cookbooks? Is his abysmal prophetic success rate in the *Almanachs* good reason for doubting his credentials as a prophet of individual recent and current events – especially when he is wheeled out by the media, as he regularly is, every time something dramatic happens?

Probably it is. True, quatrain IX.49 does *seem* to refer to a unique event – namely the beheading of King Charles I of England. Quatrain IX.16 *seems* to mention specifically Generalissimo Francisco Franco of Spain. Quatrain X.22 *begs to be* identified with the abdication of King Edward VIII in 1936. Verses VIII.70 and VI.33 *seem* to describe the Gulf War of 1991. And one passage in the Letter to Henri II *seems* to reflect the rise and fall of the Soviet Union with quite astonishing aptness, as the late Vlaicu Ionescu was the first to spot. But none of these is actually dated, astrologically or otherwise, so the identification can never be absolutely definite. Of the couple of dozen predictions that *are* dated, only V.25 (an apparent astrological pinpointing of the re-declaration of *jihad* by Osama bin Laden in August 1998), X.72 (conceivably a reference to the restoration to administrative power of European President Romano Prodi in 1999), *Sixain* 25 (a good description of the fall from office in 1998 – assuming a 'liturgical' rather than calendrical count[37, 38, 39] – of a figure remarkably reminiscent of Chancellor Helmut Kohl of Germany) and the mention in the Letter to Henri II of the perceived beginning of a new order in 1792 appear to have hit the mark at all convincingly.[38]

These apart, though, the fact that some of the *un*dated predictions have apparently managed to hit the jackpot, too, is no more than is statistically inevitable, and is certainly no more significant in respect of the future than the successful calling of a spinning coin. Any event, as Einstein should have taught us all by now, has to take place in space *and time*. It follows, therefore, that a prediction that fails to give a date or at very least an astrological 'marker' for an event is not in fact a prediction of it at all. The sheer mathematical probability of chance events means that, if I issue the prediction 'It is going to rain' – or even one as specific as 'A well-known person with brown eyes and a chronic disease is going to be murdered in Miami' – it will eventually be fulfilled. But this does not make me a prophet. Just as a dateless appointment with your dentist is no appointment at all, exactly the same applies to those supposed individual appointments with destiny that Nostradamus's prophecies are often supposed to be. Indeed, even a *dated* appointment that does not specify exactly what treatment it is for is not necessarily a prediction of the treatment that you actually receive, even though you may think so after the event!

And so what does this mean for Nostradamus's claim to be a prophet? How likely is it really that, as I cited at the beginning of this book:

> After five hundred years more heed they'll take
> Of him who was th' adornment of his age.
> Then light effulgent suddenly shall break
> Such as that time's great pleasure to engage.[52a]

Curiously, current events suggest that, for all his evident – indeed, inevitable – faults, his reputation seems unlikely to diminish dramatically in the near future. Quite the reverse, in fact.

For the truth is that, as we saw at the outset, Nostradamus was not trying to predict minor, individual events anyway. He was totally uninterested in merely predicting whatever local catastrophes may have happened in the course of our various yesterdays – however disproportionately large our chronic lack of historical and geographical perspective might tend to paint them. Nor was he trying to anticipate the winner of the next American presidential election, or the state of the present stock market, or the winner of next year's World Cup. Nor was he merely endeavoring to prove how clever he had been in retrospect, nor even how effective prophecy itself can be. Thus, he cannot reasonably be blamed if such supposed aims, which were never his, fail to materialize.

His mission was a much grander and more over-arching one. It was, as we have seen, to re-express in succinct and memorable form, and in 'a language understanded of the people' (even if only just!) the lofty message of the ancient apocalyptic prophecies in which he and his contemporaries so firmly believed. Not *his* – but those that had long been collected in books such as the *Mirabilis liber*. The end of the world was at hand – as it always is and always has been for each succeeding generation. And therefore the huge events leading up to it must inevitably happen, whether or not they were additionally amplified (as Nostradamus was prone to amplify them) with detailed analogues drawn from history and from a plethora of omens old and new.

And so the long-predicted catalogue of pre-apocalyptic disasters must surely unfold in their due season, just as I listed them in my Introduction. War, plague, famine, fire, floods, droughts, unbearable heat, earthquakes, comets, strange celestial phenomena, wholesale deaths of livestock, virtual boilings alive of fish in the rivers and seas, plagues of grasshoppers or locusts, bloody oppressions, brutal occupations, religious persecutions, murders of innocents, rapes of virgins, slaughters of infants, cannibalism, sexual depravity, official corruption, priestly immorality, monkish decadence...

It all seems so wild and improbable. Yet, strange to tell, there is not one of these catastrophes that has not *already happened* over the course of the centuries since Nostradamus's death – and repeatedly, at that. Moreover, one often has the distinct impression that such things are happening more and more frequently nowadays, and on an ever-larger scale. War, disease and famine seem to be ever more widespread. To simple inland flooding is added precisely the rise in sea -level that is on several occasions apparently predicted in the *Mirabilis liber*.

True, that increase of scale and frequency may be more perceived than real. Today we have both worldwide communications and instant, efficient and extremely dramatic media – media that are often all too prone to exaggerate and dramatize any doom and gloom that they can find. Such things, after all, are News.

But what is particularly striking is the apparent emergence, precisely in our own day, of the prime theme both identified by the *Mirabilis liber* and taken up and elaborated by Nostradamus – the predicted ultimate showdown between Islam and Christendom. *Jihad* is the catchword of the moment. Could there indeed, then, be a major Muslim invasion of Europe to come, followed by some kind of Western counter-invasion? Could the Pope be forced to flee Italy as a result? Could Christian churches throughout Europe be desecrated and destroyed? Could the Catholic Church itself decay and collapse?

Certainly, militant Islam is more rampant today than it has been for centuries, even though most Muslims are totally innocent of its more bellicose manifestations. Europe has indeed *already been* invaded by literally millions of Muslims – though these have so far been merely humble immigrants in search of work, safety and a better way of life. There have even been violent Muslim attacks on the West, to say nothing of a whole succession of apparent Antichrist-type figures of the stamp of Saddam Hussein and Osama bin Laden emerging from the East to direct them, just as predicted.

Yet, so far at least, there has been no major military invasion of the continent. Could it happen, though? And if so, would this be because it has to, or because we have failed to pay due heed to the efforts of Nostradamus and his precursors to warn us in advance? Or could it just possibly be that we have already brought it all on ourselves – the inevitable result either of our own moral shortcomings (as Nostradamus and his ilk liked to believe) or merely of centuries of conviction on the part of our major prophets that something of this kind was always bound to happen, made ten times more potent by the bitter historical legacy of the medieval European crusades against the Saracens?

Perhaps the most important thing to realize is that *nothing* is inevitable – except, as Benjamin Franklin put it, death and taxes. Even Nostradamus continually pointed out in his *Almanachs* that God can change His mind. Or, to put it another way, we are the creators of our own future. We are not bound to live out the future anticipated by our ancestors. Prophecies are not necessarily self-fulfilling. Nor are we entitled to blame fate – or Nostradamus, or the Muslims – if what happens is not what we desire.

Foreseeing the future is all very well, but we are alive *now*. The future will be decided not by the *Mirabilis liber*, nor by Nostradamus, but by what we – you and I – think and do today.

Appendix A

Nostradamus's 1552/1555 cookbook, the *Traité des fardemens et confitures* [Treatise on cosmetics and conserves] – translated extracts.

This book – much more friendly and informal than most modern cookery books, and for the most part remarkably clear and straightforward in style – is evidently based on knowledge that Nostradamus picked up here and there during his eight years as an apothecary before he entered the Montpellier Medical Faculty in 1529 with a view to taking his doctorate. It is entirely untypical of doctors of the time, who were far more concerned with theories about 'balancing the four humors' than with popular practical remedies.

The book was variously entitled *Traité des fárdemens et conserves, Excellent & Moult utile Opuscule* ('Excellent and most useful little work') and – by virtue of Part 1's concentration on cosmetics – *Le Vray et Parfaict Embellissement de la Face* ('The true and perfect beautification of the face'). It is dated '1552', but first appeared in 1555: one wonders whether the publisher couldn't understand Nostradamus's writing (about which his correspondents were always complaining) and was worried lest he get it wrong and poison somebody, with the result that Nostradamus had to get it copied up by a secretary first.

Except where otherwise indicated, the text extracts translated below are taken from the 1557 Plantin edition. While they are offered in good faith, neither I nor the publisher can make any claims for the correct identification of the various ingredients as translated, or for the safety of Nostradamus's recipes – nor, consequently, can either of us accept responsibility for readers' use of them.

Contents

A. THE COSMETICS MANUAL

Part 1 Chapter VI: *To make a perfect nutmeg oil*

Part 1 Chapter VIII [the one giving Nostradamus's famous plague remedy]: *To make the basis of a perfectly good and excellent aromatic powder*

Part 1 Chapter X: *To make a sweet-smelling, long-lasting paste*

Part 1 Chapter XI: *Another method for making aromatic balls*

Part 1 Chapter XIII: *Powder for cleaning and whitening the teeth*

Part 1 Chapter XIIII: *Another more excellent method for cleaning the teeth*

Part 1 Chapter XV: *Perfumed water for impregnating the shapes or forms mentioned above*

Part 1 Chapter XVIII (1556): *To truly make the lovers' sexual potion which the ancients used for love-making*

Part 1 Chapter XXIIII: *How to make the hair golden blond*

Part 1 Chapter XXVI [often erroneously described as for an aphrodisiac]: *A supreme and very useful composition for the health of the human body*

Part 1 Chapter XXVII: *There follows the way in which one should use the above-mentioned composition*

B. THE COOKBOOK

Part 2 Chapter III: *To make candied orange peel, using sugar or honey*

Part 2 Chapter VIII: *How to make a jam or preserve with heart-cherries*

Part 2 Chapter XV: *To make a quince jelly of superb beauty, goodness, flavor and excellence fit to set before a King*

Part 2 Chapter XXIIII: *To preserve pears*

Part 2 Chapter XXV: *To make a very fine sugar candy.*

Part 2 Chapter XXVII: *To make marzipan*

Part 2 Chapter XXIX: *To make a laxative rose syrup*

Proem (Preface) to the 1555 edition (dated 1552)

Michel de Nostredame, physician, to the Kindly Reader, salutations.

After spending most of my young years from the year 1521 to the year 1529, O KINDLY READER, on pharmaceutics and the knowledge and study of natural remedies across various lands and countries, constantly on the move to hear and find out the source and origin of plants [by a possibly Freudian error, the original text actually has *planetes* = 'planets'!] and other natural remedies involved in the purposes of the physician's craft: and having wished to imitate the lonely shade of Paulus Aigineta, *Non quod velim conferre magna minutis* [Latin: 'Not that I would wish to confer greatness on the small']: I shall merely say, *Nostradami laborem me nosse, qui plurimum terrae peragravit, Sextrophaea natus Gallia* [Latin: 'Know me (to be) the work of Nostradamus, who wandered through many countries, a native of St-Rémy in France' – the reference is to the Roman Mausoleum of Sextus just to the south of the town].

When I finally reached the end of my eight years, I found myself unable perfectly to attain the summit of the supreme doctrine [of medicine], and so I did what the one who represented the summit of the Latin tongue [Virgil] said: *Et egressus sylvis vicina coegi* [Latin: 'And having left the woods, I collected whatever I found around me'], and proceeded to complete my studies up to the present time, which is the thirty-first year of my vocation, which we know as 1552.

And having carefully and by dint of frequent and continual study perused each and every author, whether Greek, Latin or Arab [the text says *Barbare*], rendered for the most part into the Latin language, though in other cases set in the alien tongue, among other things I came across those who had left writings concerning the embellishment of the face. And because, during my stays in many countries, even those where the women because of the swiftly passing years contrived secretly and by means of a subtle skill to hide and conceal the principal part of the body, namely the head, in order to show clear evidence that substances applied to the face have succeeded in deceiving the eyes of onlookers... [Nostradamus not untypically loses the thread of his own syntax at this point]

Ladies with faces like Phryne [a famous fourth-century BC Greek courtesan] have no need to use this [book], other than for the purpose of preserving their features intact: but those who are much older, and similar to those who were at the banquet [either Plato's *Banquet* or the celebrated 15-course banquet of one Signor Trivulzio of some half a century before, a Latin account of which Nostradamus translates elsewhere in the *Traité*], truly these would be well advised carefully to read and study this – though may no such ill befall them! And I have known eminent people in various regions who continually practiced and applied most of these things to such effect that, however old they were, they did as Proteus did [mythical sea monster and son of Poseidon/Oceanus], who could change his appearance whenever he wanted to.

And even after reading all these books – at least those that my mind and ability were equal to studying – I was never able to find the things contained here, for in speaking of the beauty and embellishment of the face, one of them would say one thing and one another. But most of those who thought to commit themselves to writing have suggested unguents, liniments [printed *liminents*] and oils – even though there is nothing in the world that makes the face browner or more blotchy than applications of this type – or else they have quietly withdrawn their claims, or have said nothing about it.

I am not saying that there may not have been many who had a perfect knowledge of the entire doctrine of medicine, yet they have not known about this, just as they have excused themselves [by saying] that it was more a women's concern than a medical matter, as I myself have been able to observe.

As for those of ancient Greek times, it is quite certain that they used such [techniques] as much as, or more than today – and that the majority of women did so (without going into specifics here). And during Roman times [here Nostradamus uses the phrase *du siecle Romain*, so demonstrating the normal contemporary use of *siecle* to mean 'age'] it was [even] more frequent than it is today.

If anybody wants to assert that such needs had not yet come to light, does not Marcus Varro [Roman first-century BC writer and scholar] affirm that in the previous thousand years up to his time all the sciences and arts had been perfected, even though new discoveries are made every day, and notably in the sphere of medicine where people are constantly describing them in print – despite the fact that they [in fact] say nothing that has not already been said long before?

Many have simply taken bits from here and there, and some of them have even translated [them] from the Arabic language during the five hundred years that the real documents have been half-buried, turning them into more ornate and eloquent language – yet if you were to have them write [on their own account] without reference to the Arabs [*Barbares*] whom they quote, they would have a hard time of it. [But] the truth is that the true Attic [Greek] language has now been revived, and there are now a great number of scholars whose present erudition has scarcely been surpassed since the age of Plato.

Besides, I have not [yet] seen anyone undertake this small burden, nor anyone who – [at least] when it comes into the hands of someone who is not in the habit of denigrating everything – will vituperate in any way against this our little work.

For I have seen many who have dabbled in talking about the embellishment of the face, and they have talked about it like half-ignorant people. And as for the scents and perfumes, they have made it quite obvious that they have never used the many useless things that they have set down and committed to print, for one of them (supposed to be experienced in such things) will say that he has 'seen' it, and another that he has 'heard about' it. In consideration of which, many have been misled just by reading them, believing that the effects described were true, and have often found themselves deceived, or possibly that the one setting down in writing some guaranteed experience [has done so] without ever trying it out, recommending it as if he had actually tried it on somebody.

I have also seen many prescriptions for the inside of the human body, certified by many people of a variety of statuses, describing substances that the person involved has used in different lands, making exact distinctions computed by the [principle of] temporal symmetry concerning the duration of the illness.

It is easier to place faith in one who has studied the qualities of natural remedies after long research and dangerous experimentation digested at length than in one who has no such experience and relies on affected language, eloquent phrases and on an unusually graceful written style when in fact, by way of elaborating his teaching, he has set down as his own subtle technique only what he has found described by a whole variety of [other] authors. The fact is that he never in his life had any experience [of his own].

Speaking of those who have expressed what they had to say in writing, Pliny, who is nevertheless a most loquacious author, listed Cornelius Celsus among the ranks of the authors, but never of the Doctors – even though the truth is that the said Celsus spoke extremely well on the subject of the whole Medical discipline, and that most scholarly people have assigned to him (by Pythagorean transmutation) the very soul of Pythagoras, just as Cicero did with Longolius. And this is so whether he said good things or nothing worth repeating. Many would affirm that he [Pliny?] never practiced Medicine, even though nobody had a better command of Latin.

Let us [now] come to those of our own time. On his way back from Venice to France, Erasmus – who was, with Aldo, a great friend of Marcus Musurus, as well as of Ambrosius Leo of Nola – while passing through Ferrara spoke to Nicolas Leonicenus, a man wise and learned in all scholarship who continually translated and composed works on the craft of Medicine, and asked him why (seeing that he was so learned in the said art) he did not [actually] practice or visit the sick. He replied – sagely, as was his wont – that there was much more profit and usefulness in learning things from books than in practicing, and less aggravation too. For it is not possible for a person who has many patients to see either to study or to write anything. And it is true that those who have written a great deal in whatever discipline have hardly had need to practice, for the spirit of anyone preparing written documents needs quietness above all. Otherwise it would be a case of having to do as Julius Caesar did, who wrote down at night what he had done during the day.

Nevertheless that Phoenix of the Doctor's craft who was Hippocrates wrote so divinely that it is impossible for a mere man to know how to imitate him. Thus it is that in his works, and specifically in his *Epidemics*, he shows clearly that he had many patients to see: and yet he wrote a great deal – even though so many possible works are attributed to him that if he were still alive he would deny the greater part, despite the fact that there is not one of those works that is not redolent of the Hippocratic teaching.

Indeed, once when I was at Agen in the Agenais, a region of French Aquitaine, and with Julius Caesar Squaliger [*sic*], who was a wise and scholarly man, a second Marcilio Ficino in Platonic philosophy – in short, a person whose like I could not name, other than a Plutarch or a Marcus Varro – he affirmed that most of Galen's works had been attributed to him.

It is true that I have also often held discussions with Franois [*sic*] Valeriolla. I do not know whether the sun for thirty leagues around has ever seen a man more replete with knowledge than he – and he, too, was partially of the opinion that several works are attributed to him that he never wrote, even though Galen himself set down his catalogue in writing and the way in which his books should be read.

Among others, has not the sovereign sun produced for us and for the whole of France, including Belgium, another Galen who is Jaques Sylvius, and in Germany Leonarthus Fuchsius, who by the excellence of their studies have assured immortality for themselves, just as their works have acquired an eternal memory, such that if their shades were to descend to the Elysian Fields, Galen would recognize them as the true and perfect image of his own likeness, in that it is not possible for a human being to write in a more learned way? And there is an almost innumerable multitude [here Nostradamus pairs *plusieurs* with *innombrables*, so confirming – if confirmation were needed – that the word meant 'many' at the time, rather than 'several', as it does today] scattered throughout Christendom who continually tend to prepare some praise of this kind through their written work in order to become glorified in perpetuity.

But I doubt very much whether the time will come when there are more professors of the medical art than at present...

[The Proem goes on and on along similar lines, continually name-dropping and positively stuffed with classical allusions, until it finally concludes with the slightly confusing sign-off:]

Bidding you adieu from St-Rémy in Provence, known as Sextrophaea, this first day of April 1552, composed at Salon de Crau in Provence.

Part 1 Chapter VI

To make a perfect nutmeg oil, which not only has all the potency of nutmeg but, in addition, when applied to the stomach, is a sovereign remedy against coughs, nausea, retching and all kinds of stomach ache.

Take half a pound of nutmegs, grind them up coarsely, then boil them in a pan with a pound of spring water. When the mixture has come to the boil three or four times, remove it from the fire and put the whole thing into a little sachet of new linen, tie it up firmly, put it into a press and squeeze it hard. Put a dish underneath it to collect what runs through. You will then see the oil floating on the water like yellow wax, having a superb odor. If it is kept for a year, the yellow will turn a brownish color, and the smell will become stronger still. You will not get more than an ounce of oil from half a pound of nutmegs. Note that, since this produces such a small quantity of oil, it can also be made another way. This, though, is the proper and most natural way, confirmed by all as having all the effects of artificial balsam.

Part 1 Chapter VIII [the one giving Nostradamus's famous plague remedy]

To make the basis for a perfectly good and excellent aromatic powder whose perfume is not strange, but confers an agreeable and long-lasting sweetness, though it can only be prepared once a year.

For this famous prescription and commentary, please see Chapter 3, pages 31 to 34.

Part 1 Chapter X

To make a sweet-smelling, long-lasting paste, which is most proper and suitable for forming into aromatic balls and rosary beads because all aromatic mixtures contain roses, which are what gives them their goodly smell in the first place, and because, owing to their subtle and delicate nature, it seems quite easy. Thanks to this recipe, however, an aromatic ball or rosary retains the sweetness of its scent a long time, though it can only be made once a year.

Take some nice, clean, in-folded red roses, as many as you like – five or six hundred, more or less – and boil up as much water as you can see will be enough to cover them. When the water is boiling vigorously, put the roses into it, bring them to the boil five or six times, and then put them in a brand new earthenware pot. Then leave them to stand for twenty-four hours. The next day heat them up again, then squeeze them as hard as possible in a press until all the goodness has come out and nothing is left except the dried-out roses. Now take the liquid, put it into a pan and bring it to the boil over a low fire, starting off slowly but increasing the heat towards the end until the moisture has all gone. Finally, when you can see that it is about to reduce down completely, stir it with a stick, and when you see that it is as thick as boiled honey, drain it into a glazed earthenware dish and leave it in the sun for a few days. From this simple mixture there will now issue a sweet smell that will last for a long time, and it is suitable for forming into aromatic balls, giving a better paste than those made by infusing tragacanth in rose-water.

Part 1 Chapter XI

Another method for making aromatic balls.

Take two ounces of the purest labdanum, an ounce each of Styrax calamite and *Assae odoriferae* (which we call benzoin), half an ounce of rose tablets, one ounce of violet powder and half a dram each of amber and musk. Grind it all into a powder, knead it together with the rose mixture mentioned earlier for the space of an hour and you will have an aromatic ball of the most supreme perfume, and the longest-lasting that can be made anywhere in the world. Those who grasp the way of doing this will praise it loud and long. True, many people have added white sandalwood to it, or lemon-oil (which has no merit), and many other useless drugs that have smelt more like medicinal drugs or spices than good perfume. But it is gratuitous to excuse people who have misled others, committing to print things that they did not know and had no experience of – for such people have set down things that have neither rhyme nor reason. Be advised, then, that labdanum is very good when it is not adulterated and is the substance obtained from goats' beards in Arabia the Blest, about which Herodotus wrote in his *Thalian Muse*, which is his third book. Indeed, three years ago I searched the whole city of Genoa for it, and came away with half a pound of it on account of its excellence, taken from the beard. For in Arabia they collect it from the stomachs of goats and sheep, in the same way that sheep's wool is gathered here in Provence. So if the labdanum is of good quality and unadulterated, you can make [aromatic] balls out of it because, quite apart from their good smell, carrying them on the person offers powerful protection against infected air in times of pestilence or during outbreaks of dangerous illnesses. For it rejoices the soul, strengthens the heart and the brain, relieves fainting attacks and restores the faint heart. And it has such an exquisite perfume that the nearer you hold it to your nose, the more pleasant and attractive it is. It also strengthens the brain in cases of epilepsy to such an extent that in cases where someone might previously have had an attack once a month, he would now fall only once in three months.

Part 1 Chapter XIII

Powder for cleaning and whitening the teeth and making the breath sweet and soft, and in a few days cleaning the teeth and making them as white as ivory, however black and brown they may be.

Take three drams each of crystal, flint, white marble, glass and calcined rock salt, two drams each of cuttlefish bone and calcined sea-snail shells, half a dram each of fragmented pearls, two drams of bright riverbed stones (which form little white pebbles), one scruple of amber and twenty-two grains of musk, and grind them down thoroughly on a painter's marble slab. Rub the teeth with [the resultant powder] frequently and gently rub with a little rose honey any places where the gums have receded. In a few days you will see the flesh grow back, and the teeth clearly get whiter. [Please remember that this is Nostradamus's recipe, not mine!]

Part 1 Chapter XIIII

Another more excellent method for cleaning the teeth, even those that are really rotten and decayed – for if they have been tarnished for a long time it is impossible for them to become white again, and with this you will clearly see quick results.

Take some blue clay, of the type used for tiles that are white when fired. Take as much as you like, and knead it vigorously for a long time so that it is (above all) clean and free of gravel, and when you have kneaded it thoroughly, make it into small, long, round pieces of the type and shape that you see indicated here:

la façon & forme que vous voyez icy ſigné.
Et les ferés ſeicher au ſoleil, & quād elles ſeront bien

Dry these in the sun and, when they are completely dry, bake them in an oven used for baking clay pots or tiles: or to bake them more quickly, place them either on an iron plate, a tile or a brick and put them in a blacksmith's furnace. Then pump the bellows for half a quarter of an hour, and they will be baked as perfectly as if they had been three days in the oven. When they are well baked, prepare some water as described hereunder and soak them in it. And because the newly fired clay soaks up the water, it will retain the aroma internally. Whenever you want to clean your teeth, this will remove the stains and rottenness and unpleasant smell and give the mouth a pleasant taste for a whole day. If you persist with this, you will make them white as ivory, however black they may be. It would also be good to wet them with egg-white (after they have been treated several times with aromatic water) in which a gold leaf has been placed, in order to add luster to them [please remember, once again, that this is Nostradamus's prescription, not mine!].

Part 1 Chapter XV

Here follows the perfumed water for impregnating the shapes or forms mentioned above.

Take four ounces of Florentine violet roots, one ounce of in-folded red roses, one ounce of cloves, six drams of *cyperi* [the root of special rushes], a dram of cinnamon, half an ounce of sweet calamus, a dram of lavender, three drams of dried marjoram, two drams of orange peel, one ounce of styrax, one dram of ambergris and half a dram of musk. Let the whole of it be ground to powder and put into a glass phial with some good rose-water and some naphtha water made with orange-flowers, lime-flowers and lemon-flowers all mixed together – mainly orange-flowers, but of the other two a pound (of sixteen ounces).

Leave it there for four days, and then take a glass that is more than half the size of the original. But [before] you pour it into the glass, mix the contents vigorously by shaking the phial. Then, when you have put as much as you like in the glass, leave your shapes [sticks] to soak in it for an hour or so, as you see fit. While they are soaking, see that you keep the glass well covered, so that it does not spoil. Once they have thoroughly absorbed the water, paint them either wholly or partially with gold leaf, whichever you think best, and then clean the teeth.

Afterwards, to wash away the contamination that the shaped sticks will have produced, take the rest of the water that has remained in the phial or flask, and pass it through a straining bag, just as one does with the first straining of Hippocratic wine, squeezing out the bottom of the bag tightly, so that all the taste is washed away by the water. Then pour the water again as often as you can until it is clear. You can use this water in many ways to make pleasant odors, or for the face, the hands, the beard or as a mouthwash.

Part 1 Chapter XVIII [the rarely seen 'lost' chapter, translated from Antoine Volant's 1556 edition – seemingly the last edition in which it appeared before being quietly removed]

To truly make the lovers' sexual potion which the ancients used for love-making.

The method for making amorous potions, which the Greeks commonly called *philtres* and the Romans a *poculum amatorium*: such that, once a person had passed it from one mouth to the other, the other died of love-sickness. All the while the one continually retaining it in his mouth did not expel it by a certain time, he would die in a complete frenzy if he did not enjoy the person he was laying claim to. It was first invented by Medea. Similarly, the poet Lucretius died of it. And this potion is so powerful and efficacious that if a man were to have a little of it in his mouth, and while having it in his mouth kissed a woman, or a woman him, and expelled it with his saliva, putting some of it in the other's mouth, it would suddenly cause in her a fire that is not so much a fire as a fever without either thirst or high temperature, but a burning of her heart to perform the love-act, and that only with the one giving her the kiss and injecting it into her mouth. The love between the two remains so long and so inviolable that neither can endure not being together. And if the lovers were to be separated, their love would be like those great, passionate amours [in the past] that have been converted into madness. In those days people were obliged to make the Amulet of Venus, which we call a love-charm, with the bird that is called *cauda tremula* [literally: 'wagtail'], which appears only in the winter.

Many of those who once used sacred magic knew how to make it, such as Diotima – the woman who indoctrinated Socrates with the occult philosophy and herself used this potion from the time of her youth onwards, and in her old age tried to use it on young people but succeeded more in just fascinating or charming them. But the version that follows has magnificent power to attract one who is compatible, constraining the woman or maid to abandon herself [to you] and to taste what through [purely] artificial conjecture she is imagining in her mind.

But beware not to use it for evil ends, nor to keep it in your mouth until it fills *you*, for it could harm you. Instead, you should keep it in a tiny little glass phial, and when you are close to the person, wherever you like, put it [the mixture, presumably, not the phial!] in her mouth, inserting it while kissing her.

The poet Lucretius (and the way to make it is as hereunder) witnesses in his fourth book to having used it, saying:

> *Affligunt Amicle corpus iunguntq; salivas Oris,*
> *inspirant pressantes dentibus ora.*

[apparently a half-remembered quotation about the potion afflicting and joining friends' bodies, with the saliva forced past the teeth into the mouth...] It seems to me that it will be neither alien nor strange to this our initiative if I describe how it used to be made, despite the fact that some will not find it good that the recipe be included here, even though in truth it has not yet been committed to print by any known writer, and even though it was banned by the occult philosophy of poisons at the time of Nerva, Trajan and Hadrian, as the Platonic philosopher Apuleius explains in greater detail in his *Apology against Emylianus*, referring to it vaguely and darkly.

However, so as not to exceed our terms of reference, we shall describe the principal way in which it was made which, after its invention by Medea, spread through the whole of Thessaly, where the women used it with enthusiasm:

TAKE three mandrake apples and go and cull them as soon as you see the sun rising, and wrap them in verbena leaves and the root of the mullein herb, and leave them alone until the following morning. Then take the weight of six grains of magnetite from the point where it repels the iron, as revealed by the use of the quadrant, and pulverize it on the marble as finely as possible, sprinkling it a little with the juice of the mandrake apple. Next take the blood of seven male sparrows, bled via the left wing; of ambergris the weight of 57 barley seeds; seven grains of musk; of the core of the best cinnamon that can be found the weight of 377 barley seeds; of cloves and fine lignum aloes the weight of three deniers [pence]; of the arms of an octopus [the original French misprints this, substituting *pourpre poisson* for *poulpe poisson*, as is not impossible with dictated typesetting!] one eyelet from each, preserved and prepared in honey; of mace the weight of 21 grains; of sweet flag the weight of 500 grains; of the root of *Lyris Illyrica* or *Sclavonia* ['Illyrian or Slavonian Lyre'] the weight of 700 grains; of the root of *Apii Risus* ['Bee's Laughter'] 31 grains; of Cretan wine double the weight of the whole; of the finest sugar the weight of 700 grains, which is just a little more than an ounce. Mix all of this together and pulverize and macerate it thoroughly in a marble mortar with a wooden pestle. Ladle it out with a silver spoon and put it in a glass vessel, and set it to boil on the fire until it reduces in quantity to the point where the sugar has become like syrup, or julep. And take care above all that it is not a willow fire. Once it has boiled, strain it all carefully but vigorously, and put it in a vessel of gold, silver or glass.

And when you want to use some of it, put just a little of it in your mouth, as it were the weight of half a crown, and even if you swallow some of it, it will not harm you at all, provided that if you do not find the person to transmit it to, you do not fail that very day to have sex, wherever it seems best to you. For the increased production of semen that it produces rises to the brain and causes a madness that is called 'love-madness', as well as having other powerful effects that rejoice the person involved – indeed, if made without the magnetite, these are quite incomparable.

However, if it is to have power and efficacity for the consecration of love it is necessary that the stone be in it, for by its power the mandrake has the effect of summoning up the power of the expelled genital seed by removing the *Apii Risus*.

And note that if the person is married and the love between them has grown cold, and some divorce [is pending] by the fault of either party, especially the man (who is generally affected by the imperfection that the woman lacks), you should add oil of feces [?], 31 grains by weight of ambergris, dissolved in white dove's blood and mixed with a little *Philtre Amuleti* ['amulet potion'], which has the effect of chasing away all hate and rancor, provided that it is not for a woman who is maddened or enraged and whose nature is malign, for this might well keep her quiet for a few days, but in the end she would be just as inclined to evil malignity again, especially if she is egged on by nasty relations full of hidden malice.

It is of course possible that some students of Platonic philosophy will be inclined to class all this as frivolous. But if they think about all the reasons carefully, they will find that it has in fact escaped and emerged from their own school, ae, ae [Hee hee?], that it is pleasing to the sovereign sun, which is the true light of God, and that none was ever so bold as to try and make it other than in the context of marriage: for to use it for fraudulent and libidinous sex it would be wrong to use the knowledge of it [*sic*].

Part 1 Chapter XXIV

How to make the hair golden blond, no matter how black or white it is, making it pale yellow without losing its color for a long time, and retaining it in its entirety, and making it grow in such a way as to be that color right down to the root, just as it is to the very tip.

Take a pound of twigs of the wood called fustet, ground to a fine powder, half a pound of box-wood shavings, four ounces of fresh liquorice, four ounces of nice, dry, yellow orange peel, four ounces each of celandine root and papaver, two ounces of the leaves and flower of *glaucium* or guelder rose, half an ounce of saffron, and half a pound of paste made from finely ground wheat flour. Boil it all up in some lye made with half pounded ashes and then pour it all out [through a strainer?].

Next, take a large earthenware pot or jar, and make ten or twelve little holes in the bottom. Then afterwards take equal quantities of sacred ash [?] and pounded wood ash and put them in some large wooden mortar or something of the kind, as you please, and sprinkle them with the said concoction while pounding them vigorously for the best part of a day. Keep doing so until the ash is fairly hard, and while pounding it add a little rye- and wheat-straw, continually pounding it so that it soaks up most of the concoction. Then take the said pounded ashes and put them in the said pot or jar, and in each of the holes in the said pot stick an ear of rye that passes out to the exterior and make alternate beds of straw and ashes until the said pot is full, but leave a little room for the rest of the concoction. Then, towards evening, position another pot or jar to collect the lye that dribbles out of the holes along the ears of rye. When you want to use it in the morning, go and see what has oozed out, sponge it up and apply it to the hair by wiping. And at the end of three or four days you will have hair that is as golden-blond as a golden ducat. But before you put it on your head, wash it with another good lye, because if it were greasy it would not take so easily.

And you must understand that the contents of the present recipe are sufficient for one or two years, and are sufficient, if used properly, for the needs of ten or twelve women, for only a little of the liquor is sufficient to color the hair quickly and easily, and there is no need to wash with anything other than this for a woman whose hair was black as coal to become quickly blonde, and for a very long time.

Part 1 Chapter XXVI [often erroneously described as for an aphrodisiac]

There follows a supreme and very useful composition for the health of the human body that is of great power and efficacity.

I should like to set down here for you details of a composition which I have often prepared for the Most Reverend Monsignor the Lord Bishop of Carcassonne, Ammanien de Foys [who was in fact an appointee only, and never took up the post], which has brought life back to his body. Since the soul from the point of view of medicine is none other than natural heat, and where there is no heat there is no life, so, by means of this composition, a melancholy complexion has been changed into a sanguine one, even though the humors of the two are diametrically opposed to each other in every way – just as smoke, which is a warm, moist substance, instantly converts itself into murky soot, which is cold and dry after the manner of the earth.

So it is that this composition rejuvenates the person who uses it. If the person is sad or melancholic, it makes him bright and joyful; if he is a timid man, it makes him daring; if he is taciturn, it makes him affable by changing his qualities; if he is a malicious man, it makes him gentle and slow to anger, changing him as it were into a thirty-year-old; if the hairs of his beard are starting to turn gray, it slows down the ageing process considerably, and preserves the color no less than his youth. It rejoices the heart and whole person so entirely, that from the day when he has taken it it will make the breath smell so sweet that he will feel very pleased about it. Without overheating his nature, without changing him in any way, protecting him from headaches and pains in the side, it keeps the four humors in such balance and proportion that if the man had not been born, he would never be able to die. But he who taught us about nature also taught us that we must die.

The clarification that [this composition] brings is so restorative that it prolongs one's life, extending it to such an extent that unless some great accident or excess befalls the user, his life will be as long as that of the ancient barbarians. Anyone who is sickening for tuberculosis, be it of the first, second or third kind, will evade and escape the danger. Preserved at times of plague, he will not come to any harm, and whoever is struck by it – provided that it be within ten hours – is sure to escape it, provided that he also has a change of air by going at least three leagues from any plague carriers. Then you will be sure to escape, and will pose no risk or danger to anybody. Its powers are to be commended.

Take note, then, of how to make it, and carry out of the printed instructions exactly, for nothing [in it] is impossible to prepare.

The recipe follows [the ingredients are all in abbreviated Latin, rather like a doctor's prescription, presumably so that clients are forced to get the genuine ones from their apothecaries]:

Take the powder of sweet musk, of cold pearls, of gemstones and of master coral, 150 finely chopped gold leaves, and lapis lazuli (washed nine times and prepared in a similar way). Do not, however, use the type that the apothecaries have, for that is worthless, but rather the kind stocked by jewelers or goldsmiths. Take as much as four drams of this (if you can find so much), a dram each of best broken pearls, one dram of oak shavings, one dram of unicorn scrapings [rhinoceros horn?], two pieces of deer antler, half an ounce each of aloes wood and the heart of cinnamon, one dram each of preserved roses, alkanet and violets, six preserved nuts, half a dram of preserved lemon peel (well steeped in sugar), six drams of preserved ginger, three drams of the preserved fruit of the *mirabulanum embulicum* [?], one ounce each of finely chopped, preserved oranges, lettuce and pumpkin, four ducats' weight of the finest gold filings from golden ducats that you can find, half an ounce of occidental amber and two drams each of senna and musk.

Let the powders be put together, and the conserves and confections ground up hard in a marble mortar with the gold leaves and the filed-down gold, and all of them vigorously pounded together. Then take six ounces of fine white silk that has never been used and bring it all to the boil with two ounces of *fraissel*, which is the powder of scarlet-grains [?], together with half a pound each of the juice of good-smelling apples, rose-water and blessed edible thistles, and six ounces of fine sugar. Boil them all together with the *fraissel*, the liquids and the juice until you see that they have turned quite red, but take care that no sugar is present while you are boiling the silk. Once the silk, the juices, the water and the wine [?!!] have been well boiled, remove them from the fire, pour them out carefully [into a straining cloth?] and squeeze the liquid out as strongly as you can. Then, once it has been strained, add the sugar and boil it up like a syrup. When it is almost ready, pour two ounces of the best malmsey over it, or white wine, and boil it all a little more until it is [again] like syrup, then take it off the fire and add some ambergris to it. If it is the right stuff it will dissolve. When it has cooled, add the musk, and finally add the rest of the conserves, confections and well ground-up powders. Stir the mixture well for the space of half an hour so that it is well mixed. Then take four ounces of preserved alkanet bark and one ounce of *Doronicus Romanus* [leopard's bane?] and put it in last. Mix everything thoroughly and finally add the gold leaves. When the whole concoction is ready, put it in a tightly closed receptacle of gold, silver or glass.

Part 1 Chapter XXVII

There follows the way in which one should use the above-mentioned composition, which is equal in power and efficacity to potable gold and its power.

If one takes a dram's weight of it every morning, washed down with a little good wine or malmsey, an hour and a half before dining, it will protect against the aggravation of falling ill, strengthen the heart, the stomach and the brain, cure epilepsy in those who are not yet twenty-five years old, rejuvenate the person and slow down the ageing process. If anyone takes it during an epidemic, he will not be infected that day. A crown's weight of it provides much better nourishment than a whole capon, protects the person against leprosy, drives away melancholy and eases stomach ache.

But its greatest virtue is that if mixed with alkanet water, and taken by someone on the point of death and in his last agony, when nature and his sickness are doing battle with each other, it will so invigorate and strengthen the patient that the outcome of the crisis will be in his favor and the illness overcome [evidently it didn't work for Nostradamus himself!]. For the greatest virtue that it can have is that it benefits the heart a hundred times more than Alchermes's confection.

Also, if some woman cannot have children, it so adapts the womb that both seeds, once united, are retained in its vessels and are adapted for true child-bearing. Therefore when my lords the doctors of medicine [an interesting expression that seems to confirm that he himself wasn't one at the time] assess this composition in detail, they will bestow on it no less than the highest praise.

Again, if someone were to faint, even a little of it would restore the soul to its seat, even the soul of life.

However, this composition is not suitable for everyone, even though all humans are human. However, let anyone who wants to preserve his life and live a long time in health and happiness have some made up. But be well advised, do not trust just any apothecary: I guarantee you that for every good one there are a hundred, if not a thousand bad ones. Either they are so poor that they do not have the necessary ingredients, or they are rich and powerful, but miserly and corrupt, and so fearful of not being paid what they ask that they don't include the half – or even the third – of the prescription's ingredients.

Others are ignorant – not only not knowing, but not even wanting to know, which is a terrible evil in men of any estate – while yet others are dirty and unclean, and act dishonestly.

I will not say that there are not some among them who have it all, who have what it takes, who are conscientious, who have the know-how, but [even] they are negligent and have their medicines made up by others who do it badly. I will not deny that there are some who do well what they do, but that is very rare.

I have traveled extensively throughout the kingdom of France, or at least most of it, and have frequented and known many apothecaries and become acquainted with them, but I have seen them do so many unspeakable things that I believe one could not find any other trade in which there is more malpractice and unconscionable misuse than pharmaceutics...

[Nostradamus then goes on at considerable length about the dreadful practices he has seen in a whole variety of places – especially ones with Roman ruins to explore! – finally recommending Louis Serre at Marseille, Joseph Turel Lecurin at Aix-en-Provence and François Bérard at Salon...]

Part 2 Chapter III

To make candied orange peel, using sugar or honey, that will be excellently tasty.

Take some oranges and cut them into four or six sections, but at least four. Remove the insides, so that nothing remains except the peel, with the flesh and the pips removed. Now take your peel and leave it to soak in good clean water, on this first occasion adding a good fistful of salt, because the salt will take away the excess bitterness from the oranges. Leave the peel to stand for twenty-four hours, then change the water and replace it with fresh. Carry on changing it for nine days. At the end of nine days, boil the peel in good spring water, until, when you are ready to test it with a pin, this will go in easily. When you notice that the pin does go into the peel easily, remove the peel from the fire and use a straining spoon to put it into cold water. When the pieces have cooled, dry them a little on a white linen cloth and, when you have dried off some of the water, put them into a glass or earthenware vessel until it is full of them. Next take two or three pounds of sugar, depending on the size of the vessel, and if the sugar is of good quality do not clarify it, but dissolve it in the same weight of water as the sugar itself weighs. Once it has dissolved, let it boil until it attains the form and consistency of a syrup that has been thoroughly boiled for the first time. Then remove it from the fire and let it cool. And when it is cool, put the peel into it and let it soak well in the said syrup. The following day put the said syrup in a pan, without the peel, and bring it to the boil, just as you did before, and let it cool again. Then put it back into its vessel containing the said orange peel, and leave it to stand for three days.

And at the end of three days boil it up again as before. When you see that the syrup is boiling, throw the rind or peel into the mixture and bring it back to the boil five or six times – but no more, lest it become too hard. Then afterwards remove it from the fire, let it cool again, and put it all back into its vessel and do not touch it for a month or thereabouts. If at the end of a month you deem that it needs boiling up again, do so, or else just leave it as it is.

And if you wish, after it has all been well and truly boiled, you can add a small stick of cinnamon and some cloves pounded together – which will make a preserve of quite perfect goodness.

If, however, you wish to preserve your orange peel in honey, take as much honey as you like, put it in a pan and melt it until all the scum rises to the top, and when all the scum has risen to the top, leave it to stand until it is cold. Then remove the scum on the top with a skimmer or pierced spoon and discard it. Now take the de-scummed honey and add it to the oranges, and carry on as described for the sugar.

Part 2 Chapter VIII

How to make a jam or preserve with heart-cherries, which the Italians call amarenes, *and to prepare them in the best and most beautiful way in the world, such that [even] when they are a year old they will seem to have been prepared that day, and most tasty, too.*

Take some of the nicest heart-cherries you can find, good and ripe (for if they are not completely ripe, only skin and marrow will remain after cooking) and cut the stalks somewhat if you feel that they are too long. Take three pounds or so of them. Then take a pound-and-a-half of sugar, and let it dissolve in the juice of three or four pounds of other heart-cherries. And take care that once the juice has been extracted you add it to the sugar at once and without delay. Then place it over the fire, making sure that the sugar dissolves in no other liquid than the juice.

Boil it up as quickly as possible and when it is boiling remove all the scum that is floating on the top. When you have removed all the scum and can see that your sugar is as red as it was to start with and is thoroughly clarified, don't let it go off the boil, but immediately – without taking it off the fire – put in the heart-cherries to boil, stirring them neither too much nor too little, until they are perfect, all the while removing the scum on the top with a spatula.

Do not take them off the fire until they are cooked right through without any need to put them on the fire again. Then put one drop on a pewter plate, and once you see that it will not run down in either direction, they are ready. As soon as you see that they are done to perfection, pour them while still hot into small containers holding three or four ounces each. You will then have beautiful red, whole heart-cherries with a wonderful taste that will keep for a long time.

I have been to many different parts of the world, and have been with people who have prepared them some in this way and some in that, such that, if I were to describe what I have seen everywhere the paper would run out. I would have thought that the land of Italy would have been best at doing this, but while there (at least so far as I have observed) they go about it abysmally. I have seen it made in Toulouse, in several ways at Bordeaux and at la Rochelle – indeed, throughout the lands of Guyenne and Languedoc, and the whole of Provence, the Dauphiné and the Lyonnais. But I have never come across more beautiful nor better ones than these. In Toulouse they boil and re-boil them five or six times and several times in Bordeaux, as well as throughout the Agenais. Eventually, though, when they are five or six months old, they spoil: some go rotten, while others dry out. For if you want to preserve them properly you must use no liquid other than the juice of heart-cherries, as it increases their goodness, body and taste to such an extent that, if a sick person takes just a single one, it will be to him like a balsam or other restorative. And after a year they are just like they were on the day they were prepared.

Part 2 Chapter XV

To make a quince jelly of superb beauty, goodness, flavour and excellence fit to set before a King, and which lasts a good long time.

Take whatever quinces you like, as long as they are fully ripe and yellow. Cut them up into quarters without peeling them (for those who peel them do not know what they are doing, since the skin enhances the smell), and divide each quarter into five or six pieces. Remove the seeds, because the fruit will turn into jelly perfectly well without them. As you are cutting them up, place them in a basin full of water, for unless they are plunged into water the moment they are cut up they will turn black. Once they are cut up, boil them in a good quantity of water until they are well done, almost to the point of shriveling up. When they have boiled thoroughly, strain this liquid through a thick piece of new linen and squeeze the whole preparation through it as hard as you can. Then take this decoction, and if there are six pounds of it, take one and a half pounds of Madeira sugar and put it into the decoction, and bring it to the boil over a gentle charcoal fire until you see that, towards the end, it is reducing in volume considerably. Then damp the fire down, so that it does not burn at the edges – which would give a bad color to the jelly. Then, when it is nearly done, and so as to know when it is done perfectly, take some of it with a spatula or silver spoon and put it on a platter, and if you see that when it has cooled it comes off as a globule, without sticking either here or there, then it is done. Take it off the fire and wait for the scum on the top to settle, then pour the still-hot liquid into small wooden or glass containers. And if you want to write or gouge something on the bottom of the container, you can do so, for it will be seen easily [through the jelly]. For the color will be as diaphanous as an oriental ruby. So excellent will the color be – and the taste even more so – that it may be given to sick and healthy alike.

Part 2 Chapter XXIIII

To preserve pears.

Take as many of the best small pears, or muscatels, or others – any, in fact, that on the basis of local and regional knowledge you know to be suitable for preserving. Peel them and clean them as thoroughly as you can. And if it seems to you that the stalks are too long, cut a little off them, though it is better that they should be too long than too short, so as to be able to get hold of them when you want to. When you have peeled them as and how you can, drop them into fresh water, so that they do not turn black. When they have all been cleaned, boil them up wherever you like in good spring water – or the best that can be found – and carry on until they are sufficiently cooked (such that, when you pierce them with a pin, the pin goes in easily). And when they are sufficiently cooked, take them off the fire, remove them with a skimming-ladle and cool them down in clear water, then put them on a nice, clean, white cloth and leave them to dry by themselves for a bit. When they are dry, put them in any well-glazed earthenware vessel, or just an earthenware pot, and turn it upside down, so that any last drop of water that has failed to run out will the more easily do so. Then take as much sugar as your eye tells you is necessary, dissolve it in the same amount of water – whether more or less is neither here nor there – and, when it has dissolved, clarify it if necessary. But if the sugar is in sugar-loaf form, and particularly if it comes from Madeira, there is no need to clarify it, since it is normally whiter. This is because, when sugar is made, soft earth is piled on top of a jar whose pointed end is place in a small hole through which the sediment and all the moisture from the sugar trickles. What remains on top, at the wider end, is the most purified. When it begins to dry out, it is covered with a piece of dry clay, to cover it and absorb moisture. For this reason, take your sugar from the wide part of the sugar-loaf, and when it has melted, boil it up into a syrup, and when it is done, leave it to cool down for a bit. When it is cold, put in the pears, and if you see that the pears have been cooked too much, add a little more hot sugar, to firm it up. When the sugar-syrup has been with the pears in their pot for two days, boil it up again into a syrup and when it is completely cold, pour it back into the vessel with the pears. Leave it to stand for four days and then pour the sugar into a pan and the pears into a dish or cooking pot, and put one or two cloves and some cinnamon on each pear. This done, replace the pears back into their vessel and boil up the sugar into a proper syrup once more. Once it has boiled, pour it back over the pears and seal the pot well. You will then have a confection excellent enough to set before a prince.

Part 2 Chapter XXV

To make a very fine sugar candy.

Take nine pounds or so of nice white sugar-loaf or muscovado (for beautiful materials make for a beautiful work, and ugly ones for an ugly or nasty one) and dissolve or liquify it in a sufficient amount of water. If you do not feel, though, that the sugar is fine enough, clarify it until it has lost all its sediment such that, once clarified, you can easily run it through a strainer. Then boil it up until it takes on the consistency of a syrup. It is better to overboil, rather than underboil it, for then it would candy to a salt. As soon as it is boiled, take some specially made unglazed earthenware pots and place in each of them a little stick of pine-wood, or a length of reed, in order that the sugar may candy throughout as a result of having something to form around. When the sticks have been properly fitted inside them all, pour the still-hot sugar into each pot, put its lid on (which should be of earthenware) press it in thoroughly and seal it roughly with clay, for no other reason than to keep the heat inside for longer. Then immediately bury it under some dung – which should be warm – in some hidden or secluded place. If you see that the dung is not hot enough, warm it up with some hot water it and see that the dung is deep and that the pots are right in the middle of it. Cover them up well and leave for nine whole days and nine whole nights. At the end of nine days, take them out of the dung heap, open them and pour out the syrup which has not yet candied and you will see that out of nine pounds of sugar, five or six pounds will have candied – perhaps more, perhaps less. When you have thoroughly drained all the syrup, heat up some water until it is good and hot, then immediately wash out [each pot] two or three times, rinsing it out thoroughly, so that any syrup remaining does not get in the way, and then add the washing-water to the syrup.

Note, by the way, that when you want to prepare this you should not make less than you can easily manage, since a little costs just as much as a lot. You should also understand that if the sugar were to stay under the dung longer than nine days and the dung were hot, the sugar would de-candify because the steam from the dung contains moist fumes that would penetrate inside to some extent, and there would be as much [sugar] de-candifying itself as candying.

Note that if you want all or most of the sugar to candy, you should just boil the sugar up into a syrup and see that the pot has not been fired at too high a temperature and has not been washed (or even in contact) with water just before you put in the sugar, so that the only moisture the pot absorbs is from the sugar. Also, such pots should be made expressly for this purpose. For when you want to take the candied sugar out all in one piece, once you have removed any syrup you must place the pot over the fire directly on the charcoal while turning it a little, until you can feel the sugar moving inside. Then break the pot and remove the sugar, which will all have candied – and you will get not less than eight or nine pounds of it.

Anybody can make this, but it is disgraceful for a lot of idle chatterers to say that beautiful sugar candy can be made from an impure sugar. *Quia ex non musico non fit Musicus* [Latin: 'For you can't get good music out of a bad musician']. If, however, you mean that something beautiful can be made from a sugar which is not very nice, I will tell you how it can be done. Take a quantity of well-refined sugar, well clarified and boiled to a syrup, but only just – then put it into a large earthenware jar. Make a hole at the bottom such as one makes at the bottom of a barrel or cask, and leave the said syrup in this long, deep jar that is commensurate with the amount of syrup. Leave it there for four or five days, and at the end of five days run a good half or more of the syrup out through the hole in the bottom. What is left will then be good, for sugar acts differently from honey in that the best sugar rises to the top, as is the case with oil. The best honey, however, is that at the bottom. Thus it is possible from an impure sugar to make a fairly good sugar candy, but it will still be of inferior quality.

This, then, is how to make sugar candy as it is made in Genoa and Venice. Here at home, in fact, I have even had it made in olive-barrels once the oil has been emptied out, and this was very good and very much like that which is brought from Venice.

Part 2 Chapter XXVII

To make marzipan paste, which Hermolaus in the following letter calls Martios panes *[Latin: 'Soldiers' loaves'], and which can easily be prepared at home or in any place whatever, as you will see in the said letter.*

Take a pound of cleanly peeled almonds and pound them thoroughly in a marble mortar with half a pound of Madeira sugar. When it has all been thoroughly ground up together, add a little rose-water while still pounding, so that they do not turn oily. And once they have been well ground up, make little cakes or little round tartlets out of them and lay them out on top of wafers. Let these be of high quality. You can set them out in squares on top of the said wafers. Then bake them in the oven.

When they are half-baked, take some powdered sugar and make up a paste with egg whites and a little orange juice: make it quite runny, and when the marzipan is almost baked, take it out of the oven and, with a feather, brush on some of the liquiefied sugar, then return the marzipan to the oven simply to color it.

When it is finished, you will find that it has a really delectable and delicious taste. Any greater quantity of sugar makes it doughy and unpleasant to eat, and consequently less delicious.

If you want to bake them easily at home at any hour of the day, heat up an iron shovel, of the kind you use for the fire, until it is red-hot, and place the marzipan or little biscuits made with the said paste on a stool or table. Then pass it lightly over the marzipan without actually touching it, until you can see it starting to color up. And when it is done on one side, turn it over and do it again. When they are done, you will have the same color as mentioned above, and when made this way they are better than in the oven to the extent that they don't get smoky [the medieval equivalent of grilling!].

However, this way of making them is only for emergencies, since they are [even] more quickly baked than shaped. This is what Hermolaus Barbarus called 'soldiers' loaves', being used for medicine and for light snacks at all hours.

Some may mock me for recording such a minor detail, which all apothecaries know about. But my main aim has been to set it down in writing for common folk and for ladies who are curious to find out, and indeed for all kinds of people. In point of fact, there are [even] many of the pharmaceutical profession to whom this is unknown, even though they know a lot.

Note, though, that if you want to make a really fresh and tasty marzipan, you must make it when the almonds are freshly picked from the tree. If you taste first the one and then the other, you will find a great difference in taste and succulence.

Part 2 Chapter XXIX

To make a laxative rose syrup, of which one ounce will be wonderfully effective, and totally gentle, such that it can be given [even] to a pregnant woman of any age during her first or last months or at any time, without any danger whatsoever.

Take 900 roses that are red, blue and/or red and white (*saraceus*, as we call it), that are still in-folded, even if they are only leaves, or half-open buds, or open ones. When you have removed the leaves, let there be nearer a thousand than 900. When you have cleaned them, rub them a little between your hands, so what any whole buds disintegrate to allow the hot water to get inside them more easily.

Now put all the roses in a big, glazed, earthenware pitcher. Then take some spring water and boil it up. When it is boiling, pour it into the pitcher and stir it vigorously with a sick, so that the boiling water mixes properly with the roses. Once you have poured in enough water to cover all the roses, leave them to steep for 24 hours in the said pitcher. And at the end of 24 hours pour it all into a pan or cauldron and bring it to the boil two or three times. Then strain off the decoction and squeeze the roses as hard as you can in a press or between two pieces of wood until nothing remains except dry white roses.

Now pour the decoction – which will look as red as wine and will smell like rose-water – into a flask. Next take a further 500 roses, defoliated as previously, and put them into the pitcher. Then take the decoction in the flask, heat it until it is almost boiling, and when it is good and hot pour it over the roses. If there is not enough of the decoction, you can add a little boiling water. Leave it all to steep for another twenty-four hours. At the end of twenty-four hours bring it to the boil, then strain it and squeeze it as hard as you can and, when it has all been strained, take a pound (i.e. eighteen ounces) of sugar (without clarifying it) and put that into the decoction. Boil it until it takes on the consistency of badly prepared syrup – for the roses have a certain viscosity of their own that will thicken the syrup. When it is done, take it off the fire and, when it has cooled, pour it into a glass or glazed earthenware vessel. One ounce of this taken in the morning will have a wonderful and praiseworthy effect.

Some people enrich this with rhubarb and then it works even better and is known as *Catarticum imperiale*, which is as good as to say that it is a laxative medicine for Kings or Emperors.

This is how to do it. Take four ounces of good rhubarb and a dram of good cinnamon. Grind them to powder. When the syrup is almost done, take the said rhubarb, wrap it up in a piece of clean worsted cloth, pierce it with a thread and suspend it in the syrup while it is boiling. Squeeze it out often, and when the syrup has boiled, pour it into its vessel, hang the said rhubarb in it and seal it tightly.

This syrup should be used by noble lords who have authority over people but who are poor masters of their own anger, for one ounce of the syrup will evacuate it, curing and protecting against the Third Fever for a long time. It is numbered among the royal medicines that may be taken quite safely. It can equally well be prepared in another way that is just as good and effective.

[This is duly detailed in the following, final chapter, which then goes into great length about the varying skills of a number of medical colleagues and acquaintances whom he has met during his travels, rather as per the *Proem* of the original edition, concluding with a carefully 'tapered' text containing the words – presumably addressed to his younger brother Jean, to whom Part 2 is dedicated:]

> Therefore be pleased to receive this little Book, which I present to you as a novelty gift.

THE END

Appendix B

The *Orus Apollo* – translated extracts

The *Hieroglyphica* was a famous manuscript written apparently by a Greek priest called Horus Apollo of Menuthis, near Alexandria, in around AD 480-490, some two centuries after the true meaning of the ancient Egyptian hieroglyphs had been irretrievably forgotten. It was supposed to explain the meanings of some 182 of them, but also perpetuated a number of old wives' tales about them that had accrued in the meantime, and that then persisted until Champollion finally managed to decipher them in 1822 with the aid of the Rosetta Stone, now in the British Museum, London.

The original was in Greek, but was subsequently translated into Latin. Retranslated into French, Italian, German and English, it was commented on by Ficino, Erasmus and Rabelais. The artists Dürer, Mantegna and Raphael all drew inspiration from it.

Various Latin editions appeared between 1530 and 1542, not least from two publishers associated directly or indirectly with Nostradamus (Kerver of Paris and Gryphius of Lyon). Nostradamus's contribution was to contribute an extremely free French translation *in verse*, based on Jean Mercier's Latin-Greek version of 1551, at some point prior to 1555, when the Princess of Navarre became Queen. He also added some ten original pieces of his own. The work was never published, but its manuscript, apparently in Nostradamus's own hand, still exists in the Bibliothèque Nationale, Paris, as French manuscript No. 2594 (see page 52). The paper has been analyzed, and found to date from 1535-1539, apparently from somewhere in the general area of the Comtat Venaissin and Provence.[1, 63]

The fact that Nostradamus failed to comment in any way on what it said – other than in his Prologue and towards the end, where he disagreed violently (apparently from personal experience) with its assertions about octopuses and lobsters – suggests that he simply accepted its conclusions. Some echoes of its symbolism seem to be present in the *Sixains*, though some commentators suggest that these are not by Nostradamus.[37] The manuscript is notable for its almost total lack either of accents or of punctuation – a fact which may well reflect the way in which his later *Propheties* were originally written, too (see illustration page 52).

ORUS APOLLO, SON OF OSIRIS, KING OF EGYPT OF THE NILE

Hieroglyphic Notes – Two Books – Put Into Epigrammatical Verse.
A Work of Incredible and Admirable Erudition and Antiquity.
by Michel Nostradamus of St Remy de Provence [note in another hand]

Prologue by the translator to Madame the Princess of Navarre

As wise old nature, sympathy's true mother
By antipathy makes the facts quite other,
And having touched man's soul with her concord
Doth then destroy it after, by discord,
So it doth surely needful seem to me
To write somewhat of this deep mystery,
Even those things that pass the human brain.
I have not rendered these two books in vain,
But to show those who labor hard to know
That to good books they should more studious go.
Of secrets thus they'll know the usefulness
Whose notes, once noted, do the truth confess,
For when the learnèd shall my prologue see
Of hidden lore philologists they'll be,
And capable to marvel quite a whit
How nature works somewhat as it befit,
And know those facts no man can understand
Which Epaphus writ clearly in his hand,
Having of Memphis found each sacred sign

Whose inventory they did first define.
Thus would I know the reason and the cause
Why angry elephants daren't move their paws
And soothèd are when sheep they do behold
Yet frightened are to see within their fold
A little piglet, or its voice to hear:
Than men condemned to death they're more in fear!
Then there's the savage bull who just gives in
When tied to tree or branch, however thin,
While mighty horses cower before the whip
Whom the wolf's jaws have only just let slip
And fly along as lightly as a bird.
And when you eat the flesh (you must have heard!)
Of any beast that wolves do make their prey,
How tasty! Yet the wool you take away
All kinds of fleas and vermin doth beget.
Again, a horse will soon deteriorate
If where a wolf oft passes it doth walk.
Yet if on thorns the wolf should chance to stalk
Quite suddenly quite weak it would become.
The crafty, then, knowing that he doth come,
For fear of him, will strew thorns in the stall.
Yet e'en if man by glowworm light at all
Should wolf espy, he'll make him imbecile
And weak as water, and his voice shall steal.
In fact if man sees wolf in any way
It gets so mad it goes right off its prey.
It weakens lions and their ire provokes
If they should walk on leaves of holly oaks:
They fear the cock, and when they hear it crow
For fear of it away will quickly go.
And if hyena should by nature hap
(Which nature hereinafter I'll recap)
To walk within a doggy shade at night –
What time the slanting moon doth take its flight
And mount in beauty, sudden, up the air
As if it climbed a rope suspended there –
And it if sees a man or dog asleep
Will stretch, and make the sleeper's body creep;

And if its shadow twice as big it sees,
Disturb the sleeper through its great increase
And rend, enraged, the man who once was whole,
Yet from his hands will feed as from a bowl;
And if it sees its shadow short and brief
Will suddenly get up and quickly... leave.
Do but with both hands hold your tongue in fee
And you'll be eloquent as Mercury
And safe from dogs and hounds of any ilk
As though they puppies were, and soft as silk.
Another thing, before I let it pass –
Do but a crayfish wrap around with grass
(The *polypodes quercus*, I should say)
And all its legs and scales will fall away.
The little bat that builds its nest in rock,
If it smells ivy wood, will die of shock.
Vultures will die if ointment they should smell
And snakes if they touch anyone at all
Or if with leaves of oak you deck them o'er,
Strong though the night-wind in the ash trees roar.
A snake, once snatched up by a stork on high
And dropped, no more will wander till it die.
And if the common viper once is hit
With stick, and sees that it is trapped by it
And then recovers all its strength again –
If next the female now with might and main
You strike with any hedgerow branch that's there,
You'll see her fly up straightway in the air.
The tortoise, too, gets ill if it should taste
The flesh of snake, and looks about in haste
For marjoram, and with that herb's assistance
Obtains both health and pleasure and resistance.
And, too, the stork protects its nest, they say,
With plane tree leaves to keep the bats away,
While swallows smear with mud their little nest
Lest other birds should ever them molest.
And the ring-dove or pigeon of the wood
Puts laurel in its nest and finds it good,
While hobbies of the predatory kind

Into their nests wild lettuce seek to bind.
One bat protects its young with ivy leaves
While crow pure wool about its crowlets weaves.
The hoopoe amianthus doth install
And sometimes eats strange birds, feathers and all.
As for the rook, it often likes to eat
Vervain; and larks all kinds of grass and wheat.
And any nest that's made with such a herb
'Gainst colic is a remedy superb.
Other great cases I disdain to quote –
The partridge that on onion stalks doth dote,
The thrush on myrtle, herons crayfish too:
The eagle with its seaweed, as is due.
Much else as well which wise old nature does
We'll see from what th' Egyptians left to us.
God and his world, his seas, his earth below,
Wild beasts and tame ones, too, we'll see on show.
And other cases wonderful I'll cite –
Sea, forest, fields and places that delight.

THE FIRST BOOK OF ORUS APOLLO OF THE NILE OF EGYPT

hieroglyphic notes put into verse in the form of epigrams

How they signified Eternity

For time or for eternity immense
They did depict the moon or else the sun –
Which planets twain of time are elements –
Nor of infinity the sign did shun.
In shining gold they causèd to be done
The basilisk that with its tail so tight
Its body in a circle covers quite.
With edge of gold this circle they decked out,
Painted and formed it to impress the sight.
Their gods with serpents they did gird about.

What the Basilisk serpent denoted

Th' Egyptians did withal the serpent use
To signify of age the passing time,
Of which three species represent three views.
While some the death do die, shall fear no crime
Th' immortal whose sheer facial paradigm
Breathes death to others who are mortal made
And subject are to life and death and time.
Far, far above the gods he is portrayed.

How they represented the world

Wishing the world to show and venerate
They paint a snake with divers scales indent
Who clearly would his own tail masticate
And by his shape the world would represent.
This creature is by nature crude and bent,
Yet in its size imposing as you wish,
Like unto earth, as smooth as any fish,
That every year doth change its state and skin,
Thus ever staying young, year out, year in.
So, too, the world: and when its body it
Would fain consume, the act of God, they say
Makes weak and strong alike from out of it
Who all would fail if it should pass away.

How they signified the year

Wishing to show us how the year to write
They painted ISIS, queen and goddess too,
Who for th' Egyptians was a planet bright –
Called in their language Sothis, it is true –
Whom as ASTROMYON the Grecians knew.
Over all others strong and masterly
Now big, now small she's sometimes seen to be,

Shedding her light when first she doth appear,
And by her rising one can oft foresee
What future times shall surely summon near.

How they otherwise signified the year

Nor did their wisdom vainly give it name
Calling it ISIS as they spoke of it.
For otherwise the sense thereof to claim
Of Egypt's year, as does the name befit,
The palm they painted, whose antique remit
Of all earth's trees exceeded any yet.
Each moon another branch it doth beget
So that in twelve months twelve of them appear
Each sprouting green, and verdantly beset,
Producing one for each month of the year.

Notes on the Figure of Isis for representing her other than she is, according to the most ancient descriptions

[translated from Nostradamus's quoted Latin]

For all its beauty we are pleased to set
What in blest Araby has been undecked
As writers numerous have passed to us.
For it doth seem in Nisa, Araby,
Of ISIS and OSIRIS are the tombs
Whose columns each are carved with sacred scripts,
And that of Isis reads as now doth follow:

[Nostradamus's Latin transcription, translated below, is full of technical errors]:

I am Isis Queen of Egypt, educated by Mercury.
What I have laid down in laws.
Let none dissolve.
I am the mother of Osiris [other versions have *uxor* = 'wife']

I am the discoverer of the first of fruits.
I am the mother of king Horus.
I am resplendent in the Dog Star.
The city of Bubastis was established by me.
Rejoice, rejoice, O Egypt who hast nourished me!

The horns of Isis are added.

[Nostradamus now continues in French...]

The ancients added horns to the head in the form of a half-crescent, each horn opposite to the other, because of the aspect of the moon that appears in its first days, and for this reason it has to be so represented.

[Nostradamus's French verse-translations continue]

Interpretation of the epigram

(Dizain)

I Isis am who once was Egypt's queen
What I by law did once by statute give
(For I by Mercury long taught have been)
Shall no one ever trample while he live.
Dam of Osiris who his life did give
Am I; the first of fruits I did create;
Of royal Horus mother was and mate.
On starry Procyon I shine my rays: [wrong star in wrong constellation?]
Bubastis I once founded in my state.
Joy, joy in Egypt, who did once me raise!

How they signified the month

Wishing for us the month to signify
They paint a branch of palm all fresh and green
Or else the moon that upside-down doth fly –
The branch because of what above we've seen,
The moon aloft, for it perceiving thus
When this occurs its fifteen parts remain,
With horns turned downward over us again.

And when its form becomes occulted, soon
Its thirtieth part once more the light shall gain
Till down again shall point the hornèd moon...

How they signify the following year

And when they wish to show us all in all
The year that follows, they do write withal
A quarter field whose measurements befall
A hundred cubits, quite symmetrical.
And half an hour is reckoned, in their tongue,
As quarter, their two rising stars among.
By rising of the star that's Sothis named
The quarter part denotes a day still young.
With solar year three hundred sixty days,
Five days, five hours, if we aright but count,
Do each four quarters then depart their ways,
Which to a day each fourth time doth amount.

[*Sothis* is of course the ancient name for Sirius.]

What they meant by the eagle

When they a god in power would represent
In rank disgrace, or high and excellent,
In blood or triumph, an eagle they would paint –
A god because it is a bird potènt
Long-lived as any bird that roams the sky
And image of the sun that reigns on high,
Because the solar nature doth excel,
And o'er all birds the sun doth see full well.
For this apothecaries, sky-inspired,
Do use a herb by eagles oft required,
Whose burning eyes like rays do pierce the skies
And sun as master and as lord apprise:
Which, when applied, the power of the sight
Doth much improve, as such a product might,

Because when it would mount aloft the sky
To rise so high it takes a slanting route,
But, diving downwards, straight and true doth shoot.

[In this and the next verse, Nostradamus temporarily gives up the struggle to maintain the complex rhyme scheme, and reverts to simple rhyming couplets – except that for line 15 he can't manage to find a rhyme at all!]

How they use the eagle to signify abasement

... Abasement in that, when he would descend,
No further does he then his flight extend,
But stoops straight down in sudden passage steep
From air to earth, his vigor for to keep.
The eagle also stood for excellence
Who o'er all other birds has precedence.
Blood, too, the eagle did for them portray:
Ne'er any other drink he will essay.
Victory, too – for all can see full plain
Over all other birds he has domain.
But if she beaten is by fate adverse
She lies at once upon her back reverse,
Feet to the sky, her wings upon the soil
And, thus stretched out, to save herself doth toil
And fight whatever enemy attack
So that, seeing herself reduced, aback,
She can with ease turn round and take to flight
When man pursues her with his deadly might.

[Here it is worth noting that Nostradamus, as elsewhere in the book, offers us a *pair* of verses – thus suggesting that it is worth looking for such pairs in the *Propheties*, too, albeit for the most part widely scattered. Curiously, too, he changes from *il* to *elle* – as signified by the change from 'he' to 'she' above. Unless it is the result of sheer muddle-headedness, I cannot suggest a reason for this.]

How they showed the soul

Also the eagle for the soul they writ
And so did it interpret by their art.
The soul *Baieth* they called, which then they split,
As master-name for what they split apart.
Bai was the soul, and *Eth* the beating heart,
For heart it is encompasseth the soul,
And thus the sound of it they firmly hold
To be the soul together with it bound.
Wherefore the eagle bonds with nature's sound
As with the soul that never fades away,
Nor drinks but blood (water doth it confound),
For so the soul with blood is fed for aye.

How they signified Mars and Venus

When Mars and Venus they desired to show
They painted eagles twain in comely state,
And nearby showed for each of them a crow –
Mars for the male, and Venus for his mate.
While th' other creatures all do seem to hate
This love-match, this the eagle seems to flout.
Though from the male he'll suddenly retreat
If thirty times he hear the male call out,
He almost seems his loving to entreat.
Th' Egyptians, seeing the eagle prompt to love
Her did compare with Venus' star above
And to the sun the eagle dedicate,
By virtue of her thirty acts of love
Whereby she makes the male her loving mate.

[Once again, taking advantage of the fact that in French *aigle* can be either masculine or feminine, there is some confusion in the verse as to the eagle's true gender!]

Mars and Venus as otherwise painted by them

They Mars and Venus painted otherwise
By crows or rooks twain, carefully portrayed.
Female or male they showed them to our eyes,
For of each two eggs laid, so it is said,
One must be male, the other, though, instead
Female, as doth necessity recall.
But if it chances, rare as it befall,
That both eggs when they hatch do males produce,
Or females both, then nought can them induce
To join themselves with other meet females
Nor such females to any other males:
Therefrom emerge mere solitary birds.
And so if on your road you chance to meet
A crow as omen dogging both your feet,
A presage 'tis that you alone shall stay
As widow or as widower one day.

[Here we see Nostradamus in full omen-spotting mood!]

How they denoted a wedding

When they a wedding wanted to portray,
When it might finish and when it might start,
And how reflect man's basic nature, they
Would have well painted in the finest art
And pictured there two crows or rooks (whatever) –
For nature androgyne, which once was split,
To represent the joining back together
Of Mars and Venus, as above was writ.

How they painted Vulcan

To give us Vulcan clear to understand
A scarab and a vulture they drew in
To stand for great Minerva hidden, and
Of love the only source and origin.
By her the world's sustained through thick and thin
Without the need for males of any kind.
So we the vulture for Minerva find,
Since both these gods are, as tradition writes,
Quite different from all others of their kind,
In that they both are true hermaphrodites.

How they signified an only son

Now when they wished to show an only son,
Or father, age or generatiòn
Or human man in special form have done,
They caused to paint in great perfectiòn
A scarab by their great inventiòn.
The only son because it is begot
Without the female, such as is its lot:
When it doth please the male to make his young,
He finds the dung of ox, which when he's got
He makes into a ball of rolling dung.

How the scarab makes his ball

Then like the sky he makes it curved and round
Himself supporting by each hinder limb,
Eastwards before him rolls it o'er the ground
Using the light of dawn to vector him,
Until quite whole it is about the rim
And of the earth the roundness doth attain.
For from the east the sun the west doth gain
Then doth return to gain the east again.

The stars quite differently do move and climb,
From west to east returning over time.

[I have retranslated the last two lines rather generously, as well as changing the rhyme-scheme slightly: Nostradamus fails to point out that he is (hopefully!) talking about the way the stars appear to move from night to night, not the way they move during any one night!]

What the scarab does with his ball

Then doth the scarab afterwards his ball
Bury for eight and twenty days in all.
No longer does he shape and mould it round
But wraps it round beside the dungy mound
And for as many days as moon aloft
Circles the thing about, and just as oft.
And during this the useless beast succeeds,
For of his kind yet other ones he breeds.
His ball he opens, throws it in the flood,
Thinking that this to great conjunction leads
Between the moon and sun, or that it should.

[Here I have reverted to rhyming couplets; Nostradamus, who was obviously much more dogged than I am, in fact continues with his much more complex rhyme-scheme.]

Why the scarab signified procreation, father and mother

Of the round world, and of its procreation:
When that the ball is opened in the river
Of many scarabs it makes generation
And that is why the father, who's the giver,
Becomes the cause why it is opened there.
For the young scarab oweth all its birth
To him, the father, very like the earth
Another earth begets, of earthly shape,

Much like a man who knows not carnally
A woman, as his nature chance to be.

Of Heliopolis and the second species [of scarab]

In th' Solar City, there an image sits
Showing the god as cat with thirty toes –
A work that of the scarab, as befits,
How each month has full thirty days clear shows
As the great sun, as everybody knows,
Its course about its circling track doth ply.
The second has two horns above its eye
As 'twere a bull devoted to the moon
Because the bull ascendant in the sky
Did Egypt crown with lunar disc right soon.

[And finally, his own last verse:]

How they referred to the gods of the underworld, which they called 'manes D.M.'

When that they wished their mighty gods infernal
To signify, a face they used to paint
Sans eyes or form, and over it external,
Two eyes spaced equally, as books acquaint.
By the two eyes they showed with wisdom quaint
How that the document the gods did mean,
And by the eyeless face a passage gain'd,
As there engraved on testaments is seen.

[Compare quatrain VIII.66 of the *Propheties*. All the Roman gravestones excavated from around the city of Glanum, just to the south of Nostradamus's birthplace of St-Rémy, bore (among other things) the inscription 'D.M.' – as did (in modified form) his own tombstone. Examples of the former can still be seen in the local Musée des Alpilles (Place Favier) to this day. The legend stood in Latin for *Ditis manibus*, or 'In(to) the hands of Pluto (ruler of the underworld)' – though in the later, Christian context 'D. (O.) M.' stood for *Dei (Omnipotentis) Manibus*, or 'In(to) the hands of (Almighty) God'. However, Nostradamus is wrong to suggest that the motto was of Egyptian origin or that *manes* (Latin: 'ghosts') was an Egyptian word.]

Appendix C

Nostradamus's 1566 *Almanach* – translated extracts

NOSTRADAMUS PUBLISHED AN ANNUAL ALMANAC, PROGNOSTICATION AND/OR COLLECTION OF 'PRESAGES' every year of his life from 1550 until his death on 2 July 1566, with the sole exception of 1556 (possibly because he had been involved in a protracted visit to the Court in Paris the previous year). There was even a posthumous 1567 *Almanach*, completed (as was his wont) the previous summer, only a fortnight before he died. With the exception of only one or two of them (notably that for 1551), his secretary Jean-Aymes de Chavigny religiously recorded every prophecy they contained (all 6,338 of them) in a huge manuscript of 12 books entitled *Recueil des presages prosaïques de M. Michel de Nostradame* (1589) which has recently been restored in Paris and is currently in the Bibliothèque Municipale de Lyon.[13, 16] Since, self-evidently, each *Almanach* thus featured a set of predictions for a given year, it is possible for us to compare them with actual events at the time, and thus to gain some idea of Nostradamus's likely reliability as a prophet.

The results, alas, are not promising. In his *Recueil...*, even his secretary Chavigny – a rabid Nostradamane if ever there was one, determined to prove that his master Nostradamus was an infallible prophet – managed to identify no more than a handful as definitely accurate. Out of 154 *Presages* in verse, he succeeded in identifying only 121 as bull's-eyes (i.e. 76.1 per cent), and out of the first 1,637 prose-presages from Books 1-4 reprinted by Bernard Chevignard,[16] only 178 (i.e. 10.87 per cent) – making a total of only 299 out of 1,796, or 16.65 per cent.

In Chavigny's defense, it has to be said, of course, that the vast majority of Nostradamus's prophecies were so intentionally vague that it is impossible to identify them either as 'hits' or as 'misses' – especially when he says (as he often does) things such as 'there shall be some great affair of which I shall refrain from writing' or 'there shall be peace and not peace' (!)...

On the other hand Chavigny manages to label most of the bull's-eyes that he *does* identify only by dint of saying things like 'he really meant *this* year, not the one listed' – or even 'he really meant the opposite' (!).

Once these obvious idiocies are stripped away, the proportion of the 1,796 prophecies republished thus far by Chevignard that can be identified as having been fulfilled on the dates against which they were originally listed appears to be just 42 out of 154 (i.e. 27.27 per cent) for the verse-presages and 61 out 1,637 (i.e. 3.73 per cent) for the prose-presages.

On the basis of the data so far available, then, this makes Nostradamus's over-all success- rate for his dated prophecies (even on Chavigny's own rather optimistic estimates) no more than 103 out of 1,796 – which, alas, is only 5.73 per cent!

1566 – the historical picture

In order to assess the situation for ourselves, however, possibly we would be best advised to look more closely at *one* of the *Almanachs* in particular. The well-preserved and comprehensive 1566 one is an obvious candidate. However, given that reproducing the whole *Almanach* here is clearly out of the question, our best plan is probably to take a single month and see what we can make of it – and the obvious one to take is the fairly central one of July. This, after all, was also the month of Nostradamus's death – which is thus one thing at least that we can definitely say about it.

So, before we start, what do we in fact know about that particular month? The truth is... not much. About the year as a whole, however, quite a lot is known. For ease of reference, then, let me enumerate what we do know:

> 1. We know that religious conflict was endemic in France, with the Wars of Religion now some four years into their catalogue of horrors – though we also know that 1566 in fact fell within a relatively peaceful, if disturbed, period between the battle of Dreux of 1562 and the attempt by the Protestant faction under Condé and Coligny to stage a coup by capturing Charles IX and his mother Catherine de Médicis at Meaux in September 1567.

2. We know, indeed, that on 29 January 1566 the Privy Council actually published a decree enjoining harmony upon the various religious parties – a decree to which their leaders all assented, apparently enthusiastically.
3. We know that during the summer of 1566, in fact, the King and his mother finally arrived back in Paris with their huge government retinue at the end of a two-year pacification tour through the country in the course of which (in 1564) they had called on Nostradamus at Salon.
4. We know that workers were currently hard hit by extremely low wages, and that each town had just been made responsible for feeding its own poor – which suggests that destitution was widespread.
5. We know that the Plague and various other *maladies pestilentielles* were still rampant.
6. We know that the eminent French naturalist and physician Guillaume Rondelet, Professor of Anatomy at Nostradamus's own chosen *alma mater* of Montpellier – the man who had originally expelled him from the student body there – died on the 30th of the month, less than a month after Nostradamus himself.
7. We know that the allegedly illiterate Henri duc de Montmorency, son of the redoubtable Constable Anne de Montmorency who had allegedly welcomed Nostradamus to Paris in 1555, and a leader of the moderate Roman Catholic party, was at some point in the year made marshal of France and placed in independent charge of the Languedoc – which included Nostradamus's Provence.
8. This was also the year in which the Reformed churches in Switzerland published what was termed the 'Second Helvetic Confession' as their official statement of faith. It affirmed the supremacy of the scriptures, opposed idolatry, discussed a variety of theological issues and condemned heresies both ancient and modern.
9. On Christmas day, moreover, Jean de Chaumont, bishop of Aix, ceremonially quit his post to join the Protestants.
10. In the same year, too, the *Ordonnance de Moulins* reformed judicial procedures and stipulated the monarchy's inalienable right to various crown lands.
11. Of the daily or monthly weather we know little, except that, from 1564, the by-now fairly normal atrocious conditions had been showing some temporary signs of improvement.
12. Abroad, we know that the Muslim Ottomans were temporarily on the retreat from south-eastern Europe, as well as still licking their wounds after failing to take Malta the previous year, when the Grand Vizier Mehmet Sokollu had also fallen from power, leaving something of a power-vacuum in which factional conflicts flourished.
13. We know, indeed, that in July the Turkish Sultan Suleiman the

Magnificent was himself only a month or two away from his death, which occurred while he was besieging the Hungarian fortress of Szigetvár in September.

14. We know that in the same year the future Sultan Mehmed III was born.

15. We also know that in August the Dutch 'Beggars' started an anti-Catholic revolt against Spanish rule in the Netherlands, and that there were religious burnings in Antwerp.

16. Finally, we know that a new Pope, Pius V, had just been installed.

And so how does Nostradamus, writing in the spring of the previous year (1565), measure up to all this? With such a wealth of possible targets, surely he should have been able to score at least a few bull's-eyes?

The 1566 *Almanach* – Part 1

The first sign of an answer ought to appear in the italicized summary quatrain for the year (subsequently republished as *Presage* 118 in the *Propheties* of 1605) with which part 2 of the *Almanach* is headed – and which, like all the summary verses for this particular *Almanach*, is (unusually) in Alexandrines, or lines of 12 syllables. Since uninterrupted Alexandrines tend to sound far too 'heavy' in English, a more Drydenesque 5-5-5-6 verse-form seems appropriate for an English verse-translation. This would suggest the following:

Death to the great, fall'n honour, violence.
For who profess the faith, their sect and state:
In both their Churches, rumors, decadence,
Woes, friends at odds, and Church's slaves decapitate.

Which, it has to be said, is a good deal more bloodthirsty than history seems to record for this particular year.

The next thing to look at, then, is the brief Saints' Days calendar for July in part 1 of the *Almanach*. This is headed by another summary verse, this time for the month of July only (later republished as *Presage* 125). Sticking to the same verse-form, this translates as:

Disease and fire the orchard fruit assail;
Olives bode well; the vines, though, less well set:
Nobles shall die; but foreigners scarce fail;
Barbary raids by sea; and borders under threat.

16	F	s.Ferreol.	♊	
17	g	s.Paule vier.	♋	
18	a	s.Marcelin.	♋	● à 0.h.43.m.peu de pluie.
19	b	s.Geruais.	♌	
20	c	s.Ioachin.	♌	
21	d	s.Alban.	♍	L'air par ardeur maladif.
22	c	10000. martirs	♍	
23	F	Vigile.	♍	☽ 22.h.52 .m.Tonnerres.
24	g	s.Iean Bapti.	♎	
25	a	s.Eloy.	♎	
26	b	s.Iean.s.Paul.	♏	
27	c	sept dorman.	♏	
28	d	Vigile.	♐	
29	e	s.Pier.s.Paul	♐	
30	F	Cõm.s.Paul.	♐	

IVILLET.

Par pestilence & feu, fruits d'arbres periront:
Signe d'huile abonder: pere Denis non gueres:
Des grands mourir mais peu estrangers failliront:
Insult marin barbare: & dangers de frontieres.

1	g	Oct.s.Ioan.	♑	○ à 3.h.0.m.aer turbidus..
2	a	Visitation.	♑	
3	b	s.Tibault.	♒	
4	c	s.Vldarich.	♒	Feu du ciel en naues ardant.
5	d	Pier.de lucé.	♒	
6	e	Oct.s.Pier.	♓	
7	F	s.Pantesme.	♓	
8	g	s.Zenon.	♈	
9	a	Oct.n.dame.	♈	☾ à 17.h.20. min.
10	b	Les 7.freres.	♉	
11	c	s Pie pape.	♉	Temps diuers.
12	d	s.Nabor.	♉	
13	e	[illegible]	♌	
14	F	Bonauẽture.	♎	
15	g	Di.des apo.	♋	Naistra quelque grand.
16	a	s.Hilarin.	♋	● à 7.h.47.m. gresle ton.
17	b	s.Alexis cõf.	♌	
18	c	s.Simphoro.	♌	
19	d	s.Iuste.	♍	Le soir peu moderé.
20	e	Marguerite.	♍	
21	F	s.Praxede.	♎	
22	g	Magdaleine.	♎	
23	a	s.Apolinni.	♏	☽ à 11.h.45. min.
24	b	Vigile.	♏	
25	c	s.Iacques apo.	♏	
26	d	s.Anne.	♐	
27	e	s.Marthe.	♐	
28	F	s.Nazare.	♑	
29	g	s.Loup.	♑	
30	a	s.Abdon.	♑	
31	b	s.Germain.	♒	○ à 14.h.2.m.pluie à ppos

AOVST.

Pluies fort excessiues, & de biens abondance:
De bestail pris iuste stre: femmes hors de danger:
Gresles, pluyes, tonnerres: peuple abatu en France:
Par mort trauailleront: mort peuple corriger.

1	c	[illegible]	♒	Pluie,tonnerre,gresle.

Bibliothèque Municipale de Lyon, courtesy of Michel Chomarat
Part 1 of the 1566 Almanach*: details for July*

Once again, while agricultural and military threats to France were pretty much par for the period (the second line's original *pere Denis* refers to Dionysus, god of the vine), none seem to have been recorded for the month of July, nor even for this particular year. Could Nostradamus, then, merely be speculatively extrapolating from what he already knew about the climate of the times, rather than actually prophesying future events?

Apart from this, the month's first calendar says fairly little, apart from listing the days of the week ('a' to 'g'), the Saints' Days, the phases of the moon and the zodiacal signs through which it will be passing – in this case from Capricorn on the 1st to Aquarius (for the second time) on the 31st. The cryptic prophecies are few and far between, namely:

1st	Disturbed air/Rough winds
4th	Fire from the sky searing ships
11th	Variable weather [!]
15th	Some noble shall be born [!]
16th	Hail, thunder
19th	Immoderate evening [!]
31st	Rain should be expected

The 1566 *Almanach* – Part 2

For more in the way of actual prophecies, we need to turn to the more detailed calendar in part 2.

IVILLET.

Par pestilence & feu, fruits d'arbres periront:
Signe d'huille abonder: pere Denis non gueres:
Des grands mourir mais peu, estrangers sailliront:
Insult marin barbare: & dangers de frontieres.

Estrange transmigration.	1	g	♑	7	☉ à 5.h.o.mi. Aër turbidus.
Les grãdes & grãds differés.	2	a	♑	19	Tout reduit par le magistrat
Par religions tout trouble.	3	b	♒	1	Promulgation nõ obseruée.
Bõne fortune pour nauig.	4	c	♒	13	Feu du ciel en naues ardant.
Bons amis apparoistront,	5	d	♒	25	Deliurez de captiuité barb.
Se iettera au conflict.	6	e	♓	7	Cache dãs l'eau gelee & sorti
Mandemẽt à Roine souspi-	7	f	♓	20	Blessez en la teste, mourir.
Insipiẽtia delirans. (rer.	8	g	♈	3	Par les chemins tout halé.
Merueilleuse inflãmation.	9	a	♈	16	☾ à 17.h.20.mi.
Austrina aëris perturbatio.	10	b	♉	0	Ardore siccata omnia.
Imbres cum tonitribus.	11	c	♉	14	Temps diuers.
Conualescence de grande.	12	d	♉	28	Bon mariage & felice:
Cité maritime faschee.	13	e	♊	13	Les deux ne peuuẽt resister.
Cas incroyable de cruauté.	14	f	♊	28	Vt grex porcorũ interibunt.
Pluie de retour.	15	g	♋	13	Naistra quelque grand.
Etesiæ inualescunt.	16	a	♋	28	☉ à 7.h 47.mi. Gresle, tõner.
Abacus amoindri de peu.	17	b	♌	11	L'enfant perdu de retour.
Flat violentes aquilo.	18	c	♌	26	Le demy fort grief à passer.
Changemẽt de temps. frais.	19	d	♍	10	Le soir peu moderé.
Maladies augmenter.	20	e	♍	24	Vomissemens bons.
Flux de ventre mauuais.	21	f	♎	7	Mariages bons, & vallables.
XXI. iours en bas, bons.	22	g	♎	20	Se manifestera son mauuais
Apres lõgues malad. mort.	23	a	♏	3	☽ à 11 h.45.mi. (cœur.
Le mauuais iour passé.	24	b	♏	16	Deus in lagena. cas aduenir.
Grand conflit.	25	c	♏	28	Quere les mortelles.
Opulentiss. heredi. briguee.	26	d	♐	11	Canicularis æstus grauis.
Par religiõ querelle & mort	27	e	♐	22	Grands voiages bons à tous.
Presche faschera.	28	f	♑	4	De retour barbaraches.
Bonnes santé de Rois.	29	g	♑	16	Bonnes nouuelles à Rois.
Victoire nauale.	30	a	♑	18	Le traditeur sacré decouuert
Bonne auanture à Rois.	31	b	♒	10	● à 14.h.2.m. Pluie à ppos.

Bibliothèque Municipale de Lyon, courtesy of Michel Chomarat
Part 2 of the 1566 Almanach*: details for July*

This time the days of the week are shown, from 'a' (apparently Tuesday) to 'g' (apparently Monday), as well as the actual position of the moon within each sign. And, of course, there are two predictions for each day. They are as follows:

Strange/Foreign (trans)migration.	1	Full moon at 0300. Disturbed air.
Lords and ladies at odds.	2	Everything restored by the magistrate.
Major disturbances for religions.	3	Edict not observed.
Good luck for sailors.	4	Fire from the sky searing ships.
Good friends shall appear.	5	People delivered from barbarian captivity.
He shall throw himself into the fight.	6	Hidden in frozen water and emerges.
Instructions whispered to the Queen.	7	Wounded in the head, he shall die.
Senseless madness.	8	Everything burnt up along the roads.
Miraculous conflagration.	9	Last lunar quarter at 1720.
Rough wind from the south.	10	Everything burnt up by the heat.
Thundery showers.	11	Various weathers.
Convalescence of a noble.	12	Good marriage and happiness.
Maritime city harassed.	13	The two (leaders?) cannot resist.
Incredible case of cruelty.	14	Beware lest the herd of pigs die.
Rain back again.	15	Some noble shall be born.
Trade winds increase.	16	New moon at 0747. Hail, thunder.
Wealth not reduced much.	17	The lost child returns.
Violent north winds.	18	The minor fortress hard to get past. [?]
Change to fresh weather.	19	Little moderation in the evening.
Diseases increase.	20	Vomiting good.
Bad stomach catarrh.	21	Good, reliable marriages.
21 days in stockings recommended.	22	His reluctance shall manifest itself.
After long illnesses, death.	23	New moon at 1145.

After long illnesses, death.	23	New moon at 1145.
The worst day over.	24	God in a bottle, should the case arise. [!]
Great conflict.	25	Search for mortals.
Extremely rich heirs courted.	26	Bitches very much in heat.
Feud and death as a result of religion.	27	Long journeys good for everybody.
A sermon shall annoy.	28	Barbary pirates back.
Good health for Kings.	29	Good news for Kings.
Naval victory.	30	The priestly traitor discovered.
Good luck for Kings.	31	Full moon at 1402. Rain expected.

It has to be said that there doesn't seem to be much here to make the newspapers, let alone the history books, especially as Nostradamus doesn't actually specify exactly *where* each event will occur. Someone (it could be argued) is almost bound to fulfil each of these predictions *somewhere* on the day in question!

Perhaps the most intriguing of these predictions, in fact, is the one for the first of the month – which was, of course, to be Nostradamus's last full day on earth. Apart from remarking that he seems to have been unaware of this fact, the phrase *Estrange transmigration,* which almost certainly refers simply to a movement of foreign peoples across their frontiers, is also oddly reminiscent of the alleged transmigration of the soul at death into another body.

Probably this is purely coincidental. He quite clearly uses the same term *transmigrations* to refer to supposed invasions by 'new Italian barbarians' (Sicilians with Saracen ancestry, perhaps?) in his predictions for January, for example, as well as elsewhere in his prophecies. True, in the course of these same predictions, in which he correctly forecasts a major resumption of war for 1567 and the death and ruin of 'many great lords', he continues 'God grant me grace to live until then to describe that with which the stars threaten us!' – which might suggest that He possibly wouldn't. Again, while describing the calamities that he foresees for January 1566 (apparently incorrectly) he writes: 'While writing this a terrible horror seizes me, with cold sweat all over my body.' Could this, perhaps, represent some kind of premonition of his own death later in the year? It would, perhaps, be rather generous to assume so.

The 1566 *Almanach* – Part 3

So our best plan now seems to be to see whether we can get anything more specific out of his prose predictions for July in part 3 of the *Almanach*. These run as follows:

Predictions for July

After a quoted Latin verse which begins:

> *The celestial stars rule o'er our mortal bodies...*

and a further piece of unidentified Latin prose along the same lines, the text (here translated into English for the first time since the seer's death, with my own comments between square brackets) continues:

> At this point we shall say that the preceding conjunction of Saturn and Mars [detailed under the predictions for the last week of June] presages for the Easterners [i.e. the Ottoman Muslims] as much terrestrial as naval war, conflict and battles, more naval than terrestrial. *For he who knows the end of future war is he who knows all things, even he to whom such great weight of human affairs has been willing to reveal itself* [Latin quotation].
>
> In this month of July 1566, the full moon will be on the first day at 23 hours after noon, in 7 degrees 25 minutes of Capricorn, with the Ascendant in the eleventh degree of Libra. And it shall be windy, with some rain, thunder and violent storms. Some great affairs affecting kingdoms and some persons of great sublimity, authority and power shall be dealt with, as with a voice imperial, even affecting all those who are placed in a high position, the mother, matters pertaining to her, many who shall choose some very high position and some imperial appointment in particular, such as nobility and princeliness, and some appointment of which one shall be vain and the other very long-lasting.

The seer seems to be mercilessly hedging his bets. Could he perhaps be referring to the French Court, and to Queen Catherine de Médicis in particular? Unfortunately, there is simply no way of knowing.

> And manifestly [he continues] some great public enemy shall obstruct things, who by means of slander and [raised?] knives slashing in all

> directions shall attempt to tear everything apart. And because the abovementioned conjunction of Saturn and Mars comes to signify the divisions of sects – that is to say, the way in which citizens converted to a new sect comport themselves towards those of the religion they have discarded – *everything shall be saved* [?] *from horrible terrors* [apparently inappropriate Latin quote]. But seeing that either sect shall be in full vigor, force and power with their respective knives and cutting blades, this obliges me to keep silent about what shall result according to the perfect calculation of the stars, even [the resulting] disasters, as the great Albumazar affirms, who in matters concerning celestial revolutions in my judgment holds the foremost place among the Arabs: but my mouth has to remain firmly closed, lest I set down what I am very sure about. *For wars shall be among you and a letting of blood, but slight* [Latin phrase or quotation, seemingly designed to tantalize the ignorant by informing the educated only!]. This conjunction of Saturn and Mars signifies and threatens that the greatest ones, as much the lay monarchy as the spiritual, shall endeavor with all their might to usurp lands, domains, kingdoms, satrapies and principalities, whichever, and that this shall happen among the easterners more than in other provinces, even though those in the west shall in no wise be exempt from it.

At least Nostradamus seems to have spotted that year's *Ordonnance de Moulins* (item 10 above) – unless, of course it was already being mooted the previous year, when this particular *Almanach* was being prepared!

> The negligence of some monarchs shall permit great license for barbarian [i.e. Muslim] usurpation and spread: and among others also wars and killings on account of the preparation that has been made in the month of March last, which shall bleed somewhat in this month of July and August, and throughout the year shall scarcely be healthy [apparent medical metaphor]. And given that Mars is *in Leo* [Latin], this signifies very great detriment, ruin and innumerable losses to the Turkish nation as much in naval as in terrestrial expeditions. But towards the beginning of February it signifies some detriment happening to the Papal States, and to Roman domains. And during the whole of the month of July there is indicated great detriment to the Arabs and to all their armies. And as appears very evident from this conjunction, for 21 years, 7 months, 4 days, starting in January, there is indicated the beginning of the change [normal Nostradamian expression for 'downfall'] of Byzantium *in Thrace* [Latin] as a result of great divisions.

The kingdoms shall be bathed in much Byzantine blood.
Who out of exile came to th' kingdom shall accede [Latin quote].

Wherein is indicated the transfer of power: and thereby is indicated the decline of Islam at the end of nine hundred and sixty years [i.e. from 1582?]: and before the end of 72 years there starts some great discord between the white head and the blue, or between the whiteness and the sky-blueness [i.e. of turbans, as referred to specifically in the *Propheties* at quatrain IX.73]: and some great event shall happen to them [!].

The seer seems to be referring to the growing factionalism within a temporarily retreating Ottoman empire that everybody already knew about (item 12 above). But the *decline of Islam*?...

One who thinks to put out the eye of his adversary shall put out both of his own. In the present month shall be the cause, as a result of evil factions, wherefore many shall gather together to conclude some matter which shall partly bring them together and partly divide them, and threatens the death of many of those complaining, of two of the other nobles among them, and two of the hierarchy *mentioned above* [Latin phrase].

No doubt those involved were grateful for the advice – always assuming that they could tell who they were!

The last quarter of the moon will be on the 9th day at 1720, after noon, in 15 degrees 30 minutes of Aries, with the Ascendant in 6 degrees of Leo. And it shall be hot and dry, with the wind from the south resulting in a sudden disturbance of the air: and until the new moon the seasonal winds shall start to blow: and everything shall be converted into great heat and dryness, which shall be so vehement that it shall cause great mortality, and a great number of people shall die: and those who have escaped such a great and eminent peril shall think themselves saved, then, at the point where they have no doubt about it, shall fall, from which death shall ensue, with great tears, wails and groans, *many showers with thunder, the north wind blowing* [another apparently inappropriate Latin quotation]. Other non-infectious illnesses shall weaken many.

The states of the Kings, princes and great lords shall not go as they wish, but most shall go completely in the other direction. There is indicated here some case of flight, captivity and voluntary exile of many nobles, as well by sea as by land via hostile routes. In the direction of the Papal States there shall be great famines and privations, earthquakes; and for the Indians anguish, travails and anxiety; and in the principal cities of the

> south such as Themistitan [?] and Fez and others, the greatest ones shall die from diseases, discords and divisions. As for the deeds, acts and negotiations of Christian Kings, everything shall go forward very properly and happily, and they shall be just, equitable and reasonable, abiding in the great and praiseworthy peace of quietness, without any envy or cupidity for the possessions of their subjects, or very little.

For Nostradamus, then, with his relatively limited geographical horizons, 'the south' is no further afield than North Africa. But could there possibly be just a little case of self-contradiction here?

> Mercury being in this summer stage of the cycle in the Ascendant *signifies a good state and profit for merchants and scribes* [Latin]: and even better for all councilors' estates. All that shall be spoken about shall be people's state of health, illnesses, tiredness, how to get well, with certain secret dealings in respect of wars, embassies, legations, gifts, presents, and certain young people who have neglected their studies.
>
> The new moon will be on the 16th day at 7 hours 47 minutes after noon, in 28 degrees 12 minutes of Cancer, with the Ascendant in 10 degrees of Aquarius. And for the first few days it shall be rainy, then change to heat and unbearable burning: for towards the noonday hours great blasts shall be felt that shall all but burn human faces. In mountainous and inaccessible places, many wild, ravenous beasts, even all animals that drink with the tongue, shall become furiously enraged. Various other events shall accompany the violently burning heat. This moon with its rains, hails, tempests and furious storms shall bring with it great, burning, pestilential fevers. Furthermore, this [chart] indicates that the greatest nobles in the world shall make war on each other, others who are scarcely different shall defy each other with great bands [of men], in such wise that on either side many dead shall result. An infinity of quarrels, disputes, legal processes and divisions shall, among others, bring such continual hatreds that they shall never agree: some nobles and [even] the highest in the land shall intervene, but on either side great bloodshed shall result, but as a result of the deaths – and consequent inability to continue fighting – of the discordant parties, everything shall be agreed again for a short time at least. The happiest aspect of this summer shall be for merchants in all kinds of wares. All kinds of hoofed animals shall be in great demand, and shall sell well. Also, Mars signifies that in the houses of brothers, sisters and other near relatives, even those who are living together under a single roof, they shall disagree and quarrel with each other [!]. Friends too, and others who have associated and socialized with each other shall as September approaches become

> animated with anger and evil intent to get rid of each other, in such wise that such enforced discord shall last a very long time; and they shall agree again afterwards when the first hints of misty days arrive, with new alliances that they shall contract with each other. At the end of summer [there shall be] great wars, disputes and various disagreements, and seven in number shall die in a great cause, even two in particular, who instead of pacification resulting from their deaths, shall be the cause of a greater and mortal war between the monarchs of the eastern regions. Ambassadors shall arrive before the Christian lords, with the intention of sending giraffes. The seashore shall be pillaged in several places.

Yes, yes... all this talk of 'some', 'several', 'various' and 'many', to say nothing of the thesaurus-like lists of words that all mean virtually the same thing... But isn't it all just a clever way of actually saying nothing much at all? It needed only the odd armed set-to, after all, for Nostradamus to be able to claim that he had been 'proved right' – even though, of course, such things were almost bound to happen here or there, sooner or later, especially at the time. As for the 'long hot summer' and the almost inevitable resultant irritability and family rows, he *was* talking about Provence in July! Only in the matter of good livestock-sales and the arrival of foreign ambassadors (bearing giraffes!) has the seer really ventured to stick his neck out.

> The first quarter of the moon will be on the 23rd day at 1145 after noon, in 3 degrees 28 minutes of Scorpio, with the Ascendant in 3 degrees of Gemini. And it shall be rainy and humid, and because of the strength of the sun the earth shall be hot, and the air similarly, which shall cause great thunderbolts and lightning-flashes. In the Pyrenean mountains there shall be great danger of fire, which from a distance shall seem to be falling from them – in Sicily even more so. It is also indicated that in the towns, provinces and regions of the seventh latitude [Anatolia, the Urals, northern France and Belgium[67]] the great ladies, princesses and Queens shall see themselves in a state of the greatest honor, power, exaltation and all happy prosperity throughout all the right-hand [i.e. southern: concepts such as 'left' and 'right' normally applied to a person facing the sunrise] part of the west. Also all persons who by nature are friendly, peaceful, modest, travelers, pilgrims, ambassadors, legates, consuls and governors, as much in the cities as in the provinces, shall be raised to the highest honor, esteem and dignity. And such prosperity shall occur throughout all the land of Flanders and the neighboring regions. Also among the Christian monarchs some great hidden affair shall be prevented [!]. Here and previously the promulgations, edicts, laws, statutes

> shall be carefully observed, and to the letter. And those who shall have given advice on the law shall be [held] in the greatest honor and estimation by the greatest Kings. Furthermore some great affair is indicated during this quarter of the moon, namely concerning the death of some people on suspicion of poison, who shall be duly discovered. Also predicted is the death of many for various reasons – through treasons, through hidden events that shall be uncovered by many who through their inopportune death shall enter into the great inheritances of others who shall suddenly be raised on high by evil deeds rather than good ones, and raised to a state of unaccustomed dignity. There shall also be new actions, discords and great quarrels over the division of the possessions left behind by the dead. Many shall also be fraudulently put to death for having trusted too much, where in fact major untrustworthiness shall come to be recognized. By the agency of various great ladies many shall be recalled from banishment, exile, prison and enemy captivity, namely for various heinous crimes, larcenies, murders and sacrileges, which shall be the cause of a certain amount of murmuring. Other events shall happen as a result of omens and monsters.

We have already noted the way in which such 'monsters' (deformed births) were conventionally regarded as omens at the time, and interpreted as such by occult authorities such as Nostradamus.

> The full moon will be on the last day, at 14 hours 2 minutes after noon, in 19 degrees 15 minutes of Aquarius, with the Ascendant in 16 degrees of Cancer. The which shall be rainy withal, windy, thundery, all the while breaking down for the most part into extreme warmth, heat and burning. Men shall have more words, more aggravations, and shall find themselves more attacked than previously because of the laws and religions being too scornful of each other to agree or come to an end of their communal deliberations. Great discords shall result from such goings on, and out of indignation each shall withdraw in great discontent. Great treasures shall be discovered, great inheritances, heritages, as a result of hydrological works, ruins, other structures, and hidden things that shall be discovered. And many shall die of epidemic illnesses, fevers, incipient dropsies, high temperatures, jaundices and splenetic conditions.

But Nostradamus himself died during this very month *of the dropsy*! Could it be, then, that Nostradamus got something exactly right at last? Unfortunately not. He died on the 2nd – whereas this particular prediction is for the month's final week.

And so he concludes his predictions for the end of the month with:

> The end of the month shall be half praiseworthy, but changeable and hot. Other quite strange events shall happen, expeditions both naval and terrestrial, which so as not to go on too long we shall leave to God, who will change it all to good if it so pleases him.

All this, then, just for July!

Yet in all of it, scarcely more than a couple of what I suppose I should, on this basis, describe as the historical 'events, happenings, occurrences, manifestations or developments' outlined earlier in this chapter. Out of the 16 points that I listed, only numbers 10, 11 and 12 seem to have been correctly referred to – albeit rather vaguely – while, if anything, Nostradamus seems to have predicted the *reverse* of the important first point (the temporary lull in religious conflict).

The remainder of the *Almanach*

And what of the rest of the 1566 *Almanach*? Does it contain any more specific predictions that we can check? Was the ardent prayer truly granted that he records near the beginning of part 3? –

> O my Lord, eternal God the Father, Son and holy Ghost, at this nocturnal hour and in this moment of Sunday 15th of March 1565, when the sun is making its entry into the First Point of Aries, with hands together I come to supplicate thee in trembling supplication by thy mercy to grant me pardon, and to open my mind, memory and understanding, in order that I may faithfully explain the significations and predictions of the current year 1566.

In particular, did the 'new enemy' to whom he refers twice in his Preamble really assault the borders of France, albeit unsuccessfully? Did the famines, pestilences, earthquakes, floods, shipwrecks and wars that he foresees in the same text all really take place, not merely in Europe, but (as he says) all across North Africa and the Middle East too? Did large areas of Europe and Arabia nevertheless enjoy good harvests and pleasant weather, as described – paradoxically, it seems – in the same document? And could this be a case of Nostradamus trying to have his cake and eat it too?

Did the spring really produce large numbers of locusts and grasshoppers? Were much of Europe and the Middle East – and particularly Scotland – overrun by flies, wasps, scorpions, bird-pests and vermin generally? Did huge quantities of rain fall, as the seer quotes

Albumazar as foretelling?

And what of the ensuing monthly predictions?

Those for January, after all, include not merely a great deal of inter-religious fighting, but a large invasion of the Mediterranean shores of western Europe by *Barbares* – by whom Nostradamus normally means either Barbary pirates or the sea-borne forces of the Ottoman Empire itself – followed by the sudden deliverance, as it were at the last moment, of 'Germany, Italy, Spain and the whole of Gaul'.

Neither happened.

For February he predicts huge numbers of deaths as a result of some kind of damage to the sun, and a major take-over of the Adriatic Sea by Muslim ships.

The former, at least, did not happen.

For March he predicts a lot of fighting, huge political disagreements throughout Europe and North Africa and a massive naval victory by Christian forces over the Turks, as well as major bloodshed in Italy, accompanied by plagues and earthquakes extending into the Balkans.

None of these seems to have happened.

For April (in a section that he claims to have written atop the tower of Salon's castle) he predicts that the eastern Mediterranean will once again be full of huge Muslim invasion-fleets, from which only religious observance can save those ashore. They will in turn serve as an omen that the weather will threaten to destroy the crops.

One can only suppose, then, that people took care to be rather more religious than usual that month...

For May, already menaced by the coming conjunction of Mars and Saturn in June, he predicts (in Latin) severe disturbances throughout Egypt, Turkey, and various parts of Italy and Belgium, followed by widespread disease outbreaks throughout Europe. He also predicts *la mort de l'oriental* (presumably Suleiman himself – who in fact did die, but not until September) and – excusing himself from going into more detail by claiming (not for the first time!) to be running short of paper – a huge earthquake that will interrupt a current war, as well as a great deal of adulteration and counterfeiting of the currency (a theme to which he comes back repeatedly).

Possibly he was right about the last point.

For June, he predicts huge raids on the sea-coasts by foreign ships that will virtually lay waste the entire coastal region, as well as the discovery of buried treasure, a diminution in the various civil disputes and the rebuilding of many dilapidated defenses. A massive crime will be committed and discovered, and many portentous monsters born. Severe heat will kill much wildlife, including even the fish in the sea. Many important nobles will be killed as a result of renewed fighting.

About the first point, at very least, he seems to have been totally wrong.

The final clanger

Finally, I am unfortunately duty-bound to remind the reader of one particular prediction from the section for August. In November or early December 1564, as we saw earlier, Nostradamus had been summoned to attend King Charles IX and his formidable mother Catherine de Médicis at Arles, and had recommended the marriage of the young monarch to Queen Elizabeth of England, who was twice his age. By February she had duly dispatched her inevitable rejection, reportedly remarking at the time in typical fashion that 'My lord is too great for me, and yet too small'.

Evidently this news had not reached Nostradamus (despite his elevation to the position of Privy Councilor) by the time he wrote his 1566 *Almanach* the following spring, though (see above) – for the predictions for August actually contain what he says will be the King's wedding announcement, which 'I am assured that in this month shall be proclaimed everywhere'! We have already noted its exact wording (chapter 10, page 135).

Charles and his mother, it will be recalled, were indeed due to return from their two-year progress through the kingdom that summer (point 3 above). But of Charles IX's alleged wedding, nothing. In fact he did not marry until six years later – and four years after that he was dead.

And the predictions for the remainder of the year – wars, political marriages, international conferences and damaging naval encounters in September; foreign expeditions, religious discord, conspiracies, feuds, plague, famine, wars, earthquakes, sinkings and widespread bad health in October; pirate raids, war in the east, seditions and quarrels at home in November; a ban on astrology, some outstanding act on the part of the Imperial family, rebellions, seditions, quarrels and discoveries of buried treasure in December – were, alas, apparently no more successful, either. Only the usual seasonal climatic phenomena and the perfectly usual tendency of warfare to decline during the winter months were well described – as might, of course, be reasonably expected.

What does all this say for the 1566 *Almanach* as a whole, then? The whole thing seems, alas, to have been a catalogue of abject failures, interspersed with predictions so verbose and vague that they could never be pinned down to any actual event at all.

Could it be, then, that despite occasional flashes of possible insight – if they were not mere indications of current political awareness – Nostradamus was basically just a great flanneler, a walking thesaurus, a past master at never using one word when a hundred would do, a positive genius at saying nothing while seeming to say everything?

Was he a mere prophetic hack churning out for a gullible public what Ronsard was to describe in 1584 as:

> So many Almanacs whose words obscure
> Foretell like demons what we must endure...

– or did he reserve one level of prophecy (and a pretty mean one, at that) for the mere bread-and-butter works that were his *Almanachs*, and reserve an entirely different and much higher level of insight for the work for which he is much better known to posterity – namely his *Propheties*?

Unfortunately, thanks to the deliberately vague and imprecise – and above all, for the most part undated – nature of the latter, the latter question will probably never be finally settled to the satisfaction of everybody...

Appendix D

Specific borrowings by Nostradamus from earlier collections of prophecies

AS WE SAW IN OUR INTRODUCTION, AS WELL AS IN CHAPTER 8, many of Nostradamus's predictions in his *Propheties* and accompanying letters were based directly on ancient collections of prophecies (most of them biblically based) that were known and available long before he started writing. Numerous such anthologies were being made at the time, mainly because there was a general conviction that the End of the World was at hand. Even Columbus compiled his own anthology; indeed, to it he owed some of his ideas about a possible New World...

The first and best known of these anthologies to be published in France was the *Mirabilis liber*,[45] an early sixteenth-century collection of prophecies mainly in Latin, though partly in French – one edition of which was published in Lyon by Jehan Besson in 1523 (though it in fact bears the date '1524'). This may even (in the view of some) have been compiled by Jaume de Nostredame, Nostradamus's own father.

We have already noted many similarities of general theme. The following, however, is a comparative compendium of *specific* prophecies that can be traced back to the earlier productions.

Mirabilis liber, 1522/3:[45] There shall be earthquakes in divers places. The cities and provinces of the Islanders shall be swallowed up by floods. [Prophecy of the Tiburtine Sibyl]

Nostradamus, 1558/68:

The earth shall quake around Mortara's town,
Saint George Caltagirone half knocked down. [IX.31]

Mirabilis liber, 1522/3: After that, there shall appear in the land of Leo another prophet who shall announce astonishing things in the Roman senate. Saintly in appearance and timorous, severe as regards the sanctity of

Christian life, he shall have rooted deeply within his heart a malignant spirit that shall lead him, beneath the cloak of his hypocrisy, to the very feet of the sovereign Pontiff... He shall be called the Antichrist. The pontiffs who have honored him shall be put to death; and men shall walk in his footsteps to disgrace. [Prophecy of the Antichrist]

Nostradamus, 1557:

He who within the realm was close to rule,
A Cardinal close to the hierarchy,
Shall make himself so feared, so harsh, so cruel
When he takes o'er the sacred monarchy. [VI.57]

Mirabilis liber, 1522/3: A saintly man shall be consecrated pope. He shall reform, in a short time and in an admirable manner, all of the Church...He shall forbid the conferring of several benefices on a single person, and he shall take measures to ensure that the clergy live [only] on the tithes and offerings of the faithful. He shall forbid all pompous vestments... [Prophecy from the *Pronosticatio* of Johann Lichtenberger]

Nostradamus, 1557: All sacred pomp its wings shall soon abase... [V.79]

Nostradamus, 1555: Folk shall return their proper tithes to pay. [III.76]

Mirabilis liber, 1522/3: An extraordinary drought... shall dry up even the water of the rivers... The land shall burn in many places, and the heat shall be intense... The fishes shall perish, being themselves consumed. [Prophecy from part 3 of the *Pronosticatio* of Johann Lichtenberger]

Nostradamus, 1555:

Through the sun's heat upon the shining sea
The Black Sea's fish shall be half-cooked alive. [II.3]

Mirabilis liber, 1522/3: Flies shall spread on the wind like clouds. [Prophecy from part 3 of the *Pronosticatio* of Johann Lichtenberger]

Nostradamus, 1555:

Those Latin plains so fertile and so vast
So many flies and locusts shall produce
That the sun's light shall be quite overcast. [IV.48]

Mirabilis liber, 1522/3: Discord shall once again brandish its torch on the banks of the Rhine in Germany. [Prophecy from part 3 of the *Pronosticatio* of Johann Lichtenberger]

Nostradamus, 1555:

A flaming torch at dusk in heaven they'll spy
Near to the head and source of th' river Rhône. [II.96]

Mirabilis liber, 1522/3: Writers shall be oppressed; the most perceptive men shall be reduced to poverty. [Prophecy from part 3 of the *Pronosticatio* of Johann Lichtenberger]

Nostradamus, 1555:

Of those most learn'd of facts celestial
Shall some by ill-read princes be impeached,
By edict banned, hounded as criminal
And put to death where'er they can be reached. [IV.18]

Mirabilis liber, 1522/3: The cloisters shall be cold: no more devotion... [Prophecy from part 3 of the *Pronosticatio* of Johann Lichtenberger]

Nostradamus, 1555:

No abbots, monks, no novices to train:
Honey than candle-wax shall cost far more. [I.44]

Mirabilis liber, 1522/3: This saintly man shall break the pride of the religious, who shall all return to the fold of the primitive Church... [Prophecy on the Angelic Pope]

Nostradamus, 1555:

Of holy temples in grand Roman style
They shall the very fundaments reject,
Adopt prime human principles the while,
And many a former saintly cult eject. [II.8]

Mirabilis liber, 1522/3: Then shall appear in the celestial bodies numerous and remarkable signs which shall announce the predicted events and many others much must follow them; and as if by Divine Will the state of the world shall shortly be changed. [Prophecy of Joannes de Vatiguerro]

Nostradamus, 1555:

The chart of Lyon doth to us foretell
By fixèd stars and signs both bright and clear
That of its sudden change the age draws near,
Nor for its ill, nor yet for good and well. [III.46]

Mirabilis liber, 1522/3: Many towns... shall establish new charters, by means of which they shall isolate themselves and shall rule within their own boundaries. [Prophecy of Joannes de Vatiguerro]

Nostradamus, 1557:

A hundred leagues from where meet east and west
Amiens shall know no law and no side take. [VI.5]

Mirabilis liber, 1522/3: No one shall keep his word; but people shall deceive and betray each other. [Prophecy of Joannes de Vatiguerro]

Nostradamus, 1557:

They shall not hold to what they shall agree.
All who accept them shall be duped at will. [VI.64]

Mirabilis liber, 1522/3: ... the Catholic Church and the entire world shall mourn the capture, despoliation and devastation of the most illustrious and famous city, capital and mistress of the Kingdom of all the French. [Prophecy of Joannes de Vatiguerro]

Nostradamus, 1557:

About the mighty city there shall roam
Troops billeted in every town and farm
To strike at Paris... [V.30]

Nostradamus, 1555:

In Avignon shall all th' Imperial lords
Come to a stop, Paris being desolate. [III.93]

Mirabilis liber, 1522/3: All the Church in all the World shall be persecuted in a lamentable and grievous manner; it shall be stripped and deprived of all its temporal possessions...

Nostradamus, 1557:

Sorely the Church of God shall be oppressed,
The holy churches looted of their store... [V.73]

Mirabilis liber, 1522/3: The nuns, quitting their convents, shall flee here and there, demeaned and insulted... [Prophecy of Joannes de Vatiguerro]

Nostradamus, 1555:

The mighty city shall be desolated,
Of its inhabitants not one remain.
Church walls and orders, virgins violated,
By sword, fire, plague and gun the people slain. [III.84]

Mirabilis liber, 1522/3: The pastors of the Church and the hierarchy, hunted and stripped of their dignities and positions, shall be cruelly manhandled. [Prophecy of Joannes de Vatiguerro]

Nostradamus, 1558/68:

The blood of churchmen shall be freely shed:
As though t'were water see it flowing red!
Long time shall pass ere it shall cease to flow.
Woe, ruin, grief, the priests shall undergo. [VIII.98]

Mirabilis liber, 1522/3: The flocks and subjects shall take flight... [Prophecy

of Joannes de Vatiguerro]
Nostradamus, 1557: Reds, yellows then their flocks shall steal away... [VI.10]

Mirabilis liber, 1522/3: ... and shall remain dispersed without pastor and without leader. [Prophecy of Joannes de Vatiguerro]
Nostradamus, 1555:
Leaderless folk from Spain and Italy,
Shall die in mainland Greece, torn limb from limb. [III.68]

Mirabilis liber, 1522/3: The supreme leader of the Church shall change residence... [Prophecy of Joannes de Vatiguerro]
Nostradamus, 1558/68:
The Holy Seat shall elsewhere be removed... [VIII.99]
Nostradamus, 1555: ... When the great Pontiff shall his country fly. [II.41]

Mirabilis liber, 1522/3: The sea shall rage and shall rise against the world, and it shall swallow many ships and their crews. [Prophecy of Joannes de Vatiguerro]
Nostradamus, 1558/68:
In th' place where Jason built his famous ship
So huge a flood there'll be, and such a fount,
That there'll be neither place nor land to grip,
And waves shall climb broad-based Olympus' mount. [VIII.16]
Nostradamus, 1557:
That Attic land, foremost in wisdom's lore,
Which still remains the rose-bloom of the world,
The sea shall ruin, tumbled its fame of yore,
By waves sucked down and to destruction hurled. [V.31]
Nostradamus, 1555:
A fleet is wrecked near th' Adriatic sea,
Lifted by earthquake, cast upon the land. [II.86]

Mirabilis liber, 1522/3: Men, as well as animals, shall be struck by various infirmities and by sudden death: there shall be an unspeakable plague... [Prophecy of Joannes de Vatiguerro]
Nostradamus, 1555:
Then, Mabus shortly dying, there shall be
Of man and beast a massacre most dread. [II.62]
Nostradamus, 1558/68:
After dread war that westward is prepared
Comes pestilence with but a year's demur
So dread nor young, nor old, nor beast is spared. [IX.55]

Mirabilis liber, 1522/3: ... there shall be an astonishing and cruel famine, which shall be so great and of such an extent throughout the World and especially in the regions of the West, that since the beginning of the world no one has ever heard of the like. [Prophecy of Joannes de Vatiguerro]

Nostradamus, 1555:

The mighty famine whose approach I feel
Shall oft return, then reign from east to west,
So great, so very long that they shall steal
From trees their roots, babes from their mother's breast. [I.67]

Mirabilis liber, 1522/3: ... even the sciences and arts shall perish... [Prophecy of Joannes de Vatiguerro]

Nostradamus, 1555:

What mighty loss shall learning know, alas,
Before the cycle of the moon is done! [I.62]

Mirabilis liber, 1522/3: ... a young captive... shall regain the crown of the lily and shall spread his dominion over the whole World. [Prophecy of Joannes de Vatiguerro]

Nostradamus, 1557:

Shade-born where light is dim and sunbeams few,
With sovereign goodness he'll the scepter hold.
From th' ancient source he shall his line renew,
Replacing th' age of bronze with one of gold. [V.41]

Nostradamus, 1557: Lord over all great Chyren is acclaimed... [VI.70]

Mirabilis liber, 1522/3: When you shall hear the first ox bellow within the Church of the Lord, then the Church shall start to go lame; but when three other signs shall be presented to you, and when you shall see the Eagle joined to the Snake, and when the second ox bellows in church, it is the time of the Tribulations. [Prophecy of St Vincent]

Nostradamus, 1558/68:

When a Crusader with a mind unwhole
In holy place a hornéd ox shall see,
Then shall a pig take o'er the Virgin's role,
And king no more true order oversee. [VIII.90]

Mirabilis liber, 1522/3: Weep, Alas! sad Babylon, what miserable days await you! Like the ripened harvest, you shall be cut down, because of your iniquities. The kings of the four corners of the world shall advance against you... [Prophecy originally relating to François I]

Nostradamus, 1558/68:

Like Griffon shall the King of Europe speed,
Accompanied by forces from the North.
Of reds and whites great armies he shall lead
'Gainst Babylon's great ruler boldly forth. [X.86]

Mirabilis liber, 1522/3: The Lord shall send one of his princes against them and, in a trice, shall strike them with the fire of the thunderbolt... [Prophecy of Pseudo-Methodius]

Mirabilis liber, 1522/3: The arrow of Italy, shooting forth towards the Middle East, shall go there to dig the furrows in which to plant the vine of the true Savior...

Nostradamus, 1555:

The mighty bolt across the sky shall sprawl:
Killed in mid-sentence, many shall have died. [II.70]

Mirabilis liber, 1522/3: The same year he shall gain a double crown: then, at the head of a great army, he shall enter Greece, and shall be named king of the Greeks... [Version of the second Charlemagne Prophecy]

Nostradamus, 1555: Rested, on Epirus they'll set their sights... [I.74]

Mirabilis liber, 1522/3: He shall subjugate the Turks and Barbarians, and shall publish an edict whereby whoever will not worship the cross shall be put to death. [Version of the second Charlemagne Prophecy]

Nostradamus, 1558/68:

Ready to land, the Christian troops approach,
While Arabs watch. [IX.43]

Nostradamus, 1557:

Good heavens! Red-hats bear God's Word o'er the ocean!
Seven monks at Istanbul they'll take ashore. [VII.36]

Mirabilis liber, 1522/3: No one shall be able to resist him, because he shall always have the strong arm of the Lord beside him, Who shall bestow on him sovereignty over the entire world... [Version of the second Charlemagne Prophecy]

Nostradamus, 1557:

Lord over all great Chyren is acclaimed,
'Further beyond' they'll fear him and shall love.
His fame and praise shall soar all heaven above,
Well pleased the only victor to be named. [VI.70]

Roussat, 1549/50:[67] ... the Venerable Bede... says that the Iris [rainbow] shall not be seen for a space of 40 years preceding this cremation... [*Livre de l'estat*, Part 3]

Nostradamus, 1555: For forty years no rainbow they shall know... [I.17]

Roussat, 1549/50: Already the barque of St Peter is sore shaken and in peril... [*Livre de l'estat*, Part 4]

Nostradamus, 1558/68: His rod he'll shake and place the barque in peril... [X.58]

Roussat, 1549/50: Know, then, friendly readers, that the Kingdom of God is at hand , that is to say in the seventh millenary, the eighth sphere is about to complete one revolution and the celestial bodies shall return and cease to move at [the point where] they started. [*Livre de l'estat*, Part 3]

Nostradamus, 1555: Furthermore, we are now in the midst of the seventh count of a thousand which brings everything to a close, and approaching the eighth sphere, which is at the altitude where God eternal shall accomplish the cycle during which the patterns in the sky shall return to exert themselves [again], as well as being the superior driving-force that makes our earth stable and firm, [so that] 'non inclinabatur in saeculum saeculi' ['it shall not vary from age to age']. [*Preface to César*]

Appendix E

Translation of Nostradamus's Latin letter to François Bérard of 27 August 1562

Letter 41 of Nostradamus's private correspondence as collected and published by Jean Dupèbe[3, 21] is the one that contains most of what we know about his nocturnal esoteric practices and the sort of raw material that they produced. The copy appears to be in Chavigny's hand.

The original letter seems to have been delivered personally by the seer to François Bérard, lawyer and Procurator Fiscal to the Papal Legation at Avignon, a keen alchemist and would-be disciple and assistant of the mage of Salon, on or about 10 September 1562. It concerns (among other things) a golden 'magic' ring that the latter had recently acquired. As a magician in his own right, Nostradamus naturally had such a ring of his own (in his case, one inset with cornelian, subsequently bequeathed to his son César), and its purpose, like Bérard's, was to help bestow on him power to summon up the spirits and to assist the general alchemical *magnum opus*. Such, at all events, was the known function of such rings, and the precise methods of making them were likewise well known and in print.[8]

Not surprisingly, therefore, Nostradamus devotes most his letter to his 'reading' of Bérard's ring. Its Latin syntax is notably vague and inconsistent, but with Nostradamus this does not necessarily argue any kind of drugged or trance-like state:

> To the most learned François Bérard, Doctor of Law, from Michel Nostradamus, greetings.
>
> Most learned Bérard
> Since leaving you, I have often reflected in my mind both on your letter and on what passed between us, but was unable to satisfy all your requests in this great heat. Be advised therefore that for nine nights in

succession I have [now] sat from midnight until about four o'clock both with my brow crowned with laurel and wearing the [ring with its] sky-blue stone and, as it were on the [prophetic] tripod, have wrung out of that good spirit [everything I can] about your ring. Therefore, having plucked a swan's quill (for he thrice refused a goose one), and with the spirit dictating to me, as though carried away by a poetic frenzy I launched myself into the following lines:

For thee the suspect potions Leontine
Refused are by the voice. Thy field is free.
And PARPALUS, 'spite slain burnt offering
No ring shall grant. Yet, bare-head, now rejoice.
Crushed all your enemies. Stern spearman, he
In fluid air who lives, shall be that seer.
Shall come that ring when, splitting rocks, the ram
Colchis's fig trees shakes with furious horns,
Or cypresses on tombs far from the sun.
Bathed be the hideous limbs with blood of frog.
Enmired the nightly ghoul in Thracian gore.
Render the cedar charcoal in the censer
And seek the half-gnawed bones of fasting dog.
Ring-savèd thou from every whirling cyclone.
Dearer to gods be blood November-sprinkled.
On folk though fall Carina, now rejoice!

[Note the evidently planned and deliberate acrostic on FRANCISCO BERARDO. This, plus the fact that the poem is written in the approved Virgilian hexameters, seems suspiciously non-inspirational. The classical allusions seem even more so, so possibly putting the final seal on any suspicions one might have that the poem is not inspired at all, but a carefully-constructed artifice. On the other hand, it is not at all impossible that Nostradamus *actually started* by writing the letters of Bérard's name down the margin, precisely in order to give his intuition a jump-start and provide a kind of scaffolding for the subsequent inspiration to coalesce around. Moreover, neither the Virgilian Latin nor the classical mythology is any real surprise, since he had been steeped in both from his youth up, to the point where they possibly resurfaced regularly even in his dreams.]

Turning now to our own good spirit in person, and excellent in every point, I prayed that for the sake of his most faithful Achates [i.e. friend and follower] Francisco Berardo, an alchemist who is much esteemed in the matter of the transmutation of metals and is a supreme investigator of them, he might teach me how and in what manner he might bring forth ELICIUM and gold and purify pyrites, which we call emery.

Thus I, laurel boughs having been laid upon the pillow, and my head girt with a crown of laurel and that *daphnoides* which we call periwinkle:

"Angel who art my guardian and who guideth me in piety, grant that on matters touching the transformation of natural substances I may prophesy as on the brazen tripod, according to the courses of the stars. Grant these things, I beseech thee, through the friendly silences of the moon, and through these shadows as Mars shines at his rising. Grant them, I say, for the sake of the most good Christ and his Holy Virgin Mother, and of Michael the Archangel my invincible patron. Above all, grant that by your guidance I may increase both the resources and the favor of nature, transform with mercury the basest metals, even the slightest traces, into the veritable solar image that is gold, and make this gold itself potable for the prolongation of the lives of emperors, Kings and the greatest princes: [grant also] that these metals, along with the gold, may flow easily through the tubes of the still, without any of these liquids evaporating and [without] the gold, separated both from the watery and from the earthy, sinking to the bottom, but that all may be distilled at once by subtle artifice."

And he, in my dreams, seemed to me to reply:

Not Amaltheus' horn raise at the door:
Olenus' goats let thou not prance within.
So let the twin-born blow the fires alight.
Turbid the wind hydraulic that thee gives
Rare gold; the dewy moonstuff pour in th' cup.
***A**esgynum* press, lest aught of it escape.
Do thou add *cadmia*, some *pompholix*
All fresh; of summer myrtle add the oils.
Mix in, with sulfur, scraped molybdenum,
Upon this, burn *cucii* and *ciphii* stalks.
So shall thy fleece catch Tagus' precious lees.

Furthermore, on the subject of your destiny, of your life and its length, of your death and the manner of it, of your foes, of the spirit hidden in the ring, receive, among other jewels of your recompense, the following:

Make me some statues in a rustic place,
In gold a magic image and a wand
Carved round with mice that in these vast abodes
Have dwelling: this shall be our offering.

And mix with styrax, myrrh and purest blood
Incense, and add to sacred thymiama,
Laurel-entwined, within a bough of green.
Night shall it be when He Who Thee Rewards
Opens the age of gold, swan-quill in hand,
Stroking thy beard, though strangely hairless thou.
Then shall descend on thee, sprinkling its dew,
Rose-fingered dawn, granting the ring-empowered
Aglaia's grace by him whose spirit wild
Dwells in pyropes. Free from demons foul
And pure that solar ring! And as dread Saturn
'**M**idst Libra walks, soon shall the sprites attain
Unto thy blissful brow; then pullets' entrails,
Spring's fair burnt-offering, roast o'er steady flame.

[True, this further acrostic – this time on *MICHAIL NOSTRADAMUS* – reads more like John Keats than some mere babbler in tongues, more like the ancient Sibyl of Cumae's educated literary interpreters than her original, incoherent utterances themselves. And yet the thought *is* incoherent, the ambiance distinctly dreamlike. Possibly, then, we are as close to the source of Nostradamus's original inspiration as we are ever likely to get...]

These, then, learned Bérard, are the things that I have been able to glean from that good spirit, as from the [oracular] cave, according to the most profound judgment of the stars. And for it, in truth, I had to await the rising of Mars, which appeared in the first hour after midnight, when the moon was in conjunction with the Tail of the Dragon and the sun in auspicious conjunction with the Tail of the Lion, while Mercury was in quadrature with the right shoulder of Orion. This is why you did well, who are nevertheless outstanding in wisdom, unequalled in erudition, virtue, eloquence and knowledge of the occult, to think of addressing yourself as it were to the oracle of Apollo in respect of these questions that are exacting, difficult and remote from the common [understanding]. For in every deliberation that touches on things great and exacting it is [only] pious to implore the aid of the Gods, since without it the human [mind] can achieve little. It is meet to imitate Xenophon who called Socrates in counsel as to whether he should pursue Cyrus after his departure from Athens. For the rest, all those things that you desired to know you can easily obtain by detailed examination: for the stars promise you the greatest things. But in matters of occult philosophy, you shall not yet obtain your desires [apparently, to become Nostradamus's disciple!], for Saturn in Cancer stands most greatly in your way, and even opposes it all diametrically. But truly that recompense promises you (apart from the baldness from the ring, and apart from the good [indwelling] spirit) safety from all terrors, and shall confer on you a life of good fortune for as long as it shall last. I have recently sent you some thymiama, which some call *Vulpinacea occidentalis Arabica*, at the same time as our astrolabe which I received from the Governor of Provence, Baron [de Tende]: if this bears on your concerns, use it as you wish, I have nothing against it; otherwise see to it that everything is returned to me as soon as possible. As far as the thymiama is concerned, various people think different things – some call it amber, others something else – but be persuaded that what I have sent you is the true thymiama thanks to which Medea, once she had [gathered it], forced old men to grow young again. I hope soon to complete your birth-chart and to send it to you. And in following through your [astrological] revolutions, I have discovered that in this year of 1562, from mid-July to the beginning of August, there were serious events in your life and dangers for your honor and repute. Be therefore of good courage, since hereafter the stars promise you prosperity. Farewell and live happily. From Salon-de-Craux, 27th August 1562.

Done by M. Nostradamus 1562

Appendix F

A selection of contemporary critiques of Nostradamus

Contents

1. *The First Invective of the Lord Hercules the Frenchman against Monstradamus*[25] (*sic!*)

This pamphlet, published in Paris in 1558, had allegedly been translated into French from the Latin (but then they often said that!), and had possibly been written by Théodore de Bèze, Calvin's successor in Geneva. It is worth noting how elegant, well-modulated and clear the style is, even in English translation, if rather overblown – which totally gives the lie (even if Nostradamus's own cookbook had not already done so) to the idea that all writers at the time wrote as obscurely and clumsily as Nostradamus in his *Almanachs* and *Propheties*. One might certainly think that the author knew his Bible intimately, and may even have been even a preacher by profession. Note in particular the reference to Nostradamus's technique of divining the future on the basis of the past and present. The paragraphing is, of necessity, mine, since the technique was virtually unknown at the time.

It is to you, magnanimous Princes, reverend Prelates, noble Lords, honorable Judges, venerable Citizens, loyal Merchants and simple people; it is to you, men; it is to you, women; it is to you, girls and children of whatever age; it is to all in general and each in particular that I devote and dedicate these presents couched in but few words: the which I beseech you to accept with as good a grace as I present them to you, not out of any expectation of reward, or ambition for honor, or display on the part of their author; nor out of the wish to slander others, nor out of privy malevolence; but solely from one who is taken with a sincere and Christian desire to unmask to the world a certain monstrous abuse that is being committed to the great prejudice of the honor of God, whose honor each of us is bound to advance and maintain, to His glory. And in this error and abuse the belief and awareness of men may well interest itself, since if in the future good order and discipline be not applied to it, the said pestilence is set to infect the people and to bring about execrable heresies among the multitude.

For what can iniquity devise more detestable under heaven, and in what may the honor of Everlasting God be more trodden underfoot, than to endeavor to remove, take over and usurp the office and dignity that belong to Him alone and to no other creature? Namely the foreknowledge and awareness of predestined things to come through His holy and immutable will, the title to which He has reserved for Himself as God, as distinct from all His creatures, to whom He imparts as much or as little as seems good to Him. Therein lies the perfection of divinity, of all power and omnipotence.

The which pre-eminence and prerogative a certain brainless and lunatic idiot, who is shouting nonsense and publishing his prognostications and fantasies on the streets, would attribute and arrogate to himself when, like a man called to the consistory and privy council of God Almighty, and like a prophet of superlative degree, he predicts the states of Kings and Emperors, their lives, their deaths, the development of wars and seditions, the results thereof, peace and alliances, the government of towns and cities, the fate of Kingdoms, pestilences, famines – in short, everything that God will and can govern through His absolute power alone. Whereof he assures us twenty per cent [?], and as bold as if he could turn the world on its axis.

What? To hear him prattling and prognosticating, does he not make it thunder, rain, hail and blow, does he not make the sea flood and go down again, and calm the weather whenever he likes, on such a day, at such an hour and at so many minutes? And this refined 24-carat liar has so taken over people's simple credulity (over whom he reigns through Lucian's twin tyrants of Hope and Fear) that he has evidently beguiled many with his ambiguous babbling and double meanings into believing that the sky, the elements, even the whole universe would not fail or delay to do their duty at the hour and instant that this noble dreamer has assigned to them in his divine Almanachs; indeed, that God Himself is subject to, and sworn to follow the orders of, this sorcerer of intellects, who tells the hare-brained superstitious on which days to get married, travel, trade and put on their white shirts.

Well, if we are so dim and short of sense as to let ourselves be fooled by such charmers and charlatans, and to believe that the constellations, irradiations, aspects and influences of the stars and planets have such power over us as to change our wills and by this means to govern our souls, in that every disaster or piece of good fortune depends on their movements, is this not tantamount (as they say) to tweaking God's nose and replacing him with mere empty fate?

What does the Sovereign Lord do, after all, if not govern through His eternal and incomprehensible wisdom everything that He has created, turning and unturning them (as First Cause and Free Agent) in accordance with His will – sometimes leaving them to follow the order and course that He has assigned them ever since the beginning of their existence, then at another time, as He thinks best, suddenly making them change course and produce effects that are contrary to nature?

Who then can comprehend the admirable artifice and wisdom of God, other than to the extent that for purposes of human survival he allows men to know the natural causes and reasons apparent from observation, and not from divining [propitious astrological] moments, of which absolutely and in the last resort it is God alone who has retained for Himself all knowledge?

For all that they manage to predict or divine (exceeding the bounds of all natural philosophy, in which they are often poorly instructed) is a form of conjecture based on the interaction of the present with the past, like two Pythagorean lines or proportions which with the aid of a compass reveal the third. They, similarly, use these two aspects of time to go looking for the third, which is the future, which they [then] so boldly predict, giving everybody to believe that Astrology – an estimable enough science in itself – carries such significance and can foretell things to come. In this way they deceive people, defaming scholarship: and literate people who disagree with such sophists are held to be ignorant by those who are incapable of rational thought and do not seek to know things so far ahead, but who are nevertheless fascinated by novelty, being the sole thing that excites their easy credulity.

Wherefore, to conclude this point, what heresy can be greater that this, nor more execrable, than to attempt to introduce into human understanding a fatal necessity, and that whereas our hopes should depend totally on the goodness of Immortal God, we should attribute the good or bad fortunes of our life to the mercy and favor of the stars, or else to their malignity and contrariety? Or that in order to be the better assured that one reposes in their grace, it should be necessary to calculate the annual revolutions and draw up birth-charts in order to examine the horoscope; and as for particular incidents, to be governed by the fanatical prognostications of Monstradamus [*sic*], which from year to year he revises and changes as a serpent does its old skin.

Thus, the argument is complete, and the consequence necessary, that those who allow themselves to be thus bewitched and who believe such fantasies of divination (which overpass the limits of nature) displace, in so far as it exists within them, our God from his sovereignty over their souls, and make their goddess a Destiny and fatal necessity along with Demagoras, Lucretius, Porphyry, Lucian and such Atheist idiots who do not deserve to be mentioned. All laws, as much divine as human, ordain that such sorcerers, charmers, diviners, conjurors, mountebanks, magicians and enchanters be disgraced and punished severely, to the point of extirpating them as a pestilence and corruption of the human race. And it astonishes me greatly that those who are canny enough to refuse a counterfeit crown [golden coin] once they have put it on the touchstone (even though it seems to be true coinage, and gilded with fine ducat gold) yet cannot equally well recognize such cheats and frauds when they wrap themselves in the false cloak of philosophy, which is a science well founded and of good alloy.

Even though the Alchemists and charlatans color their work with the most useful and necessary art of medicine, do we nevertheless have unthinkingly to believe that they are what they pretend to be? Should we not test what they say against the touchstone of truth, and file it down with the file of discrimination? What idiocy befuddles and blinds people today, who take great care that nobody should cheat them of a crown, yet on the other hand co-operate in deceiving themselves in matters of such great importance for their soul and salvation, of which they seek the total ruin and destruction through their stupid credulity, and by letting the leucoma of ignorance grow in the eye of reason, which it blindfolds and dims?

O God who art light, and who causest Thy sun to shine to chase away the darkness, spread Thy eternal light to enlighten men's spirits that, seeing Thy truth, they may not blind their eyes with error, in contravention of Thy divine majesty, from which come all grace and blessing!

And you zealous enlightened ones, lovers of holy truth, do not allow such seducers and abusers of people, who are now in such vogue in the world, to set themselves up over you: keep them at arm's length, strike down their audacity and overturn their temerity: make it clear what difference there is between light and darkness, between truth and deception. And you, people, are you not aware of the long sleep to which this mountebank has subjected you? Will you not forsake your foolish credulity based on the fantastic imaginings of Monstradamus?

And you yourself, son of iniquity, conceived in lies, will you continue to feed the poor people on your fables and deceptions, cobbled together in despite of God for the damnation of those who put their trust in you? Oh how I would that you would return to reason and address yourself once again to the way of salvation, from which you have so strayed and have caused so many others to stray, too. I pray you as a Christian, if prayer has any meaning to you, to withdraw henceforth from this mire of deception in which you have been wallowing for so long. Otherwise, if you obstinately persist in your deceptions, I promise you as of this day that I shall paint you in all your true colors (since for the moment I have put down my pen) [!], and that I shall drag you out of your cave and cavern of deception as Hercules did Cacus. Thus shall I expose to everybody in the full light of day this hideous monster and sphinx, who with his tortuous and vague riddles drives stupid people out of their minds. Believe me, I shall drag you down in mid-flight, however high you have flown. I shall trim and squeeze quite dry the plumes of the liberal arts, of which you think you have taken possession.

Content yourself, then, with fulfilling the role of mathematician or astrologer without trying to play the magician and practice divining, and without counterfeiting the Gypsy and telling fortunes. Be content that people accept your Almanachs and prognostications for the changes of the seasons, the vagaries of the weather, the movements of the planets according to their natural courses, and for their effects, in so far as this can be known by observation reduced to art. Do not any longer give us to believe that you are an Icaromenippus in Lucian, who boasts of having flown up to the sky and who tells lies, like yourself, from behind an iron door. So comport yourself, that people take you for Lucan's Eryctus, or that sorceress of Heliodorus's, Myrrhina of Apuleia, or that Pythoness in the book of Kings, or Aglaonice in the commentary by Apollonius, or Ovid's Dipsas; or, indeed, for that old female diviner and magician depicted in Catullus, or in the odes of Horace. Let them not take you for a pseudo Alexander in Lucian, or a Salmoneus in Virgil – all of whom, by virtue of the fact that they knew a little astrology, wanted to be spoken of as an oracle, as do you, and bewitched and enchanted people with their cunning and malicious deceptions.

Nobody paints astrology in quite the way that you do, stuffing it with sorcery and superstition in order the better to cover up your ignorance and make people admire it, so making this science offensive to fine minds, and poisoning the simple minded who are drunk with your falsehoods dreamt up at leisure.

But, God be thanked, your game is discovered, and the Theatre of your deceptions unmasked wherein you play your farces. It thus suffices me to have said and published as much – in the first instance, purely in order to remonstrate with you. If it becomes necessary for me to put my hand to the pen again, I shall shake you up and cut you apart in quite another way: and I shall never give up until all your capers have lost their credibility. If, in short, you fail to return to the confines of philosophy and medicine (which you abuse so miserably), take these presents as your challenge and warning. You shall have plenty to suck and claw on, whereto this octet shall bear witness, serving as herald of combat:

Denounce, my muse, with clarion call
(Like silver mixed with metals base)
This sorc'rer who'd deceive us all,
False candor writ across his face.
Be sure to argue and to say
That if his prattle came to be
The world wouid work a different way,
Forged by a different Deity.

To you, my duelling partner [?],
L.V.C.M.

2. Translated extracts from Laurent Videl's *Declaration des abus, ignorances et seditions de Michel Nostradamus* of 1558[70]

Laurens Videl was a doctor and professional astrologer who taught astrology at Avignon and Lyon, and was the author of Almanacs with Claude Fabri. In 1557 he wrote (and published in 1558) a pamphlet entitled in French the *Declaration of the Deceptions, Ignorances and Seditions of Michel Nostradamus,* which on the basis of its known finances had a print-run of some 6,000. As ever, the paragraphing of my translation is not original.

> ... I can say with complete confidence that of true astrology you understand less than nothing, as is evident not merely to the learned, but to learners in astrology too, as your works amply demonstrate, you who

cannot calculate the least movement of any star whatever: and no more than knowing the movements do you understand how to use your tables. Nor do you show your knowledge of the tables when you state that the spring of this year 1557 will start on the 15th day of March when the sun enters the First Point of Aries at 0 degrees 53 minutes. See how ignorant you are... What is this First Point? Do you not show that you have no idea what this Point is? For, when the sun is at the First Point, there are consequently no minutes, given that a point is indivisible...

I ask you, Michel, what makes you say that, if not your ignorance, you who are unaware that the planets in the ephemerides are calculated for noon, and that the sun has long since passed the First Point of Aries when it gets to 52 minutes. What you ought to have said was that spring will start on the 10th of March at 3 pm when the sun enters the First Point of Aries, as calculated with *your* ephemerides, which were calculated (I believe) for the meridian of Venice, which is very different from ours, and which you wouldn't know how to adjust for...

Look, Michel, I ask you whether you aren't an even greater ignoramus and ass than I say? The full moon that you mention in your Presages for January 1557 – you say that the moon is at 37 degrees and 46 minutes of Cancer. What *are* you talking about, you great idiot – the sun in Aquarius and the moon opposite it in Cancer? Who on earth told you that Cancer was opposite Aquarius? Would even anybody who had never seen an astrology book drop a bigger clanger than yours? Aren't you a great ninny if you don't understand that Leo is opposite Aquarius, and not Cancer?...

Certainly, if I wanted to recite all the ignorances, errors and idiocies that you have been putting in your works for the last four or five years, it would need a pretty big book...

However, I see that you predicted *yourself* jolly well in January 1555, when you said that many would seduce the people by forging prophecies: for my part, the only person playing the prophet was you, and [so] I wonder whether you might not be one of the prophets of the Antichrist that are supposed to show up during the Last Times?... and I reply for all three of those [astrologers whom you have attacked] that they have forgotten more mathematics than you will ever know, for you started too late and didn't enter by the true door...

So now I would like to ask you whether you are not trying to tell everybody that you have a prophetic spirit that reveals everything to you, given that you speak as if you were assuredly God? Perhaps you will tell me that you receive revelations from a spirit, but not an evil one – but you should understand that it is the Father of Lies who tries to transform himself into an angel of light, and for every truth he tells you, he tells you

> five hundred lies, as is obvious from all your works, which are full of them...

After citing many examples of astrological inaccuracies from the 1557 *Almanach*, Videl goes on:

> Certainly it irks me to have to teach you something so easy, for I could send you the least of my disciples who would teach you that when Saturn is four signs away from the sun it is said to be neither *combuste* nor 'burning' [*combuste* meant 'next to the sun']. Perhaps you thought it was four *degrees*?
>
> Oh you ignorant muddle-head, why don't you check before you write? I don't know whether you are referring to Abbatou, who is a real liar, as I have demonstrated previously. Believe me, Michel, do a bit of study, and don't play around with these liars who give you to understand that Saturn is 'burning' when it is so far from the sun, contrary to every true rule. You said something very similar for the summer, when you even say that the sun is in Cancer, while Saturn in Taurus is *combuste*. What *are* you thinking about, you poor fool? Certainly, if a man of good sense had undertaken to stand astrology completely on its head, he could not have done worse that you in your ignorance.
>
> It irks me to demonstrate to you your major idiocies, but in order to discharge what I have been asked to do, and to fulfil my duty, I am forced to demonstrate part of your minor follies, without even mentioning your major ones, so as not to scandalize you in the eyes of the people, whom you have seduced and misled in this way, although you gave me cause, without my having ever spoken ill of you [this comment suggests that it is actually a riposte to something that Nostradamus had written or said about Videl – this was, after all, about the time when Nostradamus's quatrain against astrologers (VI.100) first appeared in print], but I would have warned you of your errors, which I perceived to be so great, if the occasion had presented itself, and would have remonstrated with you about them privately and with good will [note how Videl's style is sometimes almost as convoluted as Nostradamus's].
>
> And I am well aware that many who know me will be staggered that I have bothered to reply to somebody who deserves no such response, just as the mad are free to say whatever they like, but having been asked to do so, and for the duty that I owe to this noble science, which should not be profaned as you profane it, I have been forced to show you that I am not as stupid as you think I am...
>
> You show yourself more ignorant than it is impossible to find

anybody like you for ignorance [!]; you say that it was around half-an-hour after midnight, [yet] when you do the chart for what should be the midnight line or a little afterwards, you show it at sunrise. Look, you great ass – you want the sun to be at midnight and in the east, both at the same time: for what should be in the fourth house, you put in the first, and what should be in the first, you put in the tenth! Perhaps you will wriggle out of it for me by saying that you did it intentionally so that many should not understand you? But you shan't wriggle out of it, for in trying to wriggle out of the title of ignoramus you fall into something worse – namely that of faker, deceiver and misleader of the people.

I have just remembered that a young gentleman recounted to me that, while passing through Salon with one other, they went to call on you, in the hope that you would do the birth-chart for one of them. And you, being busy with your studies, opened your ephemerides and tried to do the birth-chart simply from where they lay open, even though that was neither the year of birth nor the year of the interrogation, such that you were reproached by them, who didn't even know anything about astrology, and who said 'What are you trying to do to us? That isn't the birth year, nor is it this year in which we are consulting you!' And in the end you tried to bluster your way out of it in your usual manner, but they refused to let you, and recognized you as the ignoramus you are, mocking you in your own presence...They certainly did their duty in recognizing how ignorant you are not to have told them anything relevant, and so they gave you nothing [for it] either.

Certainly I have seen many of your birth-charts, which you wriggled out of doing for them, but you have never had the grace to confirm that you have known how to find the true zodiacal Ascendant [this is true, as Brind'Amour demonstrates[8]]. So what reading can you possibly give us when you don't know the principal feature on which all readings have to be based? So much for your new astrology that the mathematicians can make nothing of!

It is not only in this current year that you have tried to show yourself to be the Holy Spirit [Himself], for in the Prognostication for 1552 you used words that were so definite that God himself has never used more definite ones, when you said that many great persons both lay and ecclesiastical would infallibly die. What word is this – 'infallibly'? – given that we read in the prophet Jonah that God had told him that he was going to destroy the city of Nineveh, and yet he did not; again, apparently it was said that the Prophet would die, and he didn't. Thus it is clear that the Holy Spirit never spoke with such certainty as you in your new astrology forged in your own brain, putting the world in admiration of you by your loud assertions and follies.

> Is it not the act of a madman in the said Prognostication for 1552, when you say may it please sovereign God immortal that the war, famine, sterility and death of many cattle, which will happen for sure, should not happen? Given that you say that it will happen for certain, why do you pray that it may not happen? Aren't you showing that you are contradicting yourself? First of all you say that it will happen for sure, and immediately afterwards you say that it doesn't have to happen – plus so many other idiocies that I am ashamed to point them out to you...It is certain that three days after your death your name will be just as dead [as you are]...

Obviously, then, Videl wasn't a prophet either. Or at least he was forgetting Nostradamus's undated *Propheties*. Nevertheless on page 20 he continues with his diatribe:

> That you contradict yourself, all your works bear witness: when you speak of changes in the air you say of one and the same lunar quarter that it will be hot, cold, dry and wet – who on earth taught you to speak like that? For the new moon of April 1553 you say that it will be wet and warm, and then you say dry and there is no risk of rain. *There's* a fine piece of harmony for a musician!
>
> ... I return to your errors and ignorances for the month of January 1555. You say that the full moon of the 7th will be at 6 minutes in the morning. Why do you say at six minutes, you duffer? For the full moon will occur on the said day after 8 o'clock in the evening and not at 6 minutes in the morning. Straight after that you say that you do not dare to declare what will happen that year. Why did you use such tricks – if not so that you should be summoned to the Court?
>
> ... It irks me to recount the daylight robberies you committed on the way to the said Court, in Avignon as in Lyon and Valence and Vienne and other towns [an interesting commentary on Nostradamus's route], such that I was ashamed to hear of them and you were as shameful as a dog. Among other things, I saw a woman from Lyon to whom you had issued some worthless prescription, to the extent of stinging her for 10 crowns [a huge sum equal to about $45, which we can probably multiply by 20 to get a rough modern value]. When you came out of the house of the late Lord Lieutenant Tignac she called after you 'Give me back my ten crowns, for your prescription is no good.' And like a shameless charlatan you said 'It's all right.' Even though she had realized that it was no good you refused to give her back her ten crowns: there's an honest and honorable act for you, like so many others that you performed before you left Lyon as a known charlatan ignorant of all sound knowledge!

In addition, you confessed in the presence of my lords the Doctors of Medicine that you were not a physician, but had been previously, and now you were working entirely in astrology, as if astrology stopped anyone being a physician or as if somebody had made you forget what you knew. And what response did you give Jacques Bassetin when he asked which type of domification [the division of the sky into houses] you found best? You answered his question just like (to quote the common saying) Magnificat at Matins [the Magnificat belongs in the evening service, not the morning one!]: for you just told him what fine things his epicycles were. O mighty ignorance! In short, you performed such noble, honest deeds at Lyon that on your way back from the Court you didn't dare to show yourself there, nor to let anybody know except Jean Brotot, and him forbidden expressly to tell anybody you were coming, for fear that you might be forced to pay back what you had been clever enough to trick people out of. For certainly you did such things at Lyon as merited your being thrashed or burnt. Do you really think that if the King had been told about it you wouldn't have been?

I think that your only thought is to predict all the ills that come into your head, without any other source of information – for every year you predict pestilence, famine and war. Don't you see how often you have got it wrong? Even in that same year, when provisions were so abundant and cheap everywhere, you nevertheless said at the end of March that you doubted whether this age would be renewed. But first there must come other prophets than you – for you also say 'my calculation is just and true.' How can it possibly be just and true, when you cannot calculate and don't understand the very principles of astrology, as anybody can see for themselves? You would do much better to refrain from ever talking about astrology, but if you insist on carrying on predicting as you have up to now, say that you have the spirit of prophecy and just prophesy in your own newfangled way...

You shall be frustrated in all your ambiguities and stupid threats that you keep issuing to everybody, trying to scare them with your false alarms, as you do in your Almanach for 1556 when you say 'happy he who shall walk and shall not walk on the ground, and happier he who has little or no money'. There's a fine prediction for you! But *you* weren't prepared to be one of those happy ones with little or nothing, were you? – for you were so well off as a result of your deceptions and seditions that you had acquired three or four hundred crowns [900 to 1200 pounds, or nearer $30,000 today]!

What did you mean in the said Almanach for 1556 when you said for the month of January '*Nox incubat atra* [Latin – 'Night incubates dark things'] shall be said in full daylight'? You just wanted everybody to know that you had read Virgil!

... For as Ptolemy says in his first aphorism, 'those who wish to predict in detail must needs be divinely inspired'... Believe me, leave your dreaming, which leads you to believe so many lies. Those who advised you to write against me are wishing great evil on you, for I never offended you in any way whatsoever, and yet you published insults about me. And it seemed to you that I lacked a voice to answer you with, for you thought I was dead, seeing that you had said that at the end of the year we should not have the leisure to speak. If you had been honest, and a man of good will, you would have acted differently, for if I had been in error, you should have shown me by way of good science (if you had understood it, that is) just where I have gone wrong, and not by spouting injurious words that you don't know what you mean [*sic*], unless you are joking.

... As for me, I am not at all surprised if people say you have correctly predicted and divined things that have actually happened, for inevitably among an infinite number of lies there must be *some* truth. As when you predicted the deaths of many – some did die, but others are very much alive. Even here at Avignon there is a woman whom you told that she would be dead by such-and-such a month, and she was indeed quite ill out of sheer fright. Why are you so keen to scare everybody?

... What you are so keen to promote are blasphemies, holding in such little esteem so many fine contemporary minds and the fact that the arts and sciences are currently flourishing as a result of the abundance of well-educated people that are around today.

Now Videl literally throws The Book at him...

You should take heed that you are not one of the prophets of whom Moses says at Deuteronomy 18: 'The prophet who through arrogance tries to say what I have not commanded him to say, he shall be put to death.' You say that 'prophet' means 'seer' because it is written in Samuel that 'he who today is called a prophet was formerly called a seer': but it is certain that they saw what God revealed to them through his Spirit. And you are so arrogant as to say that you have written 'in a cloudy form, more by the spirit than in any prophetic way'. What proud, stupid arrogance! Aren't you content with having yourself thought of as a prophet? Do you want to be *more* than a prophet, through revealed inspiration? Well, well, friendly reader, I beseech you to take a good look at this proud arrogance that is not content merely to con everybody with its fables and mad inventions. But on top of that to call himself a prophet, and more than a prophet – what intolerable blasphemy!

Even the Jews were thoroughly scandalized when [a certain prophet] was allowed to take on holy names when he boasted that he had received the spirit of prophecy and prophetic inspiration, and many volumes of occult philosophy that were hidden for a long time have been attributed to him. And then all his wonderful fantasies about having burned them, or 'presented them to Vulcan, and reduced them to ashes' and so on... And on top of that he says that everything that is to come he can prophesy by means of nocturnal and celestial lights, and by the spirit of prophecy. He who is totally ignorant and knows no star or celestial body proposes to invent for us a new astrology forged out of his own bacchanalian fury – and not his Mohammedan one, as he claims – in a pretence at prophecy!

So you, Michel, have composed (so you tell us) books of prophecy? You have jumbled them up obscurely and they are perpetual vaticinations? Yet never did Moses, David, Isaiah, Jeremiah, Daniel or the rest boast of such a thing – of having composed perpetual prophecies – as you do. And yet they were true prophets, having received the true gift of prophecy which is the gift of God, poured out by the Holy Spirit and not at all by any human will!! As St Paul tells the Romans in his twelfth chapter, nevertheless it is often given to the evil to prophesy – as happened to Saul when the evil spirit assailed him, and he prophesied in the middle of the house, as is written at I Samuel 8. Moreover, the term 'prophet' is applied to those who interpret the holy scriptures, as St Paul says at I Corinthians 15. So no true prophet says anything that God has not put into his mouth, as is written in the first book of Kings, chapter 22. As the prophet Micah says, 'I will speak what the Lord says to me.' In addition, a prophet is called a man of God, as is written in the second book of Kings, chapter 5. For a prophet is one who teaches what God reveals to him by His Spirit, for the glorification of the holy church, as St Paul says in the fourth chapter to the Ephesians. But *you* are rather numbered with the 400 false prophets who advised King Ahab to make war against Ramoth Gilead. But a single true prophet of God called Micheas advised the contrary, as we read in the first book of Kings, chapter 22 – the third in the Latin Bible. You are one of those lying prophetesses described in the thirteenth chapter of Ezekiel who prophesied from their own hearts, and not by the spirit of God. In St Matthew chapter 7 Jesus Christ warned us to beware of you, and of all similar false prophets: for your teaching is full of lying and avarice, unashamed to lie, disordered by your own stupidity, trying to arrogate holy names to yourself and claiming to be inspired by revelations. Take heed that you are not one of those of whom the fourth chapter of Jeremiah says that there are false prophets prophesying falsities, false vision, divination, fantasies and deceptions of their own devising, whom God has not sent, but whom he shall consume with the sword... and so on.

O great misleader of the people, you say that you have made perpetual prophecies, and then you say that they are for the period from now until 3797 [Preface to César]. Who has told you that the world will last that long? Are you not a true liar? For even the angels themselves [traditionally the guardians of the earth's successive planetary ages] know nothing of it. As it is written at St Matthew 24, 'and you would judge yourselves higher than the angels', in that you have put it about that you are more than a prophet, prophesying for the whole world.

... And afterwards in your prophecies [Preface to César] you say that before the universal end of the world there will be so many floods and deep inundations that there will be hardly any land not covered with water, and that for a long time everything will be destroyed apart from topographies. Why do you speak like that, I ask? I imagine it seems to you that everybody is as ignorant as you are in not understanding what 'topography' means. Certainly you make it perfectly clear that *you* don't know what it means, for there is no sense or reason in speaking in that way – in saying that everything will be destroyed apart from the *description of certain places*: you imagined that 'topography' meant places (*topos*) – but *graphia* means 'description', so that 'topography' is the 'description of a place'. Aren't you just showing your ignorance, you who know neither Greek nor Latin, and who in speaking French merely try to scrape off bits of Greek and Latin? Besides, you don't understand what you are writing, in that everybody can easily see your idiocy, to the extent that it is against Holy Scripture, which assures us that God will never again destroy the earth by water, as it is written in Genesis chapter 9, saying that there will henceforth be no flood to lay waste the earth. So there your doctrine and prophecies are completely contrary to Holy Scripture.

Again, you show yourself even more of an ass when you attempt to speak of secret sciences, where you say that although Mars is finishing its cycle, at the end of its final period it will take it up again. It is thirty-two years now since Mars finished [its cycle],[67] and then the moon took over rulership, which is evident and probable. But to say that it will take it up again – that is to exceed all bounds, given that even the Angels [who were said to govern the system] know nothing about it, as I said earlier. Thus it is that everybody can see that your prophecies are nasty and false, and it is hardly worth my taking the trouble to look at your works, for they are nothing but ignorance and gross deception.

And it's no use covering yourself with astrology, either, for it teaches us no such fantasies, not to fool around with going out at night to look at the stars. I realize that for those who wish to learn astrology it is necessary to observe the sky in order to recognize the fixed stars, the planets and their courses. But to say that you have to go and look at them to write Almanachs is pure deception [Nostradamus would later claim to have written part of the 1566 Almanach atop the tower of Salon's castle]. Besides, as far as doing so in order to calculate their movements is concerned, you know nothing about it. If you knew even the basics of astrology, you would know that there is no need for you to leave your study to write Almanachs. For in our own time there are plenty of learned and educated people who have already calculated for us the movements of the eight heavens. But these matters are too obscure for your brain, for it is certain that you know how to calculate neither by the heavens nor by any tables whatsoever.

True, I am not unaware that it could be objected that the tables might be badly put together. Or if I wanted to be sure that a planet was in such-and-such a sign, I could go and check with the sky. That is undoubtedly true. But when I do, I don't disguise myself by winding a great sheet about my head, nor, similarly, do I draw circles, marks or other rigmaroles beneath my feet, which are only there to pull the wool over people's eyes [an interesting sidelight on Nostradamus's possible practices]. I simply take my astrolabe or other instrument to measure the altitudes of the stars or to carry out any other necessary calculations.

Not long ago an upright man referred himself to you to ask your advice about a ulcer that he had in his bladder. And after you had stripped him completely naked you gave him a piece of advice that is worth remembering, if only so that it can be laughed at for evermore – you told him to have sex with a small black woman. This piece of advice is rather like ordering the use of turpentine or oil for putting out a raging fire [Videl, it should remembered, was a doctor]. In this way we can see that you are as good a physician as you are an astrologer for, not content with advising him to make his ulcer grow and get even worse by consorting with women, you insisted that the woman be black and small. I don't know whether you did so out of superstition, or because you meant that black women are more skilled with the weapons [of love].

Then again, I recently saw a book that you had had printed under your name [clearly the medical cookbook, or *Traité des fardemens et confitures*] containing certain recipes and cosmetics that you have gleaned from here and there, on the grounds that you had been an apothecary – or rather a sophonist [?] or chemist. At any rate you hardly understood anything about this art, for in the book there is nothing but follies and old wives' tales designed to make people dream about your cosmetics...

Now if you were a man of reason and had some grounding in some other science, I would prove to you that anyone making predictions, presages and almanacs should not use enchantments, sorcery, secret spells or similar errors, which are contrary to reason, nature and mathematics. Yet you have written publicly that you wish to harmonize occult philosophy with astrology, and in many places in your works you write that you do not dare to declare what occult philosophy says – which makes it quite clear that what you call occult philosophy is merely odds and ends that you write in the course of your great blunders...

Seeing that you have deceived and tricked the world, even many people of goodwill say, 'I don't dare read his works because of all the ills that he predicts for us.' Not only have you misled and deceived the common people, but also the great lords, whom you have caused to admire you through your disordered ramblings, and who have all let pass your tall stories or simply failed to be on their guard against them. But rather did they not think it honorable to respond to such an ignoramus – as, indeed, I did not either, even though without cause or reason you slandered me, for I knew perfectly well that what you said was false lies, given that neither I nor any of mine had accused or slandered you, whether before monarchs or anybody else, nor indeed said a word about you [had Nostradamus perhaps said unpleasant things about him to Queen Catherine de Médicis at Court in the summer of 1555?].

Therefore for the duty that I owe to science, and also so that the world should no longer be misled by your lies, deceptions, tricks and fables and other diabolical inventions – whatever truths they may contain – seeing that they argue neither from reason nor from any true science at all, but rather from various superstitions and spells which are simply not to be endured, I thought it well to warn you by this present work.

And when I consider the opinion that people have of astrology, I am reminded of what the prophet Jeremiah said: 'How the gold has darkened and changed its beauteous color!' For true knowledge has been shamed and disgraced by your ridiculous presages and idiotic fables and lies.

... For the month of February 1556 you talk about the new moon of the 10th in Aquarius. Look, you ignoramus – the sun is in Pisces and the moon in *Aquarius*? Truly, if a literate carter were to try writing almanacs, he wouldn't make as many mistakes as you do. You even say 'Saturn regarding the Lion with a sextile aspect': Saturn is in Aries, and you want it to regard Leo with a sextile?!

In truth, the more I look at your fantasies, the more I can see you are a charlatan and ignoramus. You say 'Because human reason cannot attain to heaven by means of the ancient tables of revolutions, we can get there by means of other secrets – but I absolutely do not dare to explain what must inevitably come to pass.' You want us to believe that you have more divinity than other men, because you are a prophet, or because you have *two* spirits that make you more than they are – and those are your secrets which let you attain to heaven and say that this or that will happen infallibly!

... Every year, too, you say that you wonder whether the end of the age is not truly near, but since you say that you have written your prophecies up to the year 3797, and that you are inspired by God, why are you worrying about it now, for we [evidently] still have a long way to go? Also you say that you cannot fail or err. Well, before I leave you, not for a calf, which is too small a dumb animal, but for a great bull or elephant, the biggest of dumb animals, let me assure you that I have examined very closely the revolution of this moon of 20th November 1557 at 1500 hours in the afternoon, with Mercury retrograde ascending into the sign of Aquarius, the moon conjunct with it, and afterwards Venus conjoining with Jupiter in the sign of Capricorn, the moon conjoining with the said Venus, the quartile aspect of Mars with Saturn, the conjunction of Mercury with the sun, and various other aspects during this present month of November. And among all these new phenomena I have found not one of those that you actually claimed to find through all your schemings: these may be 'new' to you, but not to those who know anything about it.

This is what I declare and make known to you, then – that you are an ignoramus, a brainless idiot, a lunatic dreamer, fleeing the company of men except when you think you can make money from them, and having no other friend than your grotty familiar [?].

Also I had forgotten to tell you that you are nothing but a Cabbalist because you don't really understand metathesis. For example, when you say in your Almanachs 'le grand Chyren', meaning 'Henry', there should be no 'C' for the purposes of metathesis, nor for orchema [?], at least if you were trying to speak French. But if you tell me that it is according to the mother-tongue of your region to say 'Henryc' for 'Henry' I accept it and admit that you win.

... Before drawing to an end this present piece I pray you, before you write any more Almanachs or Prognostications, to study the principles of astrology, for I can see quite well than in your works for the year 1558 you have still not realized your ignorance, and if I could I would persuade you to withdraw them so that you could start again from scratch. But I am not as hostile to you as you imagined, and thank God I bear you no grudge at all, and do not slander you in any way, nor have I done, and I take no pleasure in saying bad things about anybody, as those who are acquainted with me know full well. And even if I had never published any Almanachs [of my own] it would not upset me at all, given that there are many errors and idiocies written by the Arabs that are of little efficacy or usefulness.

And I advise all those who are thinking of writing predictions not to amuse themselves in this way, but rather to follow Ptolemy, who is a good author. In this way they will not exceed the limits of astrology.

Well, if it seems to you that in responding to you I have been too rude, you should know that if you ever come to speak of me again as you did, you shall know that what I have written so far has merely been the petal of the rose pricking you, and that if you eventually come back to pick it, you shall feel the thorn which will pierce you to the marrow.

From Avignon, this day when you threatened me with all kinds of ills, which is the 25th November 1557. End of the deceptions, deceptions and ignorances of Michel Nostramus [*sic*], of Salon de Craux.

ERRATA... [listed for pages 5 to 15]

Printed with the authority and permission of My Lord the Vicar General of Avignon.

3. William Fulke's *Antiprognosticon* of 1558/9

In 1559, Nostradamus's *Almanach* for that year appeared in English translation under the title *An Almanacke for the yeare of oure Lorde God, 1559, Composed by Master Michael Nostradamus, Doctour of Physike.*[P]

At that time, the religious situation in England was critical. The Catholic Queen Mary had just died, so freeing her husband Philip II of Spain to marry Elisabeth, daughter of Henri II of France, at the wedding that summer whose celebratory tournament so famously led to Henri's death – and the Protestant Queen Elizabeth had just succeeded to the throne. Catholic spies and dissidents were suspected everywhere. No wonder, then that William Fulke, denouncing either Nostradamus's work or a contemporary pirated version of it (or possibly even a quite independent forgery) in his Latin *Antiprognosticon* of that year, did so in fairly paranoid terms, which he himself translated into English the following year:

> What? Is it to be kept in sylence, howe slowlye and coldly the people in the last yeare, seduced by the foolyshe prophesye of Nostrodamus [*sic*] addressed themselfe to lette uppe the true worshippynge of GOD and hys religion? Good Lord, what tremblynge was there? What fear? What expectation? What horror? Leste all thynges sodenlye shoulde bee turned up sydowne, so that none almost of them that gave any credite to prog-

> nostications, durst be bolde to open their faythe and religion, whyche they have in theyr hartes. Yea, thys Nostrodamus reigned here so lyke a tyrant wyth hys couth saiynges, that wythout the good lucke of hys prophesies it was thought that nothyng could be broughte to effecte. What shall speake of the common peoples voyce? Thys daye the Bishoppe of Rome must be driven out of the Parliament. To morow the Queene shal take upon her the name of supreame head. After XX dayes all thyng shall ware worse. Such a day shall be the day of the last judgement. That except the true prechers of Goddes holye woords hadde sharpelye rebuked the people for credityng suche vayne prohesies, there shoulde have bene noue ende of feare and expectation. But oure craftye Nostrodamus, that coulde wrappe hys prophesyes in suche darke wryncles of obscuritye, that no man could pyke out of them, either sence or understandyng certayn. Without doubt he hath herde of the oracles of Apollo, whiche the devyll at Delphos, gave out of an ydoll to them, that asked connsel, which were obscure, double, and suche as myght chance both waies. As that whiche was aunswered to kyng Pyrrus, demaundyng of hym: I say that Aeacides the Romaynes maye overcome.[8]

All of which gives quite a good idea not merely of how Nostradamus's French translated into the English of the time, but also of how unpredictable contemporary spelling was in both languages!

4. Francis Coxe's *A short treatise declaringe the detestable wickednesses of magicall sciences, as Necromancie, Coniurations of spirites, Curiouse Astrologie and suche lyke*, 1561

In 1561, Francis Coxe joined in the attacks on the 1559 Almanach in particular, and on astrologers in general:

> Nay, they seassed not here, but so blinded and bewytched the wittes of men, that scant durst thei credit God him self, if it semed that their blinded prophesies any time woulde make contradiction. How wel this appeared in the yeare of oure Lorde God, 1559, at what time our most noble soverain began her Imperial governement & raign over us, all men maye judge, and easelye perceive. For although it was well knowen unto all men, what love and godly zeale, her most royal maiestie had and did bear to the trew prophetes of God, his afflicted flock and woorde of the crosse, yet did the people so waver, the whole realm was so troubled & so moved with the blinde enigmatical and develish prophesies of that heaven gaser Nostradamus, in such sort, that even those whiche in their heart-

es coulde have wished the glory of God and his worde most florishing to be established, were broughte into suche an extreme coldenes of faythe, that they doubted God hadde forgotten hys promise. Yea, they hong so choysly betwene the heavenly fountayne of hope, & the bottomlesse pytte of utter desperation, that in doubt it was to which they would adhere or stick, so great was thinfection of this pestilentiall poysoned lying prophesies.[8]

5. Nostradamus replies...

Evidently, then, Nostradamus was making a dramatic impact in England. But then, in his *Almanach* for 1559 Nostradamus was already replying to earlier attacks. In the English translation of the predictions for March he had written:

> The venyme of malicious tonges maketh me to staye and retire my penne from writing that which were necessary to be declared: but I have no regarde *De ignauo impetu* [Latin: 'for the unworthy attack'], of a company of vile persones, worse than Asses, which can not but speake evill if they shoulde burste, but God will make the truthe appeare, who preserve us.

Writing of the full moon of September, he had continued:

> The presages therof extende not in general causes, but in particular, whatsoever some folish calves and asses do babble whose knowledge is not perfect. *Sed perniciosa ignorantia et vanis modis noxia mortalibus* [Latin: 'but pernicious ignorance, especially of an empty type, is harmful to mortals'], and their ignoraunce shalbe as hurtfull to them that know him as this present Eclipse shalbe almoste to all the earth, principally in the particular places already declared, *Sed cum talibus pecoribus luctari non est animus* [But my mind is not about to struggle with such cattle]. It shoulde better behove them to make Soope to skoure their dull ignoraunce, and with lesse eatinge of fyshe. Now let us praye God to converte them from waye of heresie, and put them in the right path.

And finally, writing of the full moon of October:

> The seconde Cato shall furiously unsowe his woundes for sorrowe and burst for anger. The hyghe, lowe, no man knowyng the arte of Astronomy can be ignoraunt that this yeare .1559. and the yeare followynge, many shall not bee in the same limite that we bee nyghe unto the universall judgement of the worlde. I thoughte it good here to joyne Astrologie with Philosophie against those that saye I wryte *Deliramenta* [raving lunacies]: it is them selves that dote, and bee madde, and wander every where *& toto celo* [and in the whole region].[8]

Reference-Bibliography

(European/American publishers are indicated by slash-marks)

1. Allemand, J., *Nostradamus et les hiéroglyphes* (Maison de Nostradamus, Salon, 1996/).
2. Alciatus, A., *Toutes les Emblemes de M. André Alciat* [tr] (Lyon, Rouille, 1549).
3. Amadou, R., *L'Astrologie de Nostradamus* (ARRC, Poissy, 1992/).
   a Letter 30, to Johannes Rosenberger, dated 9 September 1561.
   b Letter 41, to François Bérard, dated 27 August 1562.
4 Anon, *Palinodies de Pierre de Ronsard* (1563).
5. Bellay, J. du, *La Deffense et Illustration de la Langue Françoyse* (1549).
6. Benazra, R., *Répertoire Chronologique Nostradamique (1545-1989)*, 1990.
   a page 584.
7. Breysse, J., *Adam de Craponne et son canal* (Office de Tourisme, Lamanon, 1993).
   a Quoted in the original mediaeval Latin on page 11.
8. Brind'Amour, P., *Nostradamus astrophile* (/klincksieck; University of Ottawa, 1993).
   a Quoted in Latin on page 203.
   b Quoted in Latin on page 86.
9. Brind'Amour, P., *Nostradamus: Les premières centuries ou propheties* (Droz, 1996/).
10. Britnell, J and Stubbs, D., 'The *Mirabilis liber*, its Compilation and Influence' in the *Journal of the Warburg and Courtauld Institutes*, Volume 49, 1986.
11. Chavigny, J. A. de, *Commentaires du Sieur de Chavigny Beaunois, sur les Centuries et Prognostications de feu M. Michel de Nostradamus...* (Paris, 1596) and *Les Pleiades de Sieur de Chavigny, Beaunois...* (Lyon, Pierre Rigaud, 1607).
12. Chavigny, J. A. de, *La Premiere Face du Janus François...* (Lyon, les

héritiers de Pierre Roussin, 1594).

13. Chavigny, J. A. de, *Recueil des Presages Prosaiques de M. Michel de Nostradame* (unpublished MS, 1589).
14. Cheetham, E., *The Final Prophecies of Nostradamus* (Futura/Perigree, 1989).
15. Cheetham, E., *The Prophecies of Nostradamus* (Corgi; Perigree, 1973/Berkley, 1981)).
16. Chevignard, B., *Présages de Nostradamus* (Ed. du Seuil, 1999/).
17. Chomarat, M., Dupèbe, J. & Polizzi, G., *Nostradamus ou le savoir transmis* (Chomarat, 1997/).
18. Chomarat, M. & Laroche, Dr. J. -P., *Bibliographie Nostradamus* (Koerner, 1989/).
19. Dagueniere, J., *Le Monstre d'Abus* (Paris, Barbe Regnault, 1558).
20. Dufresne, M., *Nostradamus: Première Centurie* (series) up to *Nostradamus: Septième Centurie,* 7 vols. (/Chicoutimi/JCL, 1989-97).
21. Dupèbe, J., *Nostradamus. Lettres Inédites* (Droz, 1983/).
    a Letter 30, to Johannes Rosenberger, dated 9 September 1561.
    b Letter 41, to François Bérard, dated 27 August 1562.
    c Translated in collaboration with Erin Pittenger, of the Internet Nostradamus Research Group.
    d Translated in collaboration with Samuel Oak, of the Internet Nostradamus Research Group.
22. Erickstad, H. G. B., *The Prophecies of Nostradamus in Historical Order* (Janus, 1996/Vantage, 1982).
23. Fincelius, Jobus (Fincel, Job), *De miraculis sui temporis* (1556).
24. Frytschius, Marcus (Fritsch, Markus), *De meteoris* (1555).
25. 'Hercules le François': *La Premiere Invective du Seigneur Hercules le François, contre Monstradamus...* (Paris, Simon Calvarin, 1558).
26. Hippocrates, *De aere et aqua et regionibus* in *Articella nuperrime impressa...*(de la Place, Lyon, 1515).
    Further Latin editions (1526, 1529, 1538, 1542, 1546) were also available at the time.
27. Hogue, J., *Nostradamus and the Millennium* (Bloomsbury, 1987/).
28. Hogue, J., *Nostradamus: The Complete Prophecies* (Element/Element, 1997).
29. Hogue, J., *Nostradamus: The New Revelations* (Element/Element 1994).
30. Iamblichus, *De Mysteriis Aegyptiorum, Chaldaeorum, Assyriorum*

(Lyon, De Tournes, 1549).

31. Ionescu, V., *Les dernières victoires de Nostradamus* (Filipacchi, 1993/).
32. Kidogo, Bardo (Barry Popkess), *The Keys to the Predictions of Nostradamus* (Foulsham, 1994/).
33. King, Francis X., *Nostradamus: Prophecies Fulfilled and Predictions for the Millennium and Beyond* (BCA, 1993/).
34. Laver, J., *Nostradamus or the Future Foretold* (Mann, 1942-81/).
35. Lemesurier, P., *The Essential Nostradamus* (Piatkus, 1999/).
36. Lemesurier, P., *Nostradamus Beyond 2000/Nostradamus and Beyond* (Godsfield/Sterling, 1999).
37. Lemesurier, P., *The Nostradamus Encyclopedia* (Godsfield/St Martin's, 1997).
38. Lemesurier. P., *Nostradamus in the 21st Century* (Piatkus, 2000).

a See pages 12-13. This might, of course, explain why neither in the editions of his *Propheties* published during his lifetime, nor in his correspondence with close friends, nor even on his eventual tombstone would he be described specifically as a 'doctor' – even though publishers' woodcuts would often portray him vaguely in that role. In most of his popular annual almanacs, on the other hand, in his medical cookbook, in letters to him from more remote and less well-informed correspondents and in the printed version of his letter to the Queen Mother almost at the end of his life the word would admittedly appear. It would also appear in the books subsequently written about him by his latter-day secretary and in his last will and testament. But, of the last two, the former (published at least 28 years after his death) are full of other misinformation about him, too, while the latter also describes him as an *astrophile*, or 'star-lover' – which is hardly an accredited profession, either. Meanwhile, his eventual appointment as *medecin du Roy*, or physician to the king, of course implies no more than that that was the position awarded him: it says nothing about his professional qualifications.

b Passionate efforts by latter-day commentators to link this verse with the death of Henri II unfortunately just do not fit line 3 in particular, and were not reflected at the time. The link was first suggested by César in his book of 1614.[47]

39. Lemesurier, P., *Nostradamus: The Final Reckoning* (Piatkus, 1995/Berkley, 1997).

40. Lemesurier, P., *Nostradamus – The Next 50 Years* (Piatkus, 1993/Berkley, 1994).
41. Leoni, E., *Nostradamus and His Prophecies* (/Wings, 1961-82).
a pages 780-1.
b pages 802-11.
42. Leroy, Dr. E., *Nostradamus: ses origines, sa vie, son œuvre* (Lafitte, 1993/).
a Now a mental hospital known as the *Clinique Van Gogh*, after its most famous inmate (1889-90), who painted many of his well-known pictures of the Alpilles from its grounds.
43. LeVert, L. E., *The Prophecies and Enigmas of Nostradamus* (/Firebell, 1979).
44. Lycosthenes, C., *Prodigiorum ac ostentorum chronicon* (Basel, 1557).
45. *Mirabilis liber qui prophetias revelationesque, necnon res mirandas, preteritas, presentes et futuras, aperte demonstrat...* (Paris, 1522/3: Lyon, 1523, but claiming 'Rome, 1524').
46. 'Moult, T. -J.', *Propheties Perpetuelles*, '1269' (assumed 1740 reprint of ditto by Friar Joseph Illyricus, 1530).
47. Nostradamus, C., *L'Histoire et chronique de Provence...* (Lyon, Simon Rigaud, 1614).
a page 775.
48. Nostradamus, M., *Almanach pour l'an M.D.LXVI* (Volant & Brotot, 1565).
49. Nostradamus, M., *Ein Erschecklich und Wunderbarlich Zeychen...* (Nuremberg, Heller, 1554).
50. Nostradamus, M., *Orus Apollo*, Ed. Rollet, P., as *Interprétation des hiéroglyphes de Horapollo* (Marcel Petit, 1993/).
51. Nostradamus, M., *Paraphrase de C. Galen sus l'exhortation de Menodote* (Du Rosne, 1557).
52. Nostradamus, M., *Les Propheties* (Bonhomme, 1555)
a III.94.
b IV.27.
c IV.23.
53. Nostradamus, M., *Les Propheties* (Du Rosne, September 1557).
a V.57.
b V.66.
c V.13, V.51.
d V.80, VI.42.
54. Nostradamus, M., *Les Prophéties, Lyon, 1557* (Chomarat, 1993/).

55. Nostradamus, M., *Les Prophéties, Lyon, 1568* (Chomarat, 2000).
a X.96.
b X.29.
c VIII.66.
d IX.33, X.27, X.79.
e VIII.4, VIII.44, IX.89.
56. Nostradamus, M., *Lettre à Catherine de Médicis* (Chomarat, 1996/).
57. Nostradamus, M., *'Traité des fardemens et des confitures'*, published as
a Excellent & moult utile opuscule... (Lyon, Antoine Volant, 1556).
b Le Vray et Parfaict Embellissement de la Face (Antwerp, Plantin, 1557).
58. Obsequens, Julius, *De Prodigiis* (fourth century).
59. Peucerus, Gaspar (Peucer, Kaspar), *Teratoscopia* (Book XV) in *Commentarius de praecipuis divinationum generibus* (1553).
60. Prévost, R., *Nostradamus: le mythe et la réalité* (Laffont, 1999/).
61. Rabelais, F., *Pantagrueline Prognostication pour l'an 1533* (1533).
62. Randi, J., *The Mask of Nostradamus* (/Prometheus, 1993).
63. Rollet, P. (ed), *Interprétation des hiéroglyphes de Horapollo* (Marcel Petit, 1993/).
64. Ronsard, P. de, *Discours des miseres de ce temps* (1562).
65. Ronsard, P. de, *Elegie sur les Troubles d'Amboise* (Toulouse, Jaques Colomies, 1560).
66. Ronsard, P. de, *Prognostiques sur les miseres de nostre temps* (1584).
67. Roussat, R., *Livre de l'estat et mutations des temps*, 1549/50.
68. Trithemius, J., *De Septem Secundeis...* (1508).
69. Vesalius, *De humani corporis fabrica*, 1543.
70. Videl, L., *Declaration des abus, ignorances et seditions de Michel Nostradamus* (Avignon, Roux & Tremblay, 1558).
71. Ward, C.A., *Oracles of Nostradamus* (Society of Metaphysicians [facsimile of 1891 ed.], 1990, 1995 /Modern Library [Scribner], 1940).
72. Watts, P.M., *Prophecy and Discovery: On the Spiritual Origins of Christopher Columbus's 'Enterprise of the Indies'* in: *American Historical Review*, February 1985, pages 73-102.

Index

BOOKS OF RELATED INTEREST FROM NAB

CONVERSATIONS WITH NOSTRADAMUS : His Prophecies Explained (In 3 volumes) — *Dolores Cannon*

Nostradamus believed in the theory of 'probable futures' of nexus on the lines of time with many possible courses branching off in all directions. The all three books of the *Conversations with Nostradamus* trilogy contain updates of events that already occurred since the original printing in 1989. Will the others also occur? • When will the third World War occur, and what countries will be involved? • Who is the terrible Anti-Christ that has been foreseen since Bible times? • What is the fate of the Catholic church and the last three Popes? • What natural disasters will occur before the end of this century and where? • Experimental weapons being developed by major world powers. • Who "The Great Genius" is and how he will benefit humanity after the Anti-Christ is defeated.

ISBN: 81-7822-226-4

VEDIC ASTROLOGY : A Guide to the Fundamentals of Jyotish — *Ronnie Gale Dreyer*

An excellent introductory text, covering all the basics of this centuries old predictive art. The material is well-organized, highly readable, and easily accessible to anyone with a sincere interest. Dreyer has done a beautiful job of bringing this normally cryptic and hidden material to modern life. As a practitioner of both Hindu and Western astrology, he guides newcomers away from all pitfalls and calamities.

ISBN: 81-7822-208-6

ASTROLOGY IN BUDDHISM : Buddhist Practice to Modern Astrology—*Jhampa Shaneman* and *Jan V. Angel*

While Buddhism is theologically and metaphysically compelling, it is also very practical. Within its tenets every psychological state is embraced, integrated, and brought to light. Learn how Buddhist precepts can inform and enrich your understanding of the planets, houses, and aspects, providing a holistic interpretation of the birth chart from a Buddhist perspective.

ISBN: 81-7822-167-5

FORECASTING YOUR LIFE EVENTS —*C. Rushman*

Are you likely to meet a new love soon? Are you likely to make a lot of money in your life, or will you always be challenged to make the most of what you have? The techniques presented in the book show you how to forecast upcoming trends and life events for yourself, friends and family, and astrological clients. The book will make you to predict major events and show you first hand how to practice the art of predictive astrology.

ISBN: 81-7822-109-8

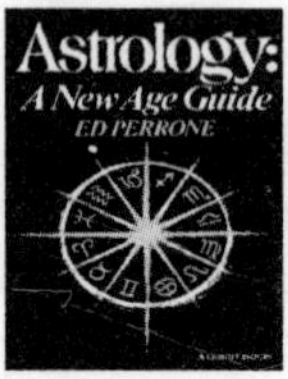

ASTROLOGY: A NEW AGE GUIDE — *E.D. Perrone*

This book is intended as a guide for all those who would use astrology's ancient wisdom to gain greater insights into themselves. *Astrology: A New Age Guide* is not aimed at advanced students of the occult, but is written for the average man and woman who seek personal answers to the timeless questions: Who am I? Why am I here? What is my personal role in the greater scheme of existence?

ISBN: 81-7822-092-x

PRACTICING THE COSMIC SCIENCE—*Stephen Arroyo*

'A Cosmic Psychology' is needed today as the new millennium begins. This book shows that this can indeed be achieved through a reformulated, modern type of astrology. Never before has there been such a practical presentation of astrology—as a valuable and therapeutic art/science. This expanded edition also includes excerpts from interviews with the author (the recipient of three international astrology awards) as well as additional new material.

ISBN: 81-7822-162-4

HUMAN HEALTH: THE NATURAL WAY— *J. Keyes*

The book merges astrological, shamanic, pagan, and healing concepts into an easy-to-read book that will help you understand the relationship between our health, the natural world, and astrology. Learn how to assess your energetic profile by looking at the elements, modalities, planets, and sign in your astrological birth chart and to address imbalances in each of these areas using simple therapies based on the four elements—earth, air, fire, and water.

ISBN: 81-7822-163-2